TRUE CRIME 2018

Homicide & True Crime Stories of 2018

Annual True Crime Anthology

By

Jack Rosewood
&
Rebecca Lo

ISBN: 9781794299887

DISCLAIMER:

This anthology of true crime stories from 2018 includes quotes from those closely involved in the cases mentioned, and it is not the author's intention to defame or intentionally hurt anyone involved. The interpretation of the events surrounding the stories are the author's as a result of researching each from a variety of different sources including newspaper stories and interviews, televised interviews and documentaries about the case. Any comments made about the psychopathic, narcissistic or sadistic behavior of the criminals arrested – some among the most prolific serial killers in the country - are the sole opinion and responsibility of the person quoted.

FREE BONUS!

Get two free books when you sign up to
my VIP newsletter at www.jackrosewood.com
150 interesting trivia about serial killers and the
story of serial killer Herbert Mullin.

Contents

Chapter 2: FEBRUARY

Chapter 5: MAY 87

Chapter 10: OCTOBER 219

Introduction

Each year, the rates of violent crime are increasing globally, but along with that come advances in technology that enable quicker resolutions. In 2018, one case that grabbed the headlines all over the world was the announcement that a serial killer, who had remained unidentified for more than 30 years, had finally been arrested. All that time, police had no idea that the killer was one of their own.

It was another year of mass shootings, particularly in the Unites States, leaving hundreds of families without a loved one. Unusually this time, there was even a mass shooting committed by a woman, which is rare. What makes these people suddenly decide to take so many lives? The answer to that question may never be known in some cases.

This book covers the most serious and violent of criminal cases throughout the year. But crime doesn't just include murder and mayhem. There is a horrific vehicle crash that found the driver criminally negligent, and resulted in the deaths of many young men. Cyberattacks in Atlanta, and Coincheck hacking feature. And of course, you can't go past the unbelievable number of sexual assault cases involving multiple victims.

Find yourself a comfortable chair, grab a coffee, and take a look back at the headlines that rocked the world in 2018.

Chapter 1:
JANUARY

Shooting Spree at Marshall County High School

Tragically, school shootings have continued to be on the rise in the United States. The year 2018 started off with yet another, resulting in the deaths of two young students, terrible wounding of nineteen others, and many who would be affected by the events of the day for the years to come.

Under Fire

Early on the morning of January 23, students were gathered before the start of their classes in an open common area, at Marshall County High School. It was just 7:57 am, and nobody knew what was about to take place.

The suspect, Gabriel Ross Parker, 15, headed to the band room at the school first to make sure his friends weren't in the open common area. He then returned to where the other students were waiting to enter their classes and opened fire, armed with a 9mm Ruger handgun.

After he opened fire on the unsuspecting students, he returned to the band room, having discarded the gun, and his friends encouraged him to hide with them, completely unaware that he was in fact the gunman on the loose.

Many of the students fled the scene, desperately seeking safety at local businesses. Some stopped to help aid those who had been wounded, attempting to get them to the hospital nearby for treatment. The scene became one of utter chaos, as students ran in all directions, dropping bags, phones and other items along the way.

At the end of the shooting, two students were dead. Bailey Nicole Holt, 15, died at the scene. Remarkably, before she died she made a phone call to her mother but due to her mortal wounding, she was unable to speak. The other young person who lost their life that day was Preston Ryan Cope, who was also 15 years old. He made it to the hospital but succumbed to his injuries shortly thereafter.

Nineteen students had been injured in the gunfire, and they suffered a range of wounds from head injuries, to arms, chest and abdomen. All were between the ages of 14 and 18 years old. Some of the wounded were transported to the hospital by fellow students and faculty members.

Unbelievably, during the chaos, suspect Parker actually rang his mother claiming that there was a shooter and that he was frightened. Once his mother found out the truth later, she was physically ill at the thought that her son had not only killed and injured so many, but that he had pretended to be a scared victim.

The Investigation

Parker was apprehended quickly and without incident, after surveillance footage at the school showed him committing the horrible crime. He was interviewed for nearly two hours before he requested a lawyer. During the interview, he claimed he had decided the night before to take the pistol belonging to his step-father. He weighed up the pros and cons of what he had planned to do before deciding to go ahead with the shooting.

Although police couldn't provide a clear motive for the shooting they did suggest that Parker had said he wanted to commit the crime as a social experiment, to see how society, the students and the faculty would react and respond. Parker also stated he had wanted to break the monotony.

Parker had been thinking about taking a gun to school and shooting people for a week before the incident took place. He went ahead with his plan to steal his stepfather's gun and hid it in the laundry basket the night before.

When he was arrested, he was carrying with him a copy of the Communist Manifesto and a large knife in a bag. He was described as being cool and calm.

Arraignment

On February 16, Parker appeared in the Marshall County Circuit Court for arraignment. He was charged with two counts of murder and fourteen counts of first-degree assault. Because he will be tried as an adult, the Kentucky Court of Appeals ordered his previously sealed records be released.

Parker and his attorney reappeared in court in March, where they attempted to have the case shifted back to Juvenile Court, but this was rejected, and he will stand trial as an adult.

Parker - Grandma's Best Friend

Those that knew Parker through school, thought of Parker as a 'grandma's boy', largely because he spent a lot of time with his grandparents. If they needed something, he would do it for them. A neighbor referred to Parker's grandmother as Parker's best friend.

Many described Parker as a good kid, quiet, and a bit of a loner. He did however talk to his friends about violence, and he had claimed he wanted to join the Mafia. There is some suggestion that Parker was bullied at school, but this has not been substantiated.

The Aftermath

In just a matter of days, the school put in place further safety methods to protect the students and staff. If a student arrived late, they would need to check in at the front office. Students were now screened by metal detector wands before they could enter the school. Further security guards were added fulltime, and in June, a rule was implemented that banned backpacks from being carried into the high school.

The community rallied around and held a benefit concert to raise money for the families of the victims. During the time following the shooting, the phrase 'Marshall Strong' became well known and well used throughout the town.

Attack at the Inter-Continental Hotel in Kabul

Although Kabul is held by the Afghan government, supported by NATO, both the Islamic State and the Taliban were still able to launch attacks on the capital. In less than a month before the attack at the Inter-Continental, a suicide bombing had taken place. It was a very unsettled time, with many different factions fighting each other.

The Attack

At approximately 9:00pm on January 20, the Inter-Continental Hotel was stormed by gunman carrying a variety of weapons, including rocket-propelled grenades. They immediately began shooting and gathering up hostages. It is thought that the gunman set their sights on foreigners staying in the hotel.

As the hotel was under attack, some of the guests of the hotel tried to escape by tying bed sheets together and climbing down the floors of the building. By this time, the hotel was on fire, but it hadn't taken full hold of the building.

Helicopters helped deploy Afghan Special Forces soldiers by lowering them on to the roof of the hotel. They were followed by soldiers from the Afghan National Army and the Norwegian Special Forces (Marinejegerkommandoen). Gunfire was exchanged with the attackers.

By the early hours of January 21, the attack was over. Four of the attackers had been shot and killed, along with 18 innocent hotel guests. The number killed included 14 foreigners. During the attack, more than 160 guests had been rescued, though many were still missing. In the hotel at the time were 16 employees of Kam Air, the Afghan airline. There had been a total of 42 employees of Kam Air at the hotel, and 11 were killed.

Security Fled Without Fighting

Three weeks prior to the attack, a private security company had taken over the security at the hotel. According to witnesses, when the attack began, the security guards fled. One employee of the hotel said, "They didn't attack. They didn't do anything to them. They had no experience."

A guest at the hotel stated he had seen four men who were dressed in army uniforms, but they were attackers. He said, "They were shouting in Pashto: 'Don't leave any of them alive, good or bad. Shoot and kill them all.'"

Ongoing Investigation

There had been many attacks in Kabul, conducted in an effort to undermine the people's confidence in the western-backed government of Afghanistan. Spokesman for the Taliban, Zabiullah Mujahid, claimed that five of the gunmen were Taliban. However, the Afghan interior ministry claimed the blame lay with the Taliban-affiliated Haqqani network. The network had been responsible for the previous 2011 attack on the hotel.

The Afghan president, Ashraf Ghani, ordered an investigation into the attack, at the same time laying blame with nearby countries for aiding militant groups. He said, "As long as the terrorist groups have secure protection and safe haven, the region will not find security, stability."

The attack on the Inter-Continental Hotel took place just a matter of days after a US security council visited the city. The purpose of the visit was to ensure that senior diplomats had the ability to assess the situation in the country. During this visit, the US embassy issued a warning that there could be possible attacks on major hotels.

Deadly Car Wash

The last thing you expect to happen at a car wash is for someone to open fire on you. Unfortunately, that is what happened in Melcroft, southeast of Pittsburgh, and it would leave four people dead and two injured.

Surprise Attack

On Sunday, January 28th at around 3:00am, William Scott Porterfield, 27, and Chelsie Cline, 25 arrived at the self-serve car wash. They had arrived in separate vehicles, and as they both exited the vehicles and walked to the side of the business, they were both shot and killed.

Shortly after, Courtney Sue Snyder, 23, and Seth William Cline, 21, also arrived at the carwash in a pickup truck. Before they had even got out of the vehicle, they were both shot and killed. As the shooter fired into the pickup from the front, a passenger in the back seat managed to hide. She survived the shooting but suffered minor injuries from broken glass.

When police arrived, they found the suspected shooter, Timothy Smith, 28, with a self-inflicted gunshot wound. He was transported to the hospital but later died.

What Was the Motive?

Because Smith died, police were unable to gain any insight from him as to why he carried out the killings. However, as they investigated, they discovered Smith had at one time been involved in a relationship with Chelsie Cline, albeit a brief involvement. She had ended the relationship months earlier though.

According to Chelsie Cline's half-sister, Smith was obsessed with Cline, even though they hadn't dated for very long. Disturbingly, a week before the shootings, Cline had put the following post on her Facebook page:

'After this week, I rlly (sic) need to get taken out...on a date or by a sniper either one is fine w me at this point.'

A friend on her Facebook page called Tim Smith had replied to the post 'I could do both.'

Could this be why Smith undertook the shootings? Had he been simply carrying out what her meme had suggested? Investigators may never really know.

Mexican Beach Resorts Violent Clashes

In the first month of 2018, the incidence of violence in Mexico reached dramatic proportions. Instead of the violence taking place in the poorer parts of the country though, it was now occurring in beach resorts near Acapulco, a popular destination for foreign travelers.

Police are Ambushed

From the night of January 6th, to the evening of January 7th, there had been a number of shootouts in the state of Guerrero, and the beach resort of San Jose del Cabo, resulting in numerous deaths.

Community police were ambushed in the early hours in the town of La Concepcion near Acapulco, resulting in eight people killed. Two of those killed were members of the community police force. As state police arrived in the area later in the morning, another shootout took place and three more people were killed.

Initial reports were unclear how the deaths occurred, but local media reported that the victims were more community police.

Police Officers Detained

As a result of the shootouts, State Attorney General Xavier Olea Pelaez stated that 30 community police officers were detained and questioned on suspicion of committing crimes. These included homicide, drug possession and carrying and use of illegal weapons.

One of the men arrested was the founder of the community force, Marco Antonio Suastegui, who was also the leader of a social movement that had fought for more than a decade against the development of a hydroelectric project in the area.

Bernandino Hernandez, a photojournalist who was covering the violent attacks, claimed that he was kicked, beaten and dragged by members of the state police. The memory cards from his camera were taken from him, and he witnessed rough treatment of several fellow journalists. He claimed he had taken photographs of police officers using force against the locals who had tried to stop the community force members from being arrested.

Increasing Violence

Guerrero has become one of the most violent states in Mexico in recent years, largely due to fighting between organized crime gangs. It is also an area where there are large amounts of opium poppy fields and marijuana cultivations, leading to an increase in violent clashes.

In 2014, 43 students from a teachers college in Guerrero went missing from Iguala after they were taken by police and handed over to a drug cartel. To this day, they have not been found.

In Baja California Sur, in the northern part of Mexico, marines had responded to gunfire reports in San Jose del Cabo on Saturday night, January 6th. As they approached, they came across men who were wearing tactical vests and were heavily armed. They were in two vehicles with license plates from California in the US.

The marines pursued the vehicles until the alleged offenders crashed. Gunfire exchanges ensued between the men in the vehicles and the marines, resulting in the deaths of all seven occupants of the two cars.

Mexico has become such a violent place that there are numerous travel warnings from countries all over the world to prospective travelers.

<u>Murder of Zainab Ansari</u>

Murders of children though horrific, occur more often than is publicized, but this murder made international headlines not just because of the horrendous trauma this young child was put through, but because of the rage and protests it incited in Kasur, Punjab, Pakistan.

Innocence Taken

Zainab Ansari, 6, disappeared on January 4th while walking to a Quran tuition class near her home. At the time, her parents were away in Saudi Arabia and Zainab's uncle was taking care of her. As soon as she went missing, her uncle Muhammad Adnan notified the Kasur District Police Office, but the family received minimal help from the authorities. Members of the family discovered CCTV footage which showed her Zainab in the company of an unknown man.

The man was dressed in white clothing and had a beard, and the CCTV video footage showed him holding Zainab's hand as they walked along Peerowala Road, Kasur. Five days later, on January 9th, her small body was discovered on a garbage pile in Shahbaz Khan Road. An autopsy was conducted which indicated Zainab had been raped before being strangled. Signs were apparent that Zainab had been kept in captivity for a period before her murder, and she had suffered some level of torture.

Finding the Suspect

On January 23rd, it was announced at a press conference that a suspect had been arrested for the murder of Zainab. The suspect was Imran Ali, 24, who worked as a mechanic and lived in the same neighborhood as Zainab. Ali was given a polygraph test, which he failed, and he was required to submit a sample of his DNA for testing.

When the results of the DNA testing came back, it linked Ali to at least 8 other young girls who had been raped in murdered in the same neighborhood. This meant that Ali was a serial killer. Ali subsequently confessed to his crimes, and it was discovered that he had taken part in the protests that had occurred following the murder of Zainab. He also knew her family.

Criminal Outcome

Ali was tried in an anti-terrorism court in Lahore Central Jail, and on February 17th, 2018, he was found guilty. His sentence included four counts of death, one life imprisonment, a further 7 year jail sentence, and a large fine.

The Protests

Following the murder of Zainab, the city of Kasur experiences violent protests. The vicious murder of the young girl prompted a national outcry, with demands of justice being sought for Zainab. As well as Kasur, protests took place in other major cities throughout Pakistan. During the protests, two people broke into a police station and were subsequently killed. Four police officers were later arrested for opening fire on the protesters.

Reactions

The Punjab chief Minister Shehbaz Sharif said the following:

"Deeply pained about brutal murder of an 8-year-old girl in a child molestation case. Those societies that cannot protect its children are eternally condemned. Not going to rest till the perpetrators of this dastardly act are apprehended & given severest possible punishment under the law."

Malala Yousafzai, Nobel Peace Prize laureate, commented on Twitter that, "This has to stop. (Government) and the concerned authorities must take action."

Former international cricketer and leader of PTI, Imran Khan, also tweeted, saying "The condemnable & horrific rape & murder of little Zainab exposes once again how vulnerable our children are in our society."

The Execution of Imran Ali

On October 17th, Imran Ali was hanged in accordance with his death sentence. Family members of Zainab, including her father, attended the execution, and afterwards, her father made a statement that he was satisfied the execution had been carried out. He had initially asked for the execution to be public, or at least televised, but both of these options were rejected by the authorities.

The Tale of the Turpins

One of the most shocking cases of alleged child abuse and claims of captivity in recent years occurred in Perris, California. The truth came out after one of the thirteen children of David and Louise Turpin made a brave dash for freedom and alerted the authorities.

Years of Abuse

According to the children following their release, their parents had not only beaten them, but also shackled them to beds and strangled them. They were only given one meal each day and each child was allowed to shower just once a year. When the children were discovered, the older ones were so malnourished that they appeared to be much younger than they really were. The oldest Turpin child, a female aged 29 years, weighed just 82 pounds (37kg).

The children were relatively uneducated about the outside world, and they had no idea what medicine was or who the police were. They were seldom allowed to leave the house, except for trick-or-treating at Halloween, and a family vacation to Las Vegas and Disneyland.

The Great Escape

The escape had been planned by the children for over two years. Finally, on January 14, two of the 13 children managed to climb out of the house through a window. However, one of them was so terrified, that they returned back to the house. The other girl, 17, continued with the escape plan and ran away.

The girl had a cell phone, and despite it being deactivated, she was able to call emergency services through 9-1-1. On arrival, the police were shown photographs the girl had of the filthy conditions in the Turpin home. Further officers were called in, and when they entered the Turpin house, they found the rest of the children. Shackled to a bed with chains was one of the children aged 22.

The police officers described the children as looking dirty, malnourished, and seemed to be younger looking than their given ages. At first they thought all of the children were minors, and were surprised to learn that the eldest child was 29 years old, and the youngest was just 2 years old. A total of 7 of the children were actually legally adults, as they were over 18 years of age. When the Turpins were questioned about the shackling of the children, they were unable to provide an answer.

The children were taken to medical facilities for examination and treatment. The minor children went to the Riverside County regional Medical Center, and were placed into foster homes once they were healthy enough to be relieved. The older adult children were taken to the Corona Regional Medical Center, and were still inpatients there as of late February.

More Disturbing Information

The girl who made the escape and notified the authorities admitted that she didn't know anything about the streets or the location where she lived. She had found a piece of paper with her mother's name and the address of the house on it, and she had read this out when she called 9-1-1.

She told officers that sometimes she would wake up and couldn't breathe because the house was so dirty. She hadn't had a bath or shower in a year or so, and when she did wash her face and hair, she did so in the sink. On examination, her skin was caked with dirt and she had a smell of being unclean and unbathed.

The brave teen told police she had not finished first grade, and so had trouble pronouncing some words. The officers noted she spoke more like a child than a 17-year-old teenager. She called her parents Father and Mother, as it was how it was done in the Bible, rather than Mom and Dad.

When she was just 12 years old, she claimed her father, David Turpin, had pulled her pants down and placed her on his lap. He was fully clothed and sitting in a recliner chair at the time. She didn't like what he was doing and pushed away from him, quickly pulling her pants back up before her mother came into the room. Her father had told her to never tell anyone about it.

The Turpins moved homes on several occasions, and at one point were living in Texas. During that time, the children were left alone for around four years, and the only care they received was their mother bringing them food.

The children were never given breakfast, and shortly before they were rescued, they were receiving one meal a day. It almost always consisted of bologna or peanut butter sandwiches, chips and a frozen burrito. They had it so often that the girl said she could no longer eat peanut butter because it caused her to gag.

The Turpins had very strict rules, and if the children disobeyed they were either slapped in the face or they would have their hair pulled by their parents. The girl who escaped claimed that her mother had caught her watching a music video a couple of years earlier and this resulted in her mother choking her and asking if she wanted to die.

David and Louise Turpin

David and Louise were married in 1985 when he was 23 and Louise was just 16 years old. Louise's father was a church pastor, and when he found out Louise and David had eloped, he was very angry.

David obtained a degree in computer engineering from Virginia Tech; Louise never finished her education, her occupation listed as a homemaker. They were members of the Quiverfull movement and Pentecostalism, and they stated they kept having children because God 'called on them to do so'. The only education the children received was learning and memorizing the Bible.

As an employee of Northrop Grumman, David's salary was around $140,000 per annum, and the total value of his assets was about $150,000. The couple was deep in debt by 2011, and they declared bankruptcy.

They had lived in Rio Vista and Fort Worth in Texas, and after they moved away in 2010, neighbors made shocking discoveries in the house they had vacated. There was feces found throughout the house, several dead dogs and cats in a trailer, large piles of garbage on the property and the beds had ropes tied to them. Despite this, the neighbors did not notify the authorities.

The Arrest and Charges Laid

Both David and Louise were arrested on January 14th, on suspicion of child endangerment and torture. They were placed in the Riverside County Jail and bail was set at $9 million. While incarcerated, police searched the Turpin house on January 17, removing numerous bags of evidence. They discovered hundreds of journals that had been written by the children, and although they may not be admissible in court, they did provide information on the experiences of the children.

On January 18, the Turpins were charged with twelve counts of false imprisonment, twelve counts of torture, six counts of child abuse and seven counts of abuse on a dependent adult. David was also charged with performing a lewd act on a child under the age of 14 years. The couple pleaded not guilty to all charges.

A brief hearing was held on January 24 in which the prosecutors requested a restraining order to forbid the Turpins from contacting their children for 3 years. The request was granted, and as a result, the Turpins cannot go within 100 yards of the children, and they are not permitted to make contact.

Further charges were added on February 23, including three more charges of child abuse, and a felony assault charge was placed against Louise. This wasn't to be the end of the charges laid against the Turpin couple however. David received eight charges of perjury on May 4, due to affidavits he had filed with the California Department of Education between 2010-2017 where he had claimed the children were receiving fulltime education in a private day school.

On June 20, a preliminary hearing took place, and the following day, it was announced that the Turpins would face trial against 50 charges of torture, false imprisonment and abuse. They remain in jail awaiting their trial.

Niels Högel - Killer Nurse

A known and established serial killer in Germany, nurse Niels Högel was initially sent to prison in 2015. What brought this case to the world media in January 2018 is the extra murder charges that were laid against Högel.

The First Arrest

In 2005, Högel was caught injecting medicine into a patient he was nursing, and he was quickly arrested and charged. At his trial, he was convicted of attempted murder and received a sentence of seven and a half years in prison in 2008.

Further Confessions 2015

A woman who had seen the media coverage of Högel's first trial became suspicious that the death of her mother at the clinic where Högel had worked may not have been natural causes after all. She went to the authorities and voiced her concerns which led to a new police investigation.

During this investigation, Högel admitted he had administered 90 injections of medicine to patients that were not authorized. As a result of these injections, 30 of the patients died and the remaining 60 were able to be resuscitated. Högel claimed he was regretful of his actions and that he hadn't killed any other patients in his care. He was subsequently charged and convicted of murders and attempted murders and was sentenced to life imprisonment.

More and More Cases Discovered

In October 2014, police embarked on a major investigation after they had identified 200 potential victims of Högel. As part of the investigation, an excess of 130 bodies were exhumed in Poland, Turkey and Germany, all from areas where Högel had worked as a nurse.

On August 28, 2017, police stated they had found Högel was responsible for at least 90 patient deaths, which included the six he had already been convicted of. Högel admitted to a number of the deaths but claimed he couldn't remember specific details in most of the murders. He stated that he was most likely responsible for all of the deaths.

By November 2017, the number of victims was increased to 106, and there were still others being investigated. In January 2018, prosecutors in Germany formally charged Högel with 97 murders and stated they also intended to file charges against other staff at the hospitals who failed to act. During the investigation, it was found that hospital authorities had failed to report the increase of fatalities that occurred while Högel was working.

The Depraved Olympic Doctor - Larry Nassar

Where once he was a highly respected national team doctor for USA Gymnastics, and an osteopathic physician at Michigan State University, allegations of sexual assault and misconduct would soon completely destroy the career and the public opinion of Larry Nassar.

Lawrence Gerard Nassar

Born in August 1963, Nassar first worked with a women's gymnastics team in 1978, at North Farmington High School. His older brother, Mike, was an athletic trainer at the school at the time, and he recommended Nassar for the role as student athletic trainer with the gymnastic team.

After graduating in 1981, Nassar attended the University of Michigan and earned an undergraduate degree in kinesiology in 1985. While he was studying, he also worked with the track and field and football teams at the university.

He began working for the USA Gymnastics National team as an athletic trainer in 1986. He continued studies at university and graduated in 1993 with a medical degree, Doctor of Osteopathic Medicine. He completed his residency at St. Lawrence Hospital, training in family practice.

In 1997, Nassar completed a sports medicine fellowship and started working as an assistant professor at Michigan State University's Department of Family and Community Medicine. During his career in medicine, Nassar was listed on several research papers on injuries in gymnasts as a co-author.

In October 1996, Nassar married Stephanie Lynn Anderson, and they went on to have three children. In 2017, following their divorce, Stephanie was granted full custody of the children.

Sexual Assault Accusations

Nassar worked as the national medical coordinator for USA Gymnastics from 1996 to 2014. In 2015, all ties with Nassar were cut after USA Gymnastics learned of concerns from some of the athletes. It was revealed in September 2016 that two gymnasts, Rachael Denhollander and another unnamed former gymnast had accused Nassar of committing sexual abuse. This resulted in Nassar being fired from the Michigan State University almost immediately.

Further accusations were revealed in February 2017, when three former gymnasts also claimed Nassar had sexually abused them. The three gymnasts, Jeanette Antolin, Jamie Dantzscher and Jessica Howard, gave an interview with television program 60 Minutes during which they made the allegations. Rachael Denhollander further stated in court in May 2017 that during five doctor's visits with Nassar in 2000, he had sexually abused her on each visit, when she was 15 years old.

McKayla Maroney, an Olympic gold medalist, stated that she had been repeatedly molested by Nassar from the age of 13, and it only stopped when she retired from gymnastics. She later filed a lawsuit against Nassar, the United States Olympic Committee, USA Gymnastics and Michigan State University, accusing USA Gymnastics of covering up the sexual abuse. The lawsuit claimed this was achieved by paying Maroney $1.25 million to sign a non-disclosure agreement.

Another Olympic gold medalist, Aly Raisman also claimed she had been abused sexually by Nassar, starting when she was 15 years old. Fellow team-mate Gabby Douglas initially criticized Raisman for 'victim shaming' but later admitted that she too was victimized by Nassar.

Maggie Nichols, a former member of the national team, documented how Nassar 'groomed' her then abused her. She claimed Nassar used Facebook to make contact with her then complimented her on her appearance on many occasions. Sarah Jantzi, Maggie Nichols' coach, overheard Maggie talking about Nassar's abuse with another gymnast, and this led to Jantzi reporting Nassar to USA Gymnastics on June 17, 2015.

Other team members Simone Biles and Jordyn Wieber followed suit and made claims that they had been abused sexually by Nassar.

On Trial

Nassar was initially indicted in November 2016, on state charges of sexual assault of a child, between the years of 1998 and 2005. The age of the child at the start was just 6 years old. He was then charged with 22 counts of first-degree criminal sexual conduct with minors. Seven of these counts pertained to Eaton County, and the other fifteen were in Ingham County.

In December 2016, Nassar was arrested by FBI agents after thousands of child pornography images were discovered along with a video of Nassar molesting underage girls. His medical license was revoked on April 6, 2017, for three years.

Nassar pleaded guilty to receiving child pornography, possession of child pornography, tampering with evidence (destruction and concealment of the images). He was sentenced to 60 years in federal prison on December 7, 2017.

The trial in Ingham County took place on November 22, 2017. Nassar pleaded guilty of seven counts of first-degree criminal sexual conduct with minors under the age of sixteen. He admitted he had molested seven girls. Then, on November 29, he pleaded guilty to a further three counts in Eaton County.

By January 18, 2018, Nassar had been accused by 135 women of sexual assault while he worked for Michigan State University and USA Gymnastics. Within a week, the number of women who came forward with accusations rose to 150.

On January 24, Nassar was sentenced to 40 to 175 years in prison. During the trial, his accusers were allowed to present victim impact statements. The Judge stated that she felt there were most likely further victims who hadn't come forward, and she said that she did not intend for Nassar to 'ever be free again'.

By the end of January, 265 complaints of sexual misconduct against Nassar had been received. Eaton County sentenced Nassar to 40 to 125 years on February 5. This sentence will run concurrently with the one imposed by Ingham County. His state sentences will start after he has completed the federal child pornography sentence. This means that Nassar will remain in prison for a minimum of 100 years.

The Aftermath

To date there have been more than 150 federal and state lawsuits filed against Nassar, the US Olympic Committee, USA Gymnastics, Michigan State University and Twistars Gymnastics Club. The entire board of USA Gymnastics, 18 members in total, all tendered their resignations. The President of Michigan State University resigned along with Mark Hollis, the Director of Athletics.

Bill Schuette, Michigan Attorney General, stated a full investigation would be undertaken to find out how Nassar was able to sexually abuse girls and young women for decades while he worked at the State University. Michigan State settled lawsuits of 332 alleged victims, agreeing to pay $500 million.

Latest Update

Nassar and his legal team announced in late July that they would be seeking a new sentencing hearing because of concerns that the previous sentencing judge was biased.

<u>Coincheck Hacking and Theft</u>

In the biggest online hack and theft to date, hackers managed to steal a staggering $535 million worth of cryptocurrency from the Japanese exchange, Coincheck.

What is Coincheck?

Headquartered in Tokyo, Coincheck is an exchange service and bitcoin wallet. It operates exchanges between fiat currencies and bitcoin/ether in Japan, and other bitcoin transactions and storage in other countries around the world.

Coincheck originated in August 2014, and by August 2016, the exchange had more than $160 million transactions in a single month. At the time, there were over 2,000 merchants utilizing the bitcoin payment solution, and that was just in Japan.

The Heist

When Coincheck was hacked in January 2018, around 500 million NEM tokens with a value of $530 million were stolen. The stolen currency was transferred through nineteen accounts, and one of these had no connection to the hacker.

Because of the robbery, two of Japan's crypto-currency trade groups merged into a new self-regulatory organization. The Financial Services Agency ordered Coincheck to improve their security practices, but didn't order the exchange to close down.

The hack was enabled by the lack of strong security measures at Coincheck. As a result, NEM has created an automated tagging system which will follow the money and tag any account that receives money which is tainted. According to Coincheck management, the NEM coins were held in what is called a 'hot wallet', which is a method of storage linked to the internet. However, Coinbase, a leading US exchange, claims that 98 percent of their digital currency holdings are in 'cold' storage or are offline.

Repaying the Losses

Coincheck stated it will repay all 260,000 users who were impacted by the theft by using their own capital. They have agreed to pay at a rate of 81 cents for each bitcoin that was lost. They also posted the following statement on their website:

"Along with the recent illegal remittance, we apologize for any inconveniences caused by customers, business partners and related parties, such as suspension of some services," the company said. "We are committed to restarting services including investigation of causes and strengthening of security system and will continue our business in the future as well as ongoing efforts to apply for registration of virtual currency exchange companies to the Financial Services Agency."

People in Planters

In Toronto, Canada, between the years 2010 and 2017, a number of men disappeared, some of whom were known to frequent Church and Wellesley, a place referred to as Toronto's gay village. The police created Project Houston to investigate whether or not the disappearances were related to each other or if a crime had actually been committed. In the summer, speculation was rife that a serial killer was behind the disappearances, and a second task force, Project Prism, was initiated. In January 2018, evidence was able to link two of the missing men to a landscaper, Bruce McArthur.

Who is Bruce McArthur?

Born Thomas Donald Bruce McArthur in 1951, McArthur was raised on a farm near Woodville in the Kawartha Lakes Region. As well as himself and his sister, McArthur's parents also took in a number of troubled foster children, with up to ten children in residence at a time.

Later, as an adult, McArthur married and had two children, a daughter named Melanie and a son named Todd. The family bought a house in Oshawa, and McArthur became active in his church. It is believed he did this to keep himself busy so he could ignore his homosexual thoughts and feelings.

In the early 1990s, McArthur started to have sexual affairs with men. A year after the affairs started, he finally admitted to his wife about his homosexuality, but despite this, they continued to live together as man and wife. Things took a turn for the worse after 1993, as a series of misfortunes affected the family. First McArthur lost his job and they were faced with financial difficulties. Part of the reason for this was because of the behavior of their son, which led to legal issues.

McArthur's son Todd became obsessed with making obscene phone calls to women that he did not personally know, while in his teenage years. To cope with the financial strain of the legal fees and the circumstances following McArthur's job loss, they mortgaged their home in 1997. Two years later, they declared bankruptcy.

McArthur left his wife and moved to Toronto in 1997, largely because of the gay community there, which was lacking in Oshawa at that time. He would frequent the bars in the gay village and eventually entered a four year relationship with a man. After that relationship ended, and during the finalization of his divorce, McArthur ended up seeing a psychiatrist and was treated for depression.

Assault on Halloween

McArthur had engaged in conversation with a male sex worker on a chat line, and then later engaged in sex with him. On October 31, shortly after noon, the man invited McArthur to his apartment so he could show him his Halloween costume. Once there, McArthur struck the man several times with an iron pipe that he often carried with him. He had struck the man from behind, and the man lost consciousness. Once he awoke, the victim called emergency services and was taken to hospital, where he was treated for injuries to his head, body and fingers. He required numerous sutures to close the wounds and underwent six weeks of physiotherapy.

McArthur turned himself in to the authorities after the attack, but claimed he couldn't remember what had happened or why. He pleaded guilty to charges of assault causing bodily harm and assault with a weapon. He received a conditional sentence of 729 days on April 11, 2003. At that time, psychiatrists suggested McArthur didn't require imprisonment as he was considered to be a low risk to reoffend.

For the first year of his sentence McArthur was under house arrest. Then, for six months he had a 10pm curfew, followed by three years of probation.

Project Houston

The Project Houston investigation lasted for 18 months, and it began in November 2012. Initially, the investigation was into the disappearance of Skandaraj 'Skanda' Navaratnam who had disappeared on September 6, 2010. The task force was created at first due to a tip about an online cannibalism ring, but this tip was eventually discounted.

Two other missing men cases were identified as being linked in June 2013. The links included geography and lifestyle, and the men were Abdulbasir 'Basir' Faizi and Majeed 'Hamid' Kayhan. They had disappeared between 2010 and 2012, and were all of South Asian origin. Both Faizi and Kayhan were leading double lives; they were married, but were involved with other men at Church and Wellesley.

Other Missing Men

Pride Toronto, the gay pride festival, took place on June 25, 2017, and the following day, Andrew Kinsman disappeared from Cabbagetown. He had last been seen near his home on Winchester Street. By the evening of June 28, his friends were concerned enough to enter his apartment. Nothing was disturbed though the cat was hungry and thirsty. The following day, they reported Kinsman's disappearance to the police.

Kinsman was an openly gay man, and had deep roots in the community, whereas the other missing men were more secretive about their homosexuality. Kinsman had been a volunteer with the Toronto People with AIDS Foundation, and he worked as a bartender, as well as being superintendent of the building he lived in. According to his friends, there was no way he would suddenly get up and leave and he certainly wouldn't leave behind his cat.

When Project Prism began in July 2017, the disappearance of Kinsman was investigated, and any possible links explored. By September, Kinsman had been linked to McArthur.

Capture of McArthur

After the link between McArthur and Kinsman was identified, police began surveilling McArthur. On January 18, 2018, police noticed a young man was about to enter McArthur's apartment, and the decision was made to arrest McArthur straight away in case the young man's life was at risk. It's just as well they did, because on entering the apartment, they found the young man tied to a bed, shaken but not suffering any injuries.

Following the arrest, police searched McArthur's van and found blood evidence, which enabled them to get a full warrant to search McArthur's apartment. What they discovered at the apartment directly lead to McArthur being charged with two counts of first degree murder, relating to the deaths of Selim Esen and Andrew Kinsman. Although the bodies hadn't been found at that stage, the evidence gave a good indication of how they had been killed.

Discovery in the Planter Boxes

It was announced on January 29 that police had found the skeletal remains of at least three men in two of the dozen planter boxes at the residence of McArthur. All of the remains showed evidence of dismemberment. Before the remains could be identified, McArthur was charged with the first degree murders of Majeed Kayhan, Soroush Mahmudi who went missing in 2015 and Dean Lisowick.

Then, on February 8, police found the remains of three more victims in planters. One of the bodies was identified as Andrew Kinsman through fingerprints.

More Charges Against McArthur

The remains of Skandaraj Navaratnam and Mahmudi were formally identified through their dental records, and McArthur was charged with another count of first degree murder for Navaratnam's death on February 23. Further identifications from the planters included Abdulbasir Faizi, Selim Esen and Dean Lisowick. On April 11, McArthur was charged with a seventh count of first degree murder.

The final set of remains found in the planters belonged to Kirushna Kumar Kanagaratnam, and on April 16, McArthur received his eighth count of first degree murder for this death.

Terrorist Attacks in Short for January

January 1

Chaman, Pakistan: Five civilians and three security officials were injured in two bomb attacks in Chaman.

Maguindanao, Philippines: Two soldiers from the 57th IB were injured when an improvised explosive device went off some 50 meters from the provincial hospital.

Pusht Rod District, Afghanistan: A district police chief has been killed in a Taliban attack in the western Farah province. Two other policemen were wounded in the attack in Pusht-e Rod district.

Madagali, Nigeria: At least three people have been confirmed killed in a blast in Nigeria's northeastern town of Madagali.

Giza, Egypt: Two Egyptian Christians were shot dead by a gunman as they celebrated the New Year at a liquor store.

January 2

Quetta, Pakistan: At least 12 Frontier Corps personnel were injured when three terrorists attacked a check post on the outskirts of Quetta in Pakistan.

Two armed attackers were killed in a heavy exchange of gunfire and the third attacker, wearing a suicide jacket, blew himself up.

Borno State, Nigeria At least 31 loggers were abducted by Boko Haram jihadists in the Nigerian state of Borno.

Mandera County, Kenya: Five Kenyan policemen were killed in an attack on their vehicle in the county of Mandera, Kenya by Al-Shabaab militants.

January 3

Nineveh Governorate, Iraq: Three Iraqi lawyers were shot dead by Islamic State militants on a Mosul road.

Gamboru, Nigeria: 14 civilians were killed when a suspected Boko Haram militant blew himself up at a mosque in Gamboru, Nigeria. Only the muezzin has survived.

January 4

Farah Province, Afghanistan: Taliban shot dead three Afghan Security personnel in western Farah province.

Kabul, Afghanistan: At least 20 people were killed in a suicide bombing that targeted a mobile police checkpoint in Kabul. As many as 30 others were injured in the incident.

January 6

Casamance, Senegal: At least 14 people were killed and seven injured when gunmen open fire in the region of Casamance, in southern Senegal.

January 7

Idlib, Syria: At least 34 people were killed and 70 others injured in four explosions in Syria's northwestern city of Idlib

Kunar Province, Afghanistan: At least three people were killed and eight others wounded when insurgents stormed a security checkpoint in Afghanistan's eastern Kunar province.

Urozgan Province, Afghanistan: At least nine Afghan army soldiers were killed and 20 others wounded after Taliban militants attacked an army camp in Urozgan province, south of Afghanistan.

January 8

Borno State, Nigeria: Gunmen on motorbikes opened fire on a group of loggers collecting firewood at Kaje village, near the Borno state capital, Maiduguri. 20 People were killed in the attack and 15 others are missing and presumed kidnapped by the attackers.

January 9

Quetta, Pakistan: A bomb went off in the center of the Pakistani city of Quetta, capital of the province of Baluchistan, killing seven people and wounding 23.

January 15

Baghdad, Iraq: 38 people were killed and at least 105 others wounded in two suicide bombings at Baghdad's al-Tayaran Square.

January 19

North Kivu, Democratic Republic of Congo: 22 soldiers were killed in Democratic Republic of Congo's volatile eastern borderlands where the army is battling Ugandan Islamist rebels. More than 20 other Congolese soldiers were also wounded after gunmen launched an attack during the night near the town of Eringeti in North Kivu province.

January 21

Gulran District, Afghanistan: A roadside bomb has killed at least 12 civilians in the western Herat province. A 13th person was wounded in the explosion, which struck a vehicle in the Gulran district.

January 23

Benghazi, Libya: A twin car bombing outside a mosque in Benghazi left at least 41 people dead and 80 injured. No group has claimed responsibility for the bombing, but many assumed it was the work of remnants of an Islamic State in Iraq and Syria group faction largely driven out of Libya.

January 25

Mopti Region, Mali: A landmine explosion blew up a civilian passenger vehicle in central Mali, killing 26 people and wounding several others.

January 27

Kabul, Afghanistan: At least 103 people were killed and 235 others injured when a Taliban suicide bomber exploded an ambulance laden with explosives near Sidarat Square in central Kabul where several government offices are located.

Soumpi, Mali: 14 people were killed and 22 wounded in an attack on a camp in Soumpi, in Mali's restive north. Two terrorists have also been killed.

January 30

Shabwah Governorate, Yemen: About 22 newly-recruited Yemeni soldiers were killed when a suicidal car bomberbombing struck a military checkpoint in the southeastern province of Shabwah. Several others were wounded in the attack.

Chapter 2:
FEBRUARY

Stoneman Douglas High School Shooting

In the second mass school shooting for the year, a gunman entered Marjory Stoneman Douglas High School in Parkland, Florida on February 14, and opened fire. By the end of the shooting, seventeen students and members of staff were dead, and a further seventeen were left with injuries.

Going Back to School

On the afternoon of February 14, former student Nikolas Cruz was dropped off at Marjory Stoneman Douglas High School at 2:19pm, just before school was due to be let out. He had traveled to the school via an Uber driver. With him he had a backpack and a duffel bag, and a staff member who recognized Cruz reported to a colleague by radio that Cruz was walking 'purposefully' towards Building 12. According to the staff member, he was only trained to report a threat, not act on it, and his colleague hid inside a closet.

Building 12 is a three-storey building that contains 30 classrooms. There would normally be up to 900 students and 30 teachers in the building at any given time. Cruz entered the building, and armed with an AR-15 style semi-automatic rifle, he first activated a fire alarm, then as the students and teachers left the classrooms, he opened fire.

A few minutes after the staff member had reported the suspicious activity, he heard gunfire so he activated a code red lockdown. On campus was an armed school resource officer from the Broward County Sheriff's Office, and he immediately took up a position between Building 12 and Building 7.

For six minutes, Cruz shot indiscriminately at anyone he saw. He was armed with multiple magazines for the rifle, which enabled him to fire multiple shots. When he had finished shooting, he dropped the rifle on the 3rd floor of Building 12, and then blended in with the students who were fleeing, and made his escape.

Cruz made his way to a Walmart store which contained a Subway restaurant and purchased a soda. He then headed to a McDonalds and stayed there until 3:01pm, when he left. Police saw Cruz in the Wyndham Lakes neighborhood of Coral Springs, located 2 miles from the school. At 3:40pm, police arrested Cruz.

The Tragic Loss

Cruz's shooting spree left seventeen people dead and a further seventeen wounded. The dead comprised fourteen students and three staff members:

Alyssa Alhadeff, 14

Scott Beigel, 35

Martin Duque, 14

Nicholas Dworet, 17

Aaron Feis, 37

Jaime Guttenberg, 14

Chris Hixon, 49

Luke Hoyer, 15

Cara Loughran, 14

Gina Montalto, 14

Joaquin Oliver, 17

Alaina Petty, 14

Meadow Pollack, 18

Helena Ramsay, 17

Alex Schachter, 14

Carmen Schentrup, 16

Peter Wang, 15

Scott Beigel, a geography teacher, was shot and killed by Cruz after unlocking a classroom for students to hide in. Assistant football coach and security guard, Aaron Feis, was fatally shot as he shielded two students from the gunfire. Chris Hixon, the athletic director, was running toward the sound of the gunfire in an effort to assist the escape of students when he was shot and killed.

Peter Wang, a student at the school and a member of the Junior Reserve Officers' Training Corps, was killed as he held doors open for students to escape through. Labelled a hero, a petition was circulated to the White House calling for him to be buried with military honors. Wang, along with victims Alaina Petty and Martin Duque, received posthumous honors from the US Army and they were awarded the ROTC Medal for Heroism.

Alyssa Alhadeff was the captain of a soccer team in Parkland when she was killed. Three weeks after her death, the United States women's national soccer team honored her before a game in Orlando. The members of her soccer team and her family were invited to attend the game and were given official jerseys bearing Alhadeff's name.

Senior student Meadow Pollack had crawled along the corridor to a classroom door but couldn't get inside the room. Cruz shot her four times. Next to her was Cara Loughran, and Pollack used her body to try and shield her. Cruz opened fire on the two girls, and they were both killed.

One of the most extraordinary stories of bravery was that of Anthony Borges, a 15-year-old student from Venezuela. Borges used his body to barricade a classroom door where 20 students were hiding inside. As a result, he was shot five times, but miraculously survived. He was given the nickname the 'real iron man' because of his strength and bravery.

What Went Wrong with Nikolas Cruz?

Nikolas Jacob Cruz, 19, had been adopted at birth by Roger and Lynda Cruz. In 2004, Roger Cruz died at the age of 67, and 13 years later, in 2017, Lynda Cruz died at the age of 68. This left Cruz an orphan at a relatively young age, and he had lived with friends and relatives following Lynda's death. Cruz had been expelled from the high school and was enrolled in a GED program at the time of his shooting rampage. He was also working at a local dollar store.

Before his expulsion, Cruz had been a member of the Junior Reserves Officers' Training Corps (JROTC). He had received multiple awards particularly for academic achievement. Cruz was also a member of the school's varsity air rifle team.

Problems with Cruz's behavior arose during middle school and he was transferred between schools six times in a three year period. He was sent to a school for children with learning or emotional disabilities in 2014. He allegedly made threats against his fellow students, so he was sent back to Stoneman Douglas High School in 2016. However, he was expelled in 2017 due to disciplinary issues. The school had sent an email to the faculty members stating Cruz had made threats against students, so the school ended up banning him from carrying a backpack while he was on campus.

In 2013, it was recommended by psychiatrists that Cruz be admitted to a residential treatment facility. In September 2016 he was investigated by the Florida Department of Children and Families following posts Cruz had put on Snapchat that showed him cutting his arms and mentioned he was planning on purchasing a gun.

At this time, a resource officer at the school recommended Cruz be examined by a psychiatrist under the Baker Act, which allows for involuntary psychiatric admission. Although two of the guidance counsellors agreed with this suggestion, the mental institution disagreed. The State investigators determined Cruz suffered from autism, attention deficit hyperactivity disorder and depression, but decided he was at low risk of hurting himself or harming others. Cruz had received previous psychiatric treatment but had not had any treatment in the year prior to the shootings.

Sheriff Scott Israel of Broward County stated that the online profiles and accounts used by Cruz were very disturbing due to the content. There were photos of Cruz with a variety of weapons including a pistol, shotgun, BB gun and long knives. His posts indicated he had 'extremist' views, and some social media accounts they believed were linked to Cruz contained anti-Muslim and anti-black slurs.

When police searched Cruz's belongings from the scene they found the gun magazines had swastikas carved into them. In a private Instagram group chat, Cruz had said he wanted 'to kill gay people and Mexicans', and discussed how black people should be kept 'in chains'. He claimed he hated Jewish people because he thought they 'wanted to destroy the world'.

Arraignment and Charges

A day after the shootings occurred, Cruz appeared in court for his initial arraignment. He was charged with 17 counts of premeditated murder and was refused bail. If he is convicted of first degree murder he could face the death penalty. Then on March 7, a grand jury indicted him on 34 charges, which included 17 counts of first degree murder and 17 counts of attempted murder.

Cruz was arraigned again on March 13, at which time the prosecution filed notice that they intend to seek the death penalty. The prosecution stated they could prove five of the aggravating factors that qualify for the death penalty in Florida. Cruz did not enter a plea, so the judge entered a 'not guilty' plea on his behalf. Previously, the defense team had said they would enter a guilty plea if the death penalty was removed. Cruz now awaits his trial.

Kidnapping of Dapchi Schoolgirls

On February 19, the Boko Haram terrorist group kidnapped 110 schoolgirls from the Government Girls Science and Technical College, Dapchi, Nigeria. The schoolgirls were aged between 11 and 19 years of age. The name 'Boko Haram' loosely translates to mean 'Western education is forbidden' in the Hausa language.

Controversy Surrounding the Withdrawal of Military Support

Army troops were withdrawn from Dapchi just hours before the schoolgirls were abducted. Neither the local police nor the state government was given any advance warning that the military was being withdrawn. Several days after the kidnapping, the army claimed it had withdrawn due to the absence of any Boko Haram activity in the general area. They also claimed they had handed the security of Dapchi over to the local police before they withdrew.

Yet on February 6, an army general was noted to express his concern over a possible attack in Damaturu, just 60 miles away from Dapchi. The state police commissioner denied the army had informed them of their intended withdrawal and the army was unable to provide any proof that they had.

The Release - Some But Not All

The Federal government of Nigeria announced on March 21 that 106 of the schoolchildren had been released by the Boko Haram terrorists. One of the kidnapped children that wasn't released was a Christian girl, and the terrorists told her parents that they would only release her if she converted to Islam.

The children who were released were dropped off in the town, transported in nine vehicles. The release was unconditional, but the Boko Haram fighters warned the parents of the children not to put them in school again.

Those children that were not released are believed to still be in the captivity of the Boko Haram.

Coach Barry Bennell - Sexual Predator

In November 2016, during an interview with The Guardian newspaper, former football player Andy Woodward alleged that he had been sexually abused as a child by his former coach at Crewe club, Barry Bennell. Within days of the interview, six other former players had made similar allegations to the police.

The Guardian reported on November 22 that another former Crewe footballer, Steve Walters, had also been a victim of sexual abuse by Barry Bennell. Two days later, manager at Crewe during the 1980s, Dario Gradi, made a statement that he had no knowledge of Bennell's alleged crimes until Bennell was arrested in the US in 1994.

David White and Paul Stewart, former players for Manchester City, made similar allegations and another coach, who was later identified as Frank Roper. Cheshire police announced that 11 people had contacted them about Bennell. Then, on November 25, two youth players came forward, Jason Dunford and Chris Unsworth, also claiming they had been sexually abused by Bennell. Dunford later made similar allegations against Roper.

Anthony Hughes, who had previously played for Crewe, stated on November 27 that he had been abused by Bennell. The next players to make allegations of sexual abuse against Bennell were Matthew Monaghan, Wales and Manchester United youth player, David Lean, former Preston North End reserve player, and Mark Williams, former Wimbledon and Northern Ireland international player.

Despite Crewe claiming to be ignorant of the allegations, this was put into doubt following November 25. Hamilton Smith, who had been the director at Crewe Alexandra between 1986 and 1990, made a statement to The Guardian that they were aware of an allegation by a junior player that

Bennell had sexually abused him. Yet Bennell was allowed to continue at the club. The chairman at the time, Norman Rowlinson, had recommended the club get rid of him, but instead, they made it so Bennell was never left alone with the boys and he was not allowed to arrange any overnight stays.

Rowlinson had asked for advice from the police about Bennell, and was told to 'move him on'. In 2001 an FA investigation into the protection of the child players was launched and it found that it had 'investigated the issues and is satisfied there is no case to answer'.

The BBC reported on December 7, 2016, that an anonymous letter was sent to Dario Gradi in 1989-90 by a mother of a youth player asking him to investigate inappropriate behavior. The incident involved a member of staff taking 'lots of boys' into his room overnight during a weekend away.

Bennell's Previous Charges

From 1992-1994 Bennell was the head coach of Staffordshire side the Stone Dominoes. During a tour with the Dominoes to the United States in 1994, a club player who was only 13 at the time claimed that he had been sexually abused by Bennell. This resulted in Bennell being arrested and charged with six counts of sexual battery, and lewd and lascivious behavior. Bennell entered a guilty plea and he was sentenced to four years in prison.

In 1996, a program on UK television highlighted the child abuse allegations against Bennell and other coaches, Keith Ketley and Bob Higgins. Ian Ackley, who was featured in the documentary, was a former player for Derbyshire youth team White Knowl, and he was one of four boys who reported the allegations to the police following Bennell's arrest in the US. However, Bennell did not serve his full sentence. But, when he returned to the UK, he was arrested.

Bennell appeared at the Mold Crown Court in northern Wales in February 1998, on charges of indecent assault, buggery and attempted buggery. The charges stemmed from incidences in the 1970s and 1980s, and up to 1992. All pertained to crimes against children aged from 9-15. Bennell pleaded not guilty and stayed in custody until his trial in June 1998. He was then found guilty of 23 offences against six boys. For this he received a nine year jail sentence.

Bennell, after his release, changed his name to Richard Jones and was living in Milton Keynes when he was arrested again. He was charged with sexual abuse against David Lean back in 1980. He pleaded guilty this time and received another two years in prison.

Gary Speed and Alan Davies had been former Manchester United players and Bennell's 'favorites'. Although there were no reports they had been abused by Bennell, they both later committed suicide. Another player, Mark Hazeldine, who had been coached by Bennell in the early 1980s at Manchester City, also committed suicide.

New Allegations in 2016-2017

On November 25, after news of further allegations broke, Bennell was found unconscious in a park and was taken to hospital. The police had been alerted by someone to a 'fear for welfare' incident, which is what lead them to find Bennell in the park. At the time, Bennell had been staying at a hotel after fleeing his home when the scandal broke.

Bennell, then 62, was charged on November 29 with eight counts of sexual assault against a boy under the age of 14, offences which occurred between 1981 and 1985. He first appeared in court via video link on December 14, then again on January 16, where he entered a plea of not guilty.

Bennell received eight further charges of child sexual abuse on March 7, 2017. On March 13, another four charges were added, and he was remanded to appear on March 22 to answer all 20 new charges. He eventually pleaded not guilty to the 14 counts of indecent assault, five counts of buggery and one count of attempted buggery.

Then, in May 2017, Bennell was charged with another 21 offences, which included 18 counts of indecent assault, two of serious sexual assault and one of attempted sexual assault. These charges pertained to four boys who were between the ages of 14 and 16 at the time, between 1983 and 1991.

But there were still more charges to come. Bennell was charged with 14 additional charges in June 2017, bringing the total of charges to 55. Ten of the new charges were for indecent assaults and four were for alleged buggery. He was remanded in custody, and his trial was set for January 8, 2018.

Trial and Conviction

When the trial began, Bennell, who now went by the name of Jones, pleaded guilty to seven of the indecent assault offences. Bennell appeared via a video link due to being ill and having to be fed through a feeding tube. The jury was asked to consider their verdict on February 8, and were instructed to return not-guilty verdicts for three indecent assault charges, as no evidence had been provided for those charges.

On February 13, Bennell was found guilty of 36 of the sex offences. The jury was given more time to ponder other counts against Bennell, and on February 15, he was convicted of another seven offences. On February 19, Bennell was sentenced on 50 offences involving 12 boys. He was sent to prison for 31 years.

Terrorist Attacks in Short for February

February 3

Kabal Tehsil, Pakistan: At least 11 security officials were killed and 13 injured in a suicide attack near a military camp in Swat district of Khyber-Pakhtunkhwa.

February 10

Nahri Saraj District, Afghanistan: A Taliban infiltrator killed 16 members of a pro-government militia force in the insurgency ridden southern province of

Helmand when he turned his gun on men who he had worked with for months.

February 10 - 13

Oruro, Bolivia: 12 people were killed and 50 others injured in two bomb attacks in the Bolivian city of Oruro.

February 16

Konduga, Nigeria: At least 21 persons were killed and 70 civilians injured as three bombers struck Konduga local government area of Borno State.

February 17

Bala Buluk District, Afghanistan: Taliban militants attacked a police checkpoint in Bala Buluk district in Farah, killing at least 10 officers.

February 18

Hawija District, Iraq: Islamic State militants ambushed a convoy of pro-government militia fighters in the Hawija district of Kirkuk province, killing at least 27 of them.

February 19

Farah Province, Afghanistan: At least 24 policemen were killed in western Farah province during coordinated attacks by the Taliban.

February 21

Al Anbar Governorate, Iraq: Islamic State militants staged an ambush on the Syrian side of the border with Iraq's western province of Anbar, killing 20 truck drivers.

February 23

Mogadishu, Somalia: At least 45 people were killed and 36 others injured in two car bombings and subsequent gunfire in Mogadishu, Somalia. Five attackers were also killed in the attack.

Bala Buluk District, Afghanistan: 25 Afghan army members died after Taliban militants attacked their checkpoint in Bala Buluk district of western Farah province. Two Taliban insurgents were also killed in the attack.

February 24

Aden, Yemen: Fourteen people were killed and 54 others injured when two car suicide bombers struck the entrance of a military base and a checkpoint near the headquarters of the Southern Transitional Council in Aden. Two other attackers wearing explosive belts also tried to climb over the external gate of the military base to reach the inside but were shot dead by guards before they could blow themselves up.

Chapter 3:
MARCH

Atlanta under Cyberattack

With the advances in computer technology, it is not surprising that cyberattacks are becoming more and more prevalent. Generally they target a specific business, corporation or person. By the Atlanta attack targeted the entire city, bringing everything to a complete halt. People couldn't pay bills online, utility services couldn't be requested, and officials in the city had to resort to filling out paper forms by hand, which had not been the normal practice for many years.

So why was this attack so notable and major newsworthy? Simply because of the vast extent of services that were affected and because Atlanta is a major economic and transportation hub in America.

Vulnerabilities and Attack

Before the attack occurred, the government in Atlanta had been criticized for not upgrading its IT infrastructure, which created multiple vulnerabilities to an online attack. An audit conducted in January 2018 found that there were up to 2,000 vulnerabilities in the city's systems, and the audit suggested that because the vulnerabilities had grown so much, the workers had become complacent.

The Virus used in the cyberattack was SamSam Ransomware. It is different from most other ransomware because it doesn't rely on phishing. Instead, it utilizes a 'brute-force' attack to guess passwords that are weak until it finds one it can break. This particular ransomware is known to specifically target weaker servers and IT infrastructures.

Since 2016, when the virus was discovered, this ransomware has been behind numerous attacks on government and medical organizations. Targets ranged from small towns, to New Mexico, to the Colorado Department of Transportation and the Erie County Medical Center. The identity of the hackers using the SamSam ransomware is currently unknown.

The Department of Atlanta Information Management first became aware of outages on a variety of internal and customer applications on March 22, at 5:40am. Shortly thereafter, the city shut down most of its digital services, including the court system database, in an effort to control the situation.

The Recovery Efforts

This was the largest breach of security in a major American city by ransomware, with the potential to affect up to 6 million people. After the attack, Atlanta city cooperated with the FBI, Secret Service and the Department of Homeland Security. The city hired security firms to investigate the hack, and the majority of government computers were to remain powered off until 5 days after the hack had occurred.

Initially, the city declared there had been no breach of personal data, but that was proven to be wrong at a later date. The breach was far worse than they had originally estimated, and in June, it was estimated that up to a third of software programs used by Atlanta city remained offline or were partially disabled. Part of the hack resulted in legal documents and police dashcam recordings being deleted, but the police were able to restore their access to the investigation files.

As a result of this cyberattack, Atlanta declared they would pay $2.7 million to contractors to recover the damage done to the IT infrastructure. However, later estimates showed it was going to cost around $9.5 million to rectify the situation caused by the cyberattack.

The Austin Serial Bomber

Between March 2 and March 20, five package bombs were sent out and exploded, leaving two people dead, and five others injured. When police identified who the bomber was, he executed himself before he could be questioned.

The Bomb Attacks

Anthony Stephan House, 39, was killed on March 2, after picking up a package at his house. The package turned out to be a bomb, and it exploded as House picked it up. At first the Austin Police Department Assistant Chief thought that perhaps House had inadvertently killed himself while making the bomb. Neighbors and nearby residents were told there was nothing to worry about and that it was an isolated incident.

Then, on March 12, young Draylen Mason, 17 was killed, and his mother was injured when they too inspected a package left at their home. That same day, Esperanza Herrera, 75, suffered serious injuries from a package bomb that was at her elderly mother's home. This second bomb was apparently addressed to another house, not the home where it was left.

In southwest Austin on March 18, two men aged 22 and 23 were seriously injured after a package exploded. This bomb was different to the others as it wasn't left on a doorstep; rather it was on the side of the road. The package had been left attached to a sign that read 'Caution: Children at Play'. Now that there had been four bomb blasts, police finally warned the public that there was likely a serial bomber in the area.

The next bombing occurred on March 20 at a FedEx Ground facility in Schertz, Texas, and one employee was injured. The package was addressed to an address in Austin. A further package bomb was identified and defused in another FedEx facility in southeast Austin the same day. Investigation showed that both packages had been sent by the same person in Sunset Valley.

Investigating the Bombings

Once the Austin police realised that House hadn't killed himself while making a bomb, they announced they were investigating his death as a possible murder. The first theory was that House was not the intended victim, and that the possible intended target was a drug dealer that lived and operated in the area.

Following the third bombing, police began to look for any possible connections between the victims. They found that House's father and Mason's grandfather were close friends, and they had both attended the same church. At the same time that this connection was made, police warned the public about opening or touching any suspicious packages. They ended up receiving 1,200 phone calls about packages by March 20.

Because the bombings were believed to be committed by a serial bomber, the FBI and the ATF became involved in assisting local police. They suggested that the bomber was a single man who was highly efficient and organized, due to the rapidity at which the bombs were created and sent. The culprit was also considered to be highly intelligent, due to the skill required to make the bombs.

The bombing on March 2 was connected after the bombings on March 12 had occurred. The first three packages were left on the doorsteps of the victims homes instead of being mailed like the remaining bombs. Two of the bombs triggered once they were picked up, while another exploded once it was opened. The fourth bomb was triggered by a tripwire, and the fifth exploded while being sorted at FedEx. The last bomb was defused.

The Main Man of Interest

The investigation into the bomb devices showed that common household ingredients had been used in the creation of them. Agents contacted stores nearby and collected all the sales records and receipts to see who may have purchased the ingredients. When these were reviewed, a suspect, Mark Anthony Conditt was identified.

What lead to Condit was that he had purchased a large amount of nails, which were the same as those used in the bombs as shrapnel. They had been purchased by Conditt at a Home Depot. The batteries used in the bombs had come from Asia, so after getting a Federal warrant, Conditt's IP address was searched. They discovered he had used Google to look for information on shipping from Asia.

While investigating the crime scene at FedEx in Sunset Valley, where the last bombs were posted from, Conditt was seen on security footage. The footage also showed a 2002 Ford Ranger, red, and even though the license plate couldn't be seen, investigators checked records for all matching vehicles in Texas that may be owned by a white male.

An Explosive End

Conditt was identified as the main person of interest, and on March 20, in the evening, a neighbor of Conditt's noted there were several parked cars in the street with people sitting in them. It is now believed they were undercover police cars carefully watching Conditt's movements. But Conditt wasn't there.

On the morning of March 21, police tracked Conditt down to a hotel in Round Rock, north of Austin. They followed him on to Interstate 35, and then pulled him over. It was around 2:00am, and as SWAT officers approached his vehicle, he detonated a bomb. Conditt was killed outright and an officer was injured. The explosion and the fact that one of their officers had been injured lead to the other officers firing on the vehicle.

While examining the scene, police were able to find Conditt's phone. It contained a video that was 25 minutes long, during which Conditt confessed to being the serial bomber. However, the video doesn't explain why he created the bombs or how he chose the victims. The police chief stated that the video was of a 'challenged young man talking about challenges in his life that led him to this point'.

The Yountville Veterans Home Shooting

A Veterans Home should be a place of peace and serenity, for those that had fought for their country in some of the most awful war situations. The Home should be where they can receive the medical treatment and care that these brave men and women deserve. But, On March 9, that peace was shattered, as a lone gunman brought the war into the Yountville Veterans Home.

The Day of the Shooting

A gunman, later identified as Albert Wong, 36, entered the Yountville Veterans Home on March 9 armed with a weapon. A US Army veteran himself of the War in Afghanistan, Wong initially released some staff members and the veterans, but he held back three staff members. They were Jennifer Gonzales Shushereba, a psychologist, Christine Loeber, the executive director of the home, and Jennifer Golick, the clinical director.

Wong had taken the three female hostages to a room on the second floor before killing them. He then killed himself with a self-inflicted shotgun wound. The standoff between Wong and the police had lasted just an hour, and the hostage negotiator had not been able to make contact with Wong at all during that time.

The Innocent Victims

All three of the victims worked for a nonprofit organization that was dedicated in providing help and services to military veterans. Tragically, Jennifer Gonzales Shushereba was 26 weeks pregnant when she was killed, and her unborn baby died from lack of oxygenated blood. They had gone to work that day with no thoughts of danger or risk, until Wong entered the building around mid-morning.

The Shooter

Wong had been a client at the Home but after he had threatened one of the three women who would later become his victims, he was kicked out of the program. Because Wong committed suicide at the scene without speaking to anyone, the true meaning behind his actions will never be known. However, because he had been removed from the program just a short time prior, it is most likely the result of revenge against those who he believed had wronged him and stopped him from getting what he wanted or needed from the program.

Russian Poisoning Saga

On March 4, two Russians residing in Salisbury, England, were poisoned with a Novichok nerve agent, also known as A-234. The nature and method of the poison used, and the background of one of the victims, opened up an international investigation involving Russia, the UK, spies and intelligence services. This international incident is still under investigation.

Sergei Skripal

Sergei Skripal, 66, had been an officer for Russia's Main Intelligence Directorate (the GRU_ in the 1990's. At the same time he was working as a double agent for the Secret Intelligence Service in the UK from 1995, until he was arrested in Russia in December 2004. He was charged with high treason in Russia, and was convicted and sentenced to serve 13 years in a penal colony.

In 2010, Skripal moved to the UK and settled through the Illegals Program spy swap. He holds both British and Russian citizenship. His daughter Yulia, 33, who became the second poisoning victim, was a Russian citizen and was in the UK visiting her father at the time of the poisoning.

How the Poisoning Occurred

Yulia Skripal flew into the UK from Russia at 14:40pm on March 4. The following morning, Skripal's vehicle was seen in the area of London Road, Churchill Way North and Wilton Road, in Salisbury. At 13:30pm the car was seen heading towards the centre of town along Devizes Road. Ten minutes later, they parked in the upper level car park a Maltings. They then went into the Bishops Mill Pub.

The Skripals dined at Zizzi Restaurant before leaving at 15:35pm. A short while later, at 16:15pm, a call was made to emergency services reporting both of the Skripals were unconscious on a public bench in the centre of Salisbury. A passing doctor and nurse had attempted to render aid while waiting for emergency services to respond. A witness reported seeing Yulia with her eyes wide open, foaming at the mouth, and her skin looked very white.

By 17:10pm both victims had been transported to Salisbury District Hospital. They were taken separately, one by air ambulance and the other by an ambulance. It was quickly identified that they had been poisoned with a nerve agent, and the police declared it a major incident due to the multiple agencies that were involved.

Health authorities checked 21 members of the public and emergency services who had come into contact with the Skripals to identify any possible symptoms. Two police officers suffered from wheezing and itchy eyes, and were treated for minor symptoms. Another police officer, Detective Sergeant Nick Bailey, who had gone to Skripal's house to look for evidence, was exposed to the agent and was in a serious condition.

Detective Sergeant Nick Bailey was discharged from hospital on March 22. He made the statement that his normal life would probably never be the same, and he was very thankful to the staff at the hospital for the treatment he had received. At that time the Skripals were still listed as critically ill.

By March 29, Yulia's condition had started to improve and she was no longer classified as critical. It took her father longer to start to recover, and he was finally removed from the critical list on April 5. Yulia was discharged on April 9 and taken to a safe and secure location. Her father was discharged on May 18.

On May 23, Yulia produced a handwritten letter to the media and made a statement via video stating that she was lucky to be alive, and that she was grateful to the staff at the hospital. Her medical treatment was described by her as slow, heavy and extremely painful. She also had a scar on her neck, most likely from a tracheotomy performed to help her breathe. Yulia also thanked the Russian embassy in her message for offering assistance but stated that she and her father were 'not ready to take it'.

International Investigation

Under the National Counter Terrorism Policing Network, it was agreed that the Counter Terrorism Command which was based within the Metropolitan Police would control the investigation. An appeal was made for witnesses to come forward by Mark Rowley, Assistant Commissioner, who is the head of Counter Terrorism Policing.

The nerve agent used in the attack was examined at the Defence Science and Technology Laboratory. It tested positive for a 'very rare' nerve agent. Experts from the military in chemical warfare defence and decontamination were deployed on March 9. The number of personnel involved were 180, and 18 vehicles were used in the deployment. They assisted the Metropolitan Police in removing objects from the Skripal home and vehicles to test for any more traces of the deadly nerve agent.

On March 11, the government advised those who had been present at the Zizzi Restaurant or The Mill pub on the same day as the Skripals should wash their possessions in case of contamination. At the same time, the advised the general public that the risk of being poisoned was low.

By March 12, the nerve agent had been identified as belonging to the Novichok family. It was understood these nerve agents had been developed by the Soviet Union in the 1980s. The agent was further identified as being A-234, which was a derivative of a previous version known as A-232.

The investigation focused largely on the Skripal home, their car, the bench in the park where they were found, the restaurant they ate at and the pub where they had drinks. The British media speculated that perhaps the nerve agent had been planted in a suitcase carried by Yulia when she left Moscow. The media in the US suggested it had been planted in their car.

Director-General of the Organization for the Prohibition of Chemical Weapons (OPCW) Ahmet Üzümcü, stated on March 20 that it would take a few more weeks before the analysis of the samples from Skripal could be finalized. The Court of Protection gave permission on March 22 for further blood samples to be taken from the Skripals.

The investigation concluded on March 28 that the Skripals were both poisoned while at Sergei Skripal's home. The highest concentration of the poison was found on his front door handle. The OPCW confirmed on April 12 that the nerve agent was what the UK had identified it as and that it was of a high purity.

A letter that had been declassified from Sir Mark Sedwill, the UK's national security adviser to Jens Stoltenbbergg, the Nato Secretary General, stated that military intelligence in Russia had hacked the email account belonging to Yulia Skripal from as early as 2013, and they had tested a variety of methods for the delivery of nerve agents, including testing it on door handles.

The nerve agent was confirmed by the Department for Environment as being in liquid form when it was delivered. They identified eight sites that required decontamination, at a cost of millions of pounds. This particular nerve agent does not disappear or evaporate, even over time, so intense cleaning with chemicals was needed to remove it. The belief was that the

Skripals survival was probably due to the weather. The high humidity and heavy fog at the time provided the moisture needed to weaken the potency of the poison.

Suspects Identified

It was reported on April 22 that a suspect had been identified. The suspect is a former FSB officer, possibly a captain, who used a variety of code names including 'Mihails Savickis' and 'Gordon'. He allegedly led a team of Russian assassins, with six members, who organized the attack on the Skripals. However, the UK national security adviser claimed on May 1 that the individual or individuals involved in the attack had not been identified.

According to the Press Association on July 19, police thought they had managed to identify several suspects, all Russians, through CCTV and border entry data. On August 6, it was reported that an extradition request to Moscow for two suspects was about to be submitted.

The Crown Prosecution Service announced on September 5 that two alleged Russian agents would be charged in absentia. It was believed the two men had traveled to the UK under aliases, even though they had legitimate Russian passports. Their names are Alexander Petrov and Ruslan Boshirov. There was enough evidence to lay charges against the two individuals but the CPS was not going to apply for extradition.

The British Prime Minister Theresa May announced that the two suspects were identified as officers in the GU Intelligence Service, formerly known as the GRU, and the attempted assassination of Skripal was most likely approved by a senior level of the Russian government.

The true identity of the man initially named as Ruslan Boshirov was finally uncovered on September 26. Colonel Anatoliy Vladimirovich Chepiga was Boshirov's real identity, and the second man, Alexander Petrov held a more junior rank in the GRU.

Russian Diplomats Expelled

A number of countries and organizations had expelled more than 150 Russian diplomats by the end of March, as a means to show their solidarity with the UK. The BBC stated it was 'the largest collective expulsion of Russian intelligence officers in history'. The UK expelled 23 diplomats from Russia on March 14, and three days later, Russia expelled the same number of British diplomats, and ordered the UK consulate in St Petersburg to be closed. The British Council in Russia was also closed.

Following the UK's lead, nine other countries expelled Russian diplomats on March 25, followed by six EU nations, Canada, USA, Albania and Ukraine. Over the ensuing days, more countries expelled their Russian diplomats. Russia then expelled the same number of diplomats of most of the countries that had expelled the Russian diplomats. Hungary, Georgia, Belgium and Montenegro expelled at least one or more Russian Diplomats.

Not all countries expelled their Russian diplomats however. Bulgaria, Malta, Luxembourg, Slovakia, Slovenia and Portugal as well as the European Union itself instead recalled their ambassadors from Russia. Iceland decided to diplomatically boycott the FIFA World Cup that was being held in Russia.

What started as the poisoning of two people became a major international outcry, with far-reaching effects, particularly for Russia and the UK. The solidarity shown by other nations in supporting the UK and decrying Russia for the attempted assassination displayed that as a world that kind of behavior was not going to be tolerated.

Investigations are still ongoing, and the Skripals are still recovering from the physical and mental toll the poisoning took on their bodies and minds.

Prison Break Attempt Results in Multiple Deaths

An attempted prison break at a prison in Venezuela erupted into violence and riots, resulting in the deaths of 68 people. Aside from the trauma experienced by those present, and the grief the families of the victims were left to bear, this incident drew attention to the appalling conditions of overcrowding in the prison, the corruption that was prevalent and the damaged infrastructure.

The Riot and Fires

On March 28, a riot broke out when an officer was shot in the leg by a detainee at the state police headquarters in Valencia, in Carabobo state. It was an attempt by the detainee to escape, and no details were provided as to how the detainee came to be armed with a weapon.

The police headquarters has a jail attached to it which was designed to hold 60 inmates, but at the time of the riot and ensuing fires, there were around 200 inmates housed there. During the riot, prisoners set their mattresses on fire in an attempt to escape. Later other reports would claim the fire broke out during a party the inmates were having. How and why they would be having a party inside the jail remains a mystery.

The fire spread quickly, and rescuers were forced to break a hole through the wall to try and free some of the prisoners. Tragically, 68 people perished, along with two women who had been spending the night at the police station. It was one of the worst jail disasters in history.

As people were rescued, photos began to be shared of victims being carried out on stretchers. Their arms and legs appeared to be frozen in strange positions, and on most their skin was peeling off.

Families Desperate for Answers

A large crowd of relatives gathered outside the police station desperately trying to find out if their loved one had died in the tragic fire. The authorities were very slow in releasing any information regarding who had died, or how they had died. The group became so angry and so large that police used tear gas to try and disperse the gathered relatives and friends. According to police, they were forced to use the tear gas because the group had tried to push their way inside the police station, and during the fracas, one officer was hit by a stone.

Arrests Made

Despite the initial silence from the authorities on what really happened that day, they did eventually take the matter seriously as a crime. During an investigation, five state police officials were arrested for their suspected role in the riot and fire.

Tarek William Saab, chief prosecutor in Venezuela, tweeted that those arrested were believed to be 'responsible for the tragic events that caused the death of 68 citizens'.

Long History of Prison Riots

There have been dozens and dozens of prison riots in the last 100 years, many of which ended with loss of lives. They don't always make major news headlines though, as in some countries, it is almost as though the inmates are not worth worrying about. Here is a list of the most notable prison riots in the last century.

1929

A prison riot occurred at Colorado State Penitentiary (renamed the Colorado Territorial Correctional Facility, Cañon City, Colorado), October 3, 1929 – In addition to the death of eight guards and five prisoners, a majority of the physical plant was destroyed during the riot.

1940s

Alcatraz Federal Penitentiary, Alcatraz Island, California, United States, May 1946 – 5 killed

1950s

Missouri State Penitentiary, United States, 1954 4 inmates killed, 29 injured, 4 guards injured.

Kingston Penitentiary riot, Canada, 1954—two-hour riot broke involving 900 inmates. Breakout attempt was foiled. Several buildings set on fire. $2 million in damages. 160 troops and a squad of police responded.

Montana State Prison Riot, United States, 16 April 1959 – 18 April 1959 – 3 people killed

1960s

Pulau Senang, Singapore, 12 July 1963 – 4 prison officers killed.

1970s

Attica Prison riot, United States, 1971 – 43 killed

Kingston Penitentiary riot, Canada, 1971 – 2 inmates killed

Oklahoma State Penitentiary riot, United States, July 1973 – lasted an entire weekend, 3 inmates killed; 24 buildings were damaged and only 4 buildings were left usable.

Idaho State Penitentiary riots, United States, 1972–1973, 1 inmate killed; many buildings destroyed.

San Quentin 1973 riot, United States, between Black Guerrilla Family and Mexican Mafia

1980s

New Mexico State Penitentiary riot, United States, 1980 – 33 killed, over 100 injured

Dick Conner Correctional Center Riot, United States, August 1983 – one inmate killed, two officers wounded

Spike Island, Republic of Ireland, August 31 – September 1, 1985 – one officer injured. Inmates took control of the island prison for a day and the civilian population was evacuated and most of the buildings burned down.

Oklahoma State Penitentiary "Disturbance", United States, December 1985 – Held a unit for a day.

Indiana Reformatory riot, Pendleton, United States. February 1, 1985. Inmates had stabbed seven correctional officers and held three employees hostage for 17 hours

West Virginia State Penitentiary Riot, United States, January 1–3, 1986

Fremantle prison riot, Western Australia, Australia, 1988

Michoacán, Mexico, July 1988 – 10 killed, 15 injured

Atlanta Prison Riots, United States, November 1987

Davao Penal Colony prison riot, April 2–3, 1989 – 16 hostages taken

Davao Metrodiscom prison riot, August 13–15, 1989 – 21 killed, including 5 civilian hostages

1990s

Strangeways Prison riot, England, April 1990 – 1 inmate killed, 194 injured (147 prison officers, 47 inmates)

Southport Correctional Facility, New York, United States, June 29, 1990 – 27 people injured

1992 Carandiru Massacre, São Paulo, Brazil, October 1992 – 111 inmates killed

1990 & 1994 Carl Robinson Correctional Institution, Enfield, Connecticut, United States, 2 dead, 36 injured in second

Southern Ohio Correctional Facility, United States, Easter Sunday, 1993 – 9 inmates killed, 1 corrections officer

Woodford Correctional Centre, Queensland, Australia 1998

2000s

Iquique, Chile, May 2001 – at least 28 inmates killed, up to 150 injured

El Porvenir prison, Honduras, April 2003 – 86 inmates killed

Camp Bucca, Iraq, January 2005 – 4 inmates killed, 6 injured

Pavon/Granja Pino Canada/El Hoyon prisons, Guatemala, August 2005 – 35 killed

San Quentin State Prison, California, United States, January 2006 – at least 25 injured

Kabul, Afghanistan, February 2006

Camp Bagong Diwa, Taguig siege in 2006 – almost all Abu Sayyaf members who rose up, including several leaders were killed along with several policemen and jail guards

North County Correctional Facility, Castaic, California, United States, February 2006 – 1 inmate killed, over 100 injured

New Castle Correctional Facility Riot, New Castle, Indiana, United States, 24 April 2007

Santa Ana prison in San Cristobal, Tachira Venezuela, December 2007 – 30 inmates killed

Ciudad Juárez riots, March 2009 – 20 killed

2009 Northpoint Training Center riot in Danville, Kentucky, United States, August 21, 2009 – 80 inmates involved, 5 buildings burned down.

2010s

El Manzano prison riot following the 2010 Chile earthquake, February 28, 2010

Chiang Mai, Thailand prison riot, April 30, 2010

Igoumenitsa, Greece prison riot, May 1, 2010

Ford Open Prison, West Sussex, United Kingdom, January 1, 2011

2011 Antofagasta riots in Antofagasta, Chile, February 20, 2011

Apodaca prison riot, Mexico, February 19, 2012

Adams County Correctional Facility, Natchez, Mississippi, United States, May 20, 2012

Yare prison riot, Venezuela, August 20, 2012

2013 Uribana prison riot, Barquisimeto, Venezuela, January 25, 2013 – 54 inmates killed, 90 injured

Willacy County Correctional Center, United States, February 20, 2015

Topo Chico prison riot, Mexico, February 10, 2016

Holman Correctional Facility, United States, March 12, 2016

2016 New Bilibid Prison riot, Philippines, September 28, 2016

Agricultural Penitentiary of Monte Cristo riot, Brazil, October 16, 2016

HMP Birmingham, England, December 16, 2016

California Correctional Center, United States, December 20, 2016

January 2017 Brazil prison riots, January 2017. At least 60 people killed at Anisio Jobim penitentiary complex in Amazonas state penitentiary complex Monte Cristo in Roraima state and Natal, Brazil, in the rebellion of Alcaçuz.

Souza-Baranowski Correctional Center, United States, January 9, 2017

James T. Vaughn Correctional Center, United States, February 1, 2017

El Dorado Correctional Facility, United States, June 30, 2017

Rivers Correctional Institution, United States, September 5, 2017

Lee Correctional Institution, United States, April 15, 2018, 7 inmates killed, 17 injured

Terrorist Attacks in Short for March

March 1

Rann, Nigeria: Boko Haram militants killed at least 11 people including three aid workers in an attack on a military barracks in the town of Rann in Borno state. Another three aid workers were wounded and one more kidnapped.

March 2

Ouagadougou, Burkina Faso: 30 people were killed and 85 wounded in terrorist attacks on the French embassy and cultural center in Burkina Faso and the country's army headquarters.

Afgooye District, Somalia: A suicide bomber rammed his explosives-laden minibus into a military camp in Afgooye, a district in Lower Shabelle region, killing at least 5 Somali soldiers and wounding several others. Six other government soldiers died after a remote-controlled landmine targeted a convoy carrying injured soldiers from Afgooye to Mogadishu.

Jowhar District, Somalia: At least three Burundian soldiers of the African Union Mission to Somalia were killed in an Al-Shabaab attack near Jowhar, Somalia. Seven others were injured, four were missing, and one armored vehicle and four trucks were damaged during the attack.

March 5

Beni Territory, Democratic Republic of Congo: Twenty people were killed in several attacks in the province of North Kivu in the Democratic Republic of Congo. More than 15 others were reported missing after the attacks and probably kidnapped by the attackers.

March 7

Jarabulus, Syria: A car bomb attack killed nine people and injured more than 60 others in Jarabulus, Syria.

March 8

Khwaja Ghar District, Afghanistan: At least seventeen security forces, including ten local policemen and seven army soldiers, were killed after the Taliban militants attacked a security post in the Khwaja Ghar district of northern Takhar province. Thirteen others, including nine local police officers, were wounded in the attack.

March 9

Kabul, Afghanistan: A suicide bomber killed 10 people and injured 22 others when he set off explosives in a crowd of Shiite Muslims near a mosque complex in Kabul.

Bala Buluk District, Afghanistan: At least 24 members of the Afghan security forces were killed and several others injured in a Taliban attack in the Balu Buluk district of western Farah province.

March 11

Kirkuk Governorate, Iraq: Islamic State terrorists, who had set up a fake roadblock on a major road, have killed 15 people and injured 5 others in Kirkuk province. In a separate attack, three people were killed while driving a car further north near the city of Daquq. The attackers then burned the car.

March 13

Aden, Yemen: At least 10 people were killed and 30 others injured in a suicide car bombing that hit a supply post belonging to a Yemeni security force backed by the United Arab Emirates in the southern port city of Aden, Yemen.

Sukma district, India: Nine paramilitary troopers of the Indian Central Reserve Police Force were killed and about ten others wounded after Naxalites targeted their vehicle with an improvised explosive device in Sukma district of the Central Indian state of Chhattisgarh.

March 14

Raiwind, Pakistan: At least ten people were killed and 35 others injured in a suicide bombing that targeted a police check post in Raiwind on the outskirts of Lahore, Pakistan.

March 18

Afrin, Syria: A bomb blast in a four-floor building in the city of Afrin in northwestern Syria killed at least 13 people and wounded 25 others.

March 20

Damascus, Syria: At least 44 people, most of them women and children, were killed when terrorists attacked with rockets on a busy market in Damascus. 35 others were wounded in the attack.

March 21

Kabul, Afghanistan: March 2018 Kabul suicide bombing: A suicide bombing near a Shiite shrine in Kabul killed at least 33 people and injured 65 others as Afghans celebrated the Persian New Year.

March 22

Mogadishu, Somalia: At least 18 people were killed and 22 others wounded in a car bomb explosion near a hotel in the Somali capital Mogadishu.

Al Anbar Governorate, Iraq: Seven Iraqi border guards were killed in an ambush by Islamic State extremists near the town of Ar-Rutbah in the western Iraqi province of Anbar. Two drivers were also killed in the attack.

March 23

Lashkargah, Afghanistan: At least 20 people were killed and 55 more injured in a suicide car bomb attack at the Ghazi Muhammad Ayub Khan stadium during a wrestling match in Lashkargah, Afghanistan.

March 27

Beni, Democratic Republic of Congo: At least 10 people are dead and 10 others are missing after militants attacked outlying areas of the eastern city of Beni. A terrorist from the Ugandan Allied Democratic Forces was also killed.

March 28

Hadhramaut Governorate, Yemen: At least 12 Yemeni soldiers were killed after Al-Qaida gunmen ambushed a military convoy in the southeastern province of Hadhramaut.

Chapter 4:
APRIL

Waffle House Shooting in Nashville

A mass shooting was carried out at a Waffle House restaurant on April 22, in Nashville, Tennessee. The shooting resulted in four victims being killed, two injured by gunshots, and two injured by broken glass. The attack only stopped when a customer decided to intervene and wrestled the weapon away.

Gunman Opens Fire

The shooter sat in his truck in the parking lot for a few minutes before he decided to enter the restaurant. He was mostly naked, wearing just a green jacket, and he carried an AR-15-style rifle. As he approached the Waffle House he shot and killed two people who were outside the building.

The gunman entered the restaurant and opened fire indiscriminately, killing a third person. The fourth victim was injured, and later died at the medical center. One of the customers, James Shaw Jr., 29, had been hiding near the bathroom when he suddenly rushed at the gunman, wrestling the rifle away. He suffered a bullet graze wound in the process, as the gunman fled the restaurant on foot.

The gunman went on the run, but was located 34 hours after the shooting on April 23. He was identified as Travis Reinking.

The names of the victims are:

Taurean C. Sanderlin, 29, of Goodlettsville. Sanderlin was an employee of the Waffle House. He was fatally wounded standing outside the restaurant.

Joe R. Perez, 20, of Nashville. Perez, a patron, was fatally wounded standing outside the restaurant.

Akilah DaSilva, 23, of Antioch. DaSilva was wounded at the restaurant and died at Vanderbilt University Medical Center.

DeEbony Groves, 21 of Gallatin. Friends say Groves was a brilliant young woman, a hard worker and a tenacious basketball player.

A Troubled Background

Reinking, originally from Morton in Illinois, had a history of experiencing delusions and displaying erratic conduct. His parents had called police in May 2016, from the parking lot of a drugstore, and on assessment by paramedics, Reinking had delusionally stated that Taylor Swift the music star was stalking him and hacking into his telephone. The report on the incident stated that Reinking was hostile towards the police and he did not recognize their authority.

In 2017, Reinking was living in an apartment above his father's business in Tremont. An employee of the business called police in June 2017 and stated the Reinking had appeared in a pink dress and carrying a rifle when he came downstairs. He swore, then tossed the rifle in the trunk of his vehicle and left the building. On another occasion, Reinking had gone to a public pool in a pink women's housecoat and had exposed himself to the lifeguards on duty.

Reinking was arrested by the Secret Service in July, after he had crossed a barrier at the White House and refused to leave the property. According to Reinking, he was trying to organize a meeting between himself and the president. He claimed he was a sovereign citizen. He was charged with the misdemeanor unlawful entry. As a result, he had to perform 32 hours of community service and was not allowed near the White House.

Following his arrest at the White House, the authorities in Illinois revoked his firearms authorization and they confiscated four of his weapons, including the rifle he would later use at the Waffle House. Reinking's father asked if he could keep the guns instead of them being confiscated and they agreed so long as they were kept securely away from Reinking. It is believed he later gave them back to his son.

In the fall of 2017, Reinking moved to Nashville and was working in construction from January 2018 - April 2018. On April 3, he was fired due to his claims that people were after him, including his fellow co-workers.

Just four days before Reinking went on the shooting rampage, he had stolen a BMW X6 vehicle from a dealership in Brentwood. The car was tracked using GPS and the key fob was found in Reinking's apartment.

Charges Laid

After Reinking was arrested for the shooting spree, he was charged with four counts of criminal homicide, along with four counts of attempted homicide and a count of having a firearm while committing a dangerous felony. A psychiatric assessment was ordered, and the forensic psychologists who examined him determined he was suffering from severe schizophrenia.

In August, with the assistance of the psychiatric report, a judge determined Reinking was incompetent to stand trial. He was subsequently committed to a mental hospital. The hope is that with treatment he will become fit and stable enough to stand trial. In the meantime, Reinking is deemed to pose a substantial threat to the general public and to himself.

YouTube HQ Shooting

A shooting occurred at the YouTube headquarters in San Bruno, California on April 3. The attack left three people wounded, and ended with the suicide of the shooter. This case was unusual because the shooter was a woman, and that is a rare occurrence with the majority of mass shootings being perpetrated by males.

YouTube under Attack

The San Bruno police were first made aware of an active shooting at the YouTube headquarters at 12:46pm. The suspect, Nasim Najafi Aghdam, 38, had entered the building through an external parking garage. She moved towards an outdoor patio then opened fire. She was using a Smith & Wesson 9 mm caliber semi-automatic pistol, which had a 10 round capacity.

Initial reports to the police claimed that it was a domestic dispute, and that Aghdam had shot her boyfriend before killing herself. When police arrived on the scene, they warned the public to steer clear of the area. Many employees of YouTube shared live updates on their Snapchat and Twitter accounts. Once it was established that the shooting had stopped and the gunwoman was dead, the wounded were transported to the San Francisco General Hospital and the Stanford University Medical Center. The victims included a 36-year-old man, a 27-year-old woman and a 32-year-old woman. A fourth person suffered an ankle injury as the fled the scene.

Who Was Nasim Najafi Aghdam?

Aghdam was born in Urmia, Iran, and immigrated with her family to the United States in 1996. A registered member of the Baha'i Faith, Aghdam agreed with how her religion was aligned with veganism, but she didn't agree with the Middle Eastern cultural practices, and the Baha'is and Muslims who ate meat. A frequent poster on Facebook, Telegram, Instagram and YouTube, a lot of her content went viral on Iranian social media, and this drew a lot of attention.

On January 16, 2018, Aghdam legally bought the pistol she would later use to shoot up the YouTube headquarters. Her family reported her missing to the police on March 31, and her father had stated she hated YouTube and they were worried she was heading to their office.

Police found Aghdam the day before the shooting, asleep in her car in a parking lot at Walmart in Mountain View. At that time, the police officers who came into contact with her did not consider her to be a threat to anyone or to herself. It is unknown if they knew about her father's concerns or not. That same day, Aghdam went to a shooting range to practice.

The Big Question is Why

Although she cannot be asked why she carried out the shooting that day, police do believe her issues with YouTube were the motivation. She disagreed with the policies and procedures YouTube had on censorship with the channels that Aghdam ran. On her website she had complained about the company, stating "YouTube filtered my channels to keep them from getting views!" She also claimed that YouTube had demonetized many of her videos she posted.

It seems most likely that this was the motive behind her actions, and it is clear that her thoughts were not those of a normal person. It is just fortunate that she didn't kill more people that day.

Of note, at her autopsy, there were no drugs or alcohol in her body, and she died from a self-inflicted gunshot wound to the chest.

The Toronto Van Attack

On an April day in Toronto, Canada, pedestrians were innocently going about their business in the North York City Centre business district when a madman behind the wheel of a van ploughed into them. The attack left 10 people dead and 16 injured, and is the deadliest vehicle-ramming attack in the history of Canada.

Pedestrians under Attack

The first call received by emergency responders came through at 1:25pm on April 23. A white Chevrolet Express van was driving along Finch Avenue, and then ran a red light before driving along the sidewalk of Yonge Street. Multiple pedestrians were struck and the van continued along the sidewalk for several blocks, continuously hitting people as he drove along. The van was shown on security camera video reaching Tolman Street, one block south of Finch, at 1:24pm.

According to a witness, the driver looked directly at the victims as he struck them. It seemed as though he was trying to kill as many people as possible. The van left the sidewalk for a short distance then mounted the sidewalk again in front of Mel Lastman Square. Pedestrians were still being struck, and the van had now travelled 0.87miles south of Finch Avenue.

Immediately on receiving the reports, paramedics were sent to the scene, and nearby Sunnybrook Health Sciences Centre was set up as an emergency center. When paramedics arrived, they found nine people dead at the scene, and 15 injured. By that evening, a tenth person had died from their injuries. Ten victims had been treated at Sunnybrook, and two were pronounced dead on arrival. Five of the victims were critical, two were in a serious condition, and another was in a fair condition.

Meanwhile, there was one police officer in traffic control capacity. This was Constable Ken Lam, and he intercepted the killer van while it was stopped on Poyntz Avenue, west of Yonge Street, and 1.4 miles from where the whole attack had begun. The driver of the van, Alek Minassian was standing near the open driver door when Lam pulled up and confronted him.

During the interaction between Lam and Minassian, the suspect kept pulling his hand from his back pocket, pointing a dark object towards Lam. It seemed Minassian was trying to get Lam to shoot him, and this was confirmed when Minassian kept demanding to be shot in the head. Lam ordered him on to the ground, which Minassian disobeyed. Lam turned his siren off in the cruiser, and as the two men moved towards each other, Lam was able to ascertain that the dark object in Minassian's hand was not a gun. Lam put his pistol in its holster, and took his baton out instead. Minassian dropped the object and lay down, surrendering to Lam. His arrest occurred at 1:32pm.

The names of the victims killed in the attack were as follows:

Beutis Renuka Amarasinghe, 45, who worked as a nutritionist

Andrea Bradden, 33, an account executive

Geraldine Brady, 83, an Avon saleswoman

So He Chung, 22, a student at university

Anne Marie D'Amico, 30, a financial analyst

Mary Elizabeth Forsyth, 94, retiree

Chul Min "Eddie" Kang, 45, a chef

Ji Hun Kim, 22, a student from South Korea

Munir Najjar, 85, Jordanian retiree who was visiting family

Dorothy Sewell, 80, retiree

As well as murder charges for those he killed, Minassian was also charged with the attempted murders of the following survivors:

Robert Anderson

Amir Kiumarsi

Aleksandra Kozhevinikova

Mavis Justino

Morgan McDougall

Jun Seok Park

Samantha Peart

So Ra

Catherine Riddell

Samantha Samson

Beverly Smith

Amaresh Tesfamariam

Yunsheng Tian

There were two other survivors that left the scene before they could be identified, but their identities were later determined from dashcam footage in the police car. It is expected Minassian will receive another 3 attempted murder charges.

The Man Behind the Wheel

Alek Minassian, 25, had no prior criminal record, and he was a student at Seneca College in North York. He had previously been in a special education class for students with Autism Spectrum Disorder while at elementary and secondary school, but had eventually become a software and mobile app developer. He was described by classmates as not being very social, but was harmless.

Minassian enlisted with the Canadian Armed Forces in late 2017, but requested release after only 16 days of training. According to a senior official, Minassian couldn't adapt to military life, particularly with the uniform dress, group interactions in a military setting and deportment. However, there were no indications that he would eventually drive a van into multiple people.

After the attack, a post on Facebook attributed to Minassian was circulated widely online. The post indicated he could have identified as being an incel, which is an involuntary celibate. The subculture of incel is mainly made up of males, and is limited to online communities. The post, which had appeared shortly before the attack read as follows:

Private (Recruit) Minassian Infantry 00010, wishing to speak to Sgt 4chan please. C23249161. The Incel Rebellion has already begun! We will overthrow all the Chads and Stacys! All hail the Supreme Gentleman Elliot Rodger!

Incel Rebellion is used interchangeably sometimes with the term 'Beta Uprising', or 'Beta Male Uprising'. This refers to a violent response to sexlessness, viewed as sexual deprivation by the incels. Elliot Rodger, mentioned in the post, was a mass murderer who orchestrated the Isla Vista killings in California in 2014. Rodger had planned to target attractive women as well as men who were sexually successful.

Facebook eventually verified that the account the post had appeared on was in fact Minassian's. According to the Department of National Defence, the number stated, C23249161 was the military identification number assigned to Minassian during his short period in the military.

First Degree Murder Charges

Minassian appeared in court without legal representation on April 24. He received charges of 10 counts of first degree murder and 13 counts of attempted murder. Minassian was ordered to have no contact with any of the alleged attempted murder victims. On May 10, he received three more charges of attempted murder, bringing the total to 16 counts. He is awaiting trial.

The Hart Family Tragedy

What started as a tragic family car accident in March 2018 was later determined to be an intentional act by the driver of the vehicle. At least six of the family members were killed after the vehicle they were in plunged over a California cliff. This case falls under April because of the discovery of another body.

Over a Cliff

Jennifer and Sarah Hart, both 38, were a married lesbian couple who lived in Washington. They had adopted six children, and to all intents and purposes were considered to be a happy family on the outside. But things weren't so good at all, and this speculation is what has led to the theory that the crash wasn't an accident at all.

After the car plummeted over the 100 foot cliff on the Mendocino coast, County Sheriff Tom Allman said there was every indication that all of the children had been in the vehicle. The bodies of Jennifer and Sarah, son Markis, 19, Jeremiah, 14, Abigail, 14, were recovered from the scene after the crash. The body of Sierra, 12, was later found on April 8.

The bodies of two of the children, Devonte, 15, and Hannah, 15, have not been located.

The Investigation

When the speedometer of the vehicle was examined, it showed that the vehicle had been traveling at a speed of 90 mph when it crashed over the cliff. There were no skid marks, and the evidence showed that the car had stopped before the cliff, and then sped up towards the edge. Nobody in the vehicle was wearing a seatbelt.

The home of the Hart family was searched thoroughly, and officers removed computers, credit card statements and bank records from the house. Although no suicide note has been found, the data from the vehicle itself indicated it was an intentional act.

Toxicology tests on the family members recovered from the crash showed that Jennifer, who was the driver of the vehicle, had an alcohol level of .102. Sarah, her wife, along with two of the children had significant levels of a chemical that is found in Benadryl cough medicine which can make the consumer very sleepy.

Troubled Family

There had been indications recently before the tragedy that all was not well within the family. Their neighbors, Bruce and Donna Dekalb, had called child protective services following a visit from one of the children, Devonte. He had knocked on their door and asked for food because he was being starved to death. One of the other children, Hannah, had also come to the neighbors and asked them not to send her back to the family.

An investigation was launched by the child protective services on the same day the Dekalbs had called them, March 23. Three attempts were made to contact the family with no success. The family had already crossed paths with legal services after Sarah Hart was charged and convicted of domestic assault in 2011. She had left bruises on the stomach and back of her 6-year-old daughter. She was given a three-month suspended jail sentence and a year of probation.

Final Note

It seems that for some reason or another, Jennifer decided that day to end the lives of her entire family. With some of the bodies showing evidence of drugs in their systems, perhaps Jennifer drugged them so they wouldn't be aware of what was going on. It seems strange that her wife Sarah didn't put up some kind of fight.

The motive remains unclear, but it is easy to speculate that the couple was struggling to raise their adopted children. Maybe they thought it would be easier than it really was to take on all these children. Six kids are a handful, and with most of them being teenagers, they would need more food and probably other things that younger children wouldn't require.

Perhaps Jennifer killed everyone because she was worried that the child protection services would find them negligent, and she didn't want to go to prison. The inability to care for the children appropriately may have just been too much of a failure for her to bear. After all, people that adopt children do it because they want to care for someone.

Monster in Munster

Another case where a van was used as a battering ram against pedestrians occurred in Munster, Germany on April 7. Initially there were two persons killed and 20 injured. One of the injured passed away four months later on July 29, bringing the number killed to three.

Camper Van Attack

While people were seated outside a restaurant in a square in Munster on April 7, a man drove a camper van into the restaurant and café terraces, knocking down innocent people. When police approached the van after it had come to a stop, they discovered the suspect had shot himself and he was dead. Inside the van they found a booby trap device with a wire connected to a pistol.

The Perpetrator

The driver of the deadly van was identified as Jens Alexander Rüther, a German national. He had suffered from a psychiatric illness in the past. Once described as a wealthy furniture designer who owned four homes, he was later to become a small time criminal, stealing car radios and cell phones. This was purely to fund his drug habit. Although it was believed he had been in touch with far-right groups, he was not an extremist. He had stated before that he wanted to die by suicide in a 'spectacular way'. There had been relationship troubles leading up to the attack as well, and the final determination was that the attack was to do with Rüther's life and his feelings of guilt.

Suicide Note Left Behind

Rüther, 48, had left a lengthy suicide note behind, some of which was subsequently published in the German press. The note seemed to confirm that he was suffering from psychological problems and there was no indication that he was politically motivated to perform the attack.

In the note he said he had been conspired against his whole life, including by his parents and doctors who had once operated on his back following an injury, leaving him with constant pain. He claimed he had wanted to die since he was as young as 7 years old. He blamed his parents for the emotional outbursts he suffered from as a young child, and he felt his parents had mistreated him. Rüther believed that this lead to him being impotent, and as a result, he was terrified that people would think he was homosexual.

Although the letter provided hints that he was considering committing suicide, there was nothing to suggest he was planning the van attack or any other sort of mass attack.

<u>Lee Correctional Institute Riot</u>

Riots are not unheard of in the prison system, but occasionally they become so severely violent that they result in deaths. This was the case at the Lee Correctional Institute in Bishopville, SC, in April, which left seven inmates dead and 17 more requiring medical treatment.

Rioting Among Inmates

At 7:15pm on April 15, fighting began between inmates at the Lee Correctional Institute. The fighting spread to three housing units with multiple 'inmate on inmate' fights occurring. Shortly before midnight, the SLED (South Carolina Law Enforcement) agents were joined by police services from the corrections department, in the hope of regaining control.

It wasn't until 2:55am the next morning that the institution was finally secured and order had been regained. Because of the number of injuries and fatalities, fire crews assisted by the Florence County EMS, the Kershaw County EMS, the Darlington County EMS, the Lexington County EMS and Hartsville Rescue to assist with the mass casualties. A private service called Med One also assisted.

All of the corrections staff and law enforcement officers who responded on the night came through unscathed.

The Victims

Those inmates who were killed during the riot were Raymond Angelo Scott, Michael Milledge, Damonte Marquez Rivera, Eddie Casey Jay Gaskins, Joshua Svwin Jenkins, Corey Scott, and Cornelius Quantral McClary.

Raymind Angelo Scott was in prison on convictions for assault and battery and weapons. He had been housed at Lee Correctional Institute since October 2017.

Michael Milledge had been convicted of assault and battery, drug and gun offences. He had been at Lee since November 2017.

Damonte Marquez Rivera had been convicted of murder, armed robbery, kidnapping and burglary. He had been at Lee since November 2017.

Eddie Casey Jay Gaskins was transferred to Lee just three days before the riot took place. He had been convicted on domestic violence.

Joshua Svwin Jenkins had been convicted of attempted murder, voluntary manslaughter and burglary. He had been at Lee since January 2016.

Corey Scott was imprisoned for armed robbery, kidnapping, assault and battery and carjacking. He had been transferred to Lee in November 2017.

Cornelius Quantral McClary had been at Lee since October 2017. He had been convicted of assault and battery, weapons and burglary.

Autopsies on those killed had shown the same cause of death for each inmate, which was exsanguination. In simple terms, exsanguination means severe blood loss. The inmates had received multiple sharp force injuries due to stabbing wounds and major lacerations.

Response by Authorities

According to Bryan Stirling, Director of the South Carolina Department of Corrections, the riot was the product of fighting between inmates over territory and contraband, particularly cell phones. Stirling said the officers had acted how they were trained to, despite being outnumbered by inmates and the need to be extremely cautious in such a violent situation.

Governor Henry McMaster stated that the inmates are violent people, and when they are sent to prison, that violent attitude comes with them. The governor said that until the law is changed to allow blocked cell phone accessibility, they would continue to fight over the sought-after contraband.

Golden State Killer Finally Identified

For more than 40 years, the identity of the Golden State Killer had remained a mystery. It was known that he was a serial killer, rapist and burglar who was responsible for at least 13 murders, over 50 rapes and more than 100 burglaries in California between 1974 and 1986.

A Man of Many Names

In Sacramento, the killer was labelled the East Area Rapist, and his modus operandi had linked him to further attacks in Contra Costa County, Modesto and Stockton. In southern California he had been given the moniker the Original Night Stalker. The girls and women he raped ranged from age 13 to 41. It is believed he started out as a burglar before moving on to the violent crimes, as links have been made with multiple cases and evidence in a variety of areas.

It is believed the killer had moved to Sacramento in mid-1976, at which point his crimes moved from burglary to violence. The crimes were originally centered on areas of Citrus Heights, Carmichael and Rancho Cordova. In the early years, his MO was to stalk the middle-class neighborhoods at night to seek out women. He looked for those that were alone, in one-story homes for easier access, and preferred those next to a creek, trail, school or open space, so he could make a rapid escape.

Many of the victims had either heard or seen a prowler on their property prior to the attacks, and some had been subjected to break-ins. The police believed he was conducting in-depth reconnaissance on several houses in a neighborhood before choosing his next one for attack. He would prowl the yards and look in the windows for several days before he would attack.

On some occasions, it was suspected that the killer broke into the homes of his selected future targets so he could make sure windows were unlocked and guns were unloaded. He would also leave ligatures in hiding places so they were on hand when he needed them. He would phone his target sometimes for months before hand and would claim he had the wrong number or would simply hang up. This was to learn more about the intended victim's lifestyle and routine.

Eventually he moved on to attacking couples instead of lone women. He would break in to the home through a sliding glass door or a window, and wake the couple up with a flashlight while threatening them with a gun. He would then tie the victims up with the ligatures, blindfold them and use towels to gag them. Normally he would make the woman tie up the man before tying her up. He would then separate the couple, and would put breakable dishes on the man's back so he could hear if the man moved.

He would then take the woman in to another room and repeatedly rape her, sometimes over a period of several hours. The killer would ransack the home, eat the food and drink any beer he found. Sometimes victims would think he had left, only to be terrorized again when he jumped out of the darkness at them. He would steal personal objects that weren't worth a lot and firearms and any cash that he found in the house.

Quietly he would slip way, so the victims were left uncertain whether he had actually left or not. He would then run through his escape route before using a car or bicycle. He chose pathways that would keep him off the main streets.

The Murders

On the night of February 2, 1978, Brian and Katie Maggiore were walking their dog in the Rancho Cordova area. They were confronted by a man and attempted to flee, but the offender chased them and shot them, killing the couple. Because it was near the area where the East Area Rapist had been operating, police suspected that the cases were connected.

A Goleta couple was confronted by an intruder in their home on the night of October 1, 1979. They heard the man say "I'll kill 'em" which alarmed them enough to make them try and escape. The woman screamed, and realizing the couple was alerted to his presence, the intruder took off into the night on a bicycle. A neighbor, who happened to be an FBI agent, responded to the screaming and chased the intruder, who abandoned a knife and the bicycle before fleeing through the backyards of homes. The shoeprints he left behind and the twine he had left at the house linked the perpetrator to the Offerman-Manning murders.

December 30, 1979, Robert Offerman, 44, and Debra Alexandra Manning, 35, were shot to death at Offerman's condominium on Avenida Pequena in Goleta. The bindings used on Offerman were untied which suggested he had attempted to lunge at his attacker. The neighbors had heard gunshots but didn't think anything of it, so they didn't report it. When police searched the home, they found the paw prints of a large dog, which they believed had been brought to the scene by the offender. A bicycle had also been stolen from a vacant residence next door, and it was found away from the scene.

The next couple killed was Lyman (43) and Charlene (33) Smith, who were found on March 13, 1980, in their home. Charlene had been raped before she was killed. Investigators found a log of wood in the house that had been used to bludgeon the couple to death. The log had apparently come from their own woodpile beside the house. Both had been bound at the wrists and ankles with a drapery cord. The knot used, the Chinese knot, was also used in one of the cases of the East Area Rapist.

On August 19, 1980, Keith Eli Harrington, 24, and Patrice Briscoe Harrington, 27, were found in their home after being bludgeoned to death. Their home was in a gated community, yet the killer was able to gain access. Patrice Harrington had been raped, and there was no evidence that the couple had been bound. No ligatures or weapons were found at the home. At the time of their deaths, the couple had only been married for three months. Keith was a medical student and Patrice was a nurse.

Manuela Witthuhn, 28, was raped and killed at her home in Irvine on February 6, 1981. There were signs on her body that she had been bound, but the ligatures had been removed and taken away. She had been bludgeoned to death. Her husband was in hospital at the time of the murder, so Manuela was at home alone at the time of the vicious attack. A television belonging to the couple was found in the backyard, and police suspected the killer had tried to make it look like a robbery gone wrong.

Gregory Sanchez, 27, and Cheri Domingo, 35, were killed in Domingo's home on July 27, 1981. The killer had gained access to the house by entering a small window in the bathroom. Sanchez had not been bound, and had been shot in the cheek before being bludgeoned to death with a garden implement. His head was covered with clothing that had been pulled out of the closet. Domingo was raped before she was bludgeoned and bruising on her ankles and wrists showed she had been tied up, despite no ligatures being found at the scene.

On May 4, 1986, Janelle Lisa Cruz, 18, was found in her Irvine home after she had been raped and bludgeoned to death. At the time of the attack, her family was away on vacation. It was believed she was killed with a pipe wrench that had belonged to her stepfather, that was missing after the murder.

Identifying the Killer

The Golden State Killer was eventually identified through DNA. The DNA evidence had linked him to eight murders, and two others were linked by his modus operandi. During the investigation of the rapes and murders, many suspects were eventually eliminated through the DNA evidence, an alibi, or for other reasons. In 2001 it was established through DNA that the East Area Rapist and the Original Night Stalker were the same man.

A news conference was held in 2016 to announce that authorities were renewing their efforts in solving the cases. A reward was offered for information leading to the arrest of a suspect. The Golden State Killer case was a contributing factor in the development of a DNA database in California, where DNA is collected from all accused and convicted felons.

The name the Golden State Killer was penned by crime writer Michelle McNamara to heighten the public's awareness that this killer remained unidentified and uncaught and he had operated throughout California.

On April 24, 2018, authorities had finally identified their man and charged him. Joseph James DeAngelo, now 72, was a Navy veteran and former police officer. He was found to be a DNA match to all the samples pertaining to the Golden State Killer case. He was charged with eight counts of first degree murder. Because of the statute of limitations in California for rape cases occurring prior to 2017, he cannot be charged with any of the rapes. He was however charged with 13 counts of kidnapping and abduction attempts. The Santa Barbara County District Attorney's office charged DeAngelo with four more counts of first degree murder on May 10.

How the Match was Made

Four months before his arrest, the efforts to identify DeAngelo increased. DNA profile from a rape kit was uploaded to a website called GEDmatch. The website then identified up to 20 distant relatives of the killer. Five investigators worked with a genealogist, Barbara Rae-Venter, who helped to construct a large family tree. Through this, they identified two suspects, one of whom was subsequently ruled out, which only left DeAngelo as the prime suspect.

Officers managed to carefully collect a DNA sample from De Angelo from his car's door handle on April 18, without his knowledge. They then collected a tissue from a garbage can DeAngelo had left on the curb for collection. When the samples were analyzed, they were a match.

DeAngelo's Background

Born in 1945, in New York, DeAngelo had two sisters and one brother. When he was around the age of 10, he witnessed his sister Connie being raped. He went through school and graduated in June 1964, at which time he enlisted with the US Navy the same year. He served during the Vietnam War as a damage control man, on the cruiser USS Canberra.

After he left the Navy, DeAngelo attended college and graduated in 1970 with an associate degree in police science. He had become engaged to his girlfriend Bonnie Colwell, but they never married. He returned to university in 1971 and gained a bachelor's degree in criminal justice. He then undertook post-graduate work before doing police training at the College of the Sequoias. He then completed a 32 week internship at the Roseville Police Department.

DeAngelo served as a police officer in Exeter from May 1973 until August 1976. He was married in 1973 to Sharon Marie Huddle. The marriage produced three girls, and the union ended in 1991.

DeAngelo remained with the police force until 1979, when he was caught and convicted of shoplifting, which ended his career. He received six months' probation for the crime. Little is known about DeAngelo until 1990, when he began working as a truck mechanic. He continued this work until he retired in 2017. At the time of his arrest, he was living with his daughter and granddaughter.

Legal Proceedings

DeAngelo was charged with 13 counts of murder and 13 counts of kidnapping. He returned to court on August 13, following which it was announced that he will also be charged for the murder of Claude Snelling in 1975.

In charge of prosecuting the case are a number of district attorneys from Contra Costa County, Orange County, Sacramento County, Santa Barbara County, Tulare County, Ventura County, and the Supervisor of the 5th District. These all represent the areas in which DeAngelo committed his crimes.

On August 23, he was arraigned in Sacramento, and several of the DAs were present in the courtroom.

Terrorist Attacks in Short for April

April 1

Bulo Marer, Somalia: Al-Shabaab terrorists attacked an African Union military camp in the Bulo Marer area of Lower Shebelle, where Ugandan peacekeepers are stationed, killing at least 59 people. 14 militants died in the attack.

Jere, Nigeria: Boko Haram fighters attacked a military base and two surrounding villages near the Nigerian city of Maiduguri in the Jere Local Government Area, killing at least 20 people and wounding 84.

Shopian district and Anantnag district, India: In three anti-terrorist operations, three members of the army and 13 terrorists were killed in the districts of Shopian and Anantnag in South Kashmir. Several others were injured in the encounters.

April 6

Mohnyin District, Myanmar: 18 Tatmadaw soldiers were killed and 13 injured when armed rebels attacked a Tatmadaw's Battalion 86 military base in Hpakant Township.

April 7

Al-Bab, Syria: Ten civilians were killed and 20 others injured when a car bomb exploded near a mosque in the city of Al-Bab in northern Syria.

Hajjah, Yemen: 12 Sudanese Armed Forces were killed during an ambush in the northern province of Hajjah before dawn on Friday, according to military sources. This is the worst attack against the Sudanese army in Yemen since troops deployed to war-torn country in 2015.

April 12

Khwaja Umari District, Afghanistan: Fourteen people, including a district governor, were killed in a Taliban attack in the Khwaja Umari district of the southeastern province of Ghazni in Afghanistan. In addition, five people were injured.

Al-Shirqat District, Iraq: 25 people were killed and 18 wounded when explosives exploded at a funeral for Sunni Muslim tribal fighters in the village of Asdira near the northern Iraqi town of Al-Shirqat.

April 14

Sancharak District, Afghanistan: In Sancharak district, in the northern province of Sar-i-Pul, two government checkpoints in the west were attacked by Taliban fighters with night vision devices and sniper rifles, initially killing a security guard. When local pro-government militiamen tried to counter the assault, they fell into a Taliban ambush and 10 more were killed.

North Sinai Governorate, Egypt: Militants wearing explosive belts blew themselves up as they tried to infiltrate a military base in Egypt's central Sinai, killing 30 soldiers and injuring 40 others.

April 16

Nasarawa State, Nigeria: 32 people were killed and another 19 were injured when Fulani herdsmen carried out the attacks simultaneously in Awe, Keana, Obi and Doma Local Government Areas of the state.

April 18

Mayadin District, Syria: Islamic state militants launched an attack in the Mayadin region in the southeast of the Syrian province of Deir ez-Zor and killed 25 Syrian government forces. At least 13 militants were also killed in the attack.

April 21

Guma, Nigeria: 15 people were killed during an attack in the villages of Uzughul, Tse Ginde, in Guma Local Government Area of Benue state. The attackers burnt houses and looted the villages.

April 22

Kabul, Afghanistan: A suicide bomb attack at a voter registration centre in the Afghan capital Kabul killed at least 69 people and injured 120 others. The casualties were all civilians, most of whom had been waiting outside the office to apply for their IDs in order to register to vote in the upcoming elections

Ngala, Nigeria: Boko Haram jihadists shot dead 18 forest workers who had been collecting firewood in Borno State, near the town of Gamboru, on the border with Cameroon. In another incident, a vehicle carrying civilians travelling in a nearby army convoy hit a mine placed by insurgents, killing three people and wounding eleven others near the village of Wumbi.

April 24

Quetta, Pakistan: At least eight policemen were killed and 23 others injured in three suicide bombings targeting security personnel in Quetta, the provincial capital of Baluchistan.

April 25

Almar District, Afghanistan: At least nine Afghan security force members were killed and fifteen others injured in a Taliban attack in the Almar district of the Afghan province of Faryab.

April 26

Ménaka Region, Mali: At least 47 people were killed and two injured in two armed attacks on the settlements of Aklaz and Awakassa in the Ménaka region of Mali.

April 30

Kabul, Afghanistan: 30 April 2018 Kabul suicide bombings: At least 29 people were killed and 50 others injured in two suicide bombings in the Afghan capital Kabul, including several journalists documenting the scene.

Daman District, Afghanistan: At least 11 students were killed and 16 other people, including five Romanian soldiers, were injured in a suicide car bombing in Daman district in the southern province of Kandahar.

Chapter 5:
MAY

Santa Fe High School Shooting

On May 18, ten people were shot to death and thirteen others wounded after a shooting spree at Santa Fe High School in Santa Fe, Texas. This was the second deadliest school shooting in the US for 2018, after the previously mentioned shooting at Stoneman Douglas High School.

Teachers and Students Under Fire

At around 7:40am, shots were fired into an art class at the school. The shooter appeared to target two classrooms that were connected by a ceramics room, and it seemed the shooter had gained access by damaging the window of a door to get in. As the shooter walked into the classroom, he allegedly pointed at someone and said he was going to kill them.

Some of the students were able to barricade themselves in the storage closet of the classroom, but the shooter used a shotgun to shoot through the door. When he left the room, the students thought it was safe to leave the closet, and they tried to barricade the classroom door but were unsuccessful. The shooter pushed the door open, and on seeing a student he knew, he yelled 'surprise' and shot the student in the chest.

The school had police officers stationed on the property, and when the shooting began, those officers engaged with the shooter. This resulted in one officer being shot and wounded. The shooter opened fire into the ceramics room and was then confronted by a school police officer and a Texas State Trooper who tried to get him to surrender peacefully.

Instead he threatened to shoot the officers while he fired rounds. After arguing for a while, he eventually did surrender, partly because he had been wounded during the shooting. The shooting had lasted for nearly 25 minutes, and he told the police he had wanted to kill the classmates he had shot and spare the ones he liked so they could tell his story.

The weapon used by the shooter was a pump-action Remington Model 870 shotgun and a .38-caliber revolver. Both weapons were owned legally by the shooter's father. Authorities also found other weapons on and off campus including a Molotov cocktail.

Those Who Were Taken

Eight students and two teachers were killed in the shooting spree, and they were as follows:

Jared Conrad Black, 17

Shana Fisher, 16

Christian Riley Garcia, 15

Aaron Kyle McLeod, 15

Glenda Ann Perkins, 64 (teacher)

Angelique Ramirez, 15

Sabika Sheikh, 17 - an exchange student from Pakistan

Christopher Stone, 17

Cynthia Tisdale, 63 (teacher)

Kimberly Vaughan, 14

Suspect Identified

Following his surrender, the suspect was identified as Dimitrios Pagourtzis, 17, who was a student at the school at the time of the shooting. One witness claimed Pagourtzis had been the victim of bullying from both students and coaches at the school. However, the school denied the bullying by any of their faculty. A teacher described him as quiet, but not in a weird way, and that she had never seen him write or draw anything alarming or unusual. Pagourtzis was on the honor roll and was a member of the school football team.

When police looked at his journals he had kept on his cell phone and computer, they discovered he had clearly wanted to commit the shooting, and his original plan was to commit suicide afterwards. He had planned on doing this for quite some time.

The day before the shooting, classmates didn't notice anything different about Pagourtzis and that he seemed normal, friendly and funny. He had quite a strong presence on social media, and newspapers were quick to point out that in one photo, posted on April 30, Pagourtzis was wearing a shirt that had 'Born to Kill' emblazoned on it. There were also photos of him wearing a black duster coat, and the accompanying caption read"

"Hammer and Sickle=Rebellion. Rising Sun=Kamikaze Tactics. Iron Cross=Bravery. Baphomet=Evil. Cthulu=Power."

Family Makes a Statement

The Pagourtzis family released a statement in which they extended their condolences and prayers to the victims and also thanked the first responders for their assistance at the scene. They were just as shocked as everyone else at what had taken place, and they were cooperating fully with the authorities.

Charges Laid

Pagourtzis was charged with ten counts of capital murder and multiple counts of aggravated assault, and he was ordered to be held without bond. Because of his age, Pagourtzis is not eligible for the death penalty, even though the crime was so severe. In 2005, a Supreme Court ruling declared that imposing the death penalty on minors constituted cruel and unusual punishment.

Other Lawsuits Filed

The parents of Chris Stone filed a lawsuit against the parents of Pagourtzis, stating that the guns had not been properly secured and that the parents were negligent in allowing their son to handle the firearms. It is against the law in Texas to allow a minor access to a gun unless it is under parental supervision or is being used for hunting. If convicted, the penalty can be as much as a year in prison and a fine of $4,000. The parents of another victim, Aaron McLeod, joined in with the lawsuit and made further allegations against the family. These include failure to obtain mental health counselling and support and failure to warn the public of the dangerous propensities of their son.

Aftermath - The School's Response

The school has an active shooter plan and there are two armed police officers on campus. The school district leadership had made plans in the year prior to the incident to arm the staff and teachers through the Texas School Marshal Program. Following the shooting, the president of the school district's Board of Trustees stated that the policies and procedures worked, and that what happened was not a failure of the procedures. If someone was intent on entering the school in such a manner, they would do so regardless.

As a direct result of the shooting, the district planned to renovate the area of the campus where the shooting occurred. This includes sealing off he art rooms and the hallway adjacent to them. A new counselor's office and hallway would be installed. A protection plan for 2018-2019 involved the installation of metal detectors at each entrance, and the police officers would patrol campus with donated AR-15s equipped with rifle optics.

The Scottsdale Spree Shootings

From May 30 to June 4, a shooting spree was undertaken in Scottsdale, Arizona. By the time the shooter killed himself, six people were dead.

The Shootings

Within the first 24 hours, four victims were shot and killed within a 10 mile radius in Scottsdale and Phoenix. The first was Steven Pitt, 59, who was a notable forensic psychiatrist. He was shot on May 31 at 5:20pm as he left his office. He had previously examined the perpetrator during a bitter divorce. Pitt was known for helping police in 2006 identify the Baseline killer, a serial rapist and murderer in Phoenix.

The next two victims were Veleria Sharp, 48 and Laura Anderson, 49, both of whom were paralegals. They were killed on June 1 at 2:15pm, in the offices of the law firm they worked for, Burt, Feldman and Grenier. One of the lawyers at the firm had also been involved in the divorce proceedings of the suspect. By late that night, police knew that the three murders were committed using the same weapon.

Just after midnight, the first hour of June 2, the body of psychologist and counselor Marshall Levine, 72, was found in his office. Unbeknown to the shooter, Levine was subletting the office from the woman who was the real target, as she had provided counseling to the shooter's son during the divorce.

The last two victims, Mary Simmons, 70, and Bryon Thomas, 72, were not discovered until June 4. They were killed inside a home in Fountin Hills.

The Investigation

The suspect, Dwight Jones, was brought to the attention of the police by a retired Phoenix police detective who was now married to Jones' ex-wife. The detective identified the connection to the divorce of his wife to the three crime scenes and notified the violent crime unit on June 2. Police then obtained a DNA sample from a relative of Jones and matched it to a sample taken from a shell casing from one of the scenes.

On the morning of June 4, police cornered Jones at the extended stay hotel where he had been staying. While officers cleared guests out of the surrounding rooms, Jones fired several shots at the officers. As they moved forward, the gunfire ceased, and the officers eventually found that Jones had killed himself by gunshot.

The Perpetrator - Dwight Lamon Jones

Dwight Lamon Jones, 56, had previously been arrested on charges of domestic violence, due to the mistreatment of his child and his wife. For the nine years since, he had been residing at Extended Stay hotels. His former wife claimed that she had been living in fear for all those years, as he was a 'very emotionally disturbed person as the court records will confirm'.

Days before the spree killings, Jones had attempted to make allegations that his ex-wife was the abuser not him, by using his social media. He created nearly 10 hours of content on the page outlining what he said was a conspiracy by his ex-wife, the lawyers, psychiatrists and the judicial system to rig the divorce and enable his ex-wife to gain custody of his son.

Miles Family Murders

The Miles family was well known in Margaret River, Australia, and were well respected and well liked. People were left to wonder what could have gone so horribly wrong that would result in the deaths of three adults and four children in one family.

Community Reeling

WA Police Commissioner Chris Dawson confirmed that after attending a triple-0 call made by a man connected to the property at 5:15 a.m., May 11, they found seven people dead from gunshot wounds, with six of the victims considered to be homicide victims, and the seventh to be a suicide.

In a shed on the property that had been converted into a living area, police located the bodies of one adult and four children, all of whom had died from gunshot wounds. In the main house they found the body of a woman, also shot to death.

The last body found was that of an older man, on the veranda of the main house. He was slumped in a chair, and it was believed that he was the shooter and had died from a self-inflicted gunshot wound.

The victims were Cynda Miles, 58, Katrina Miles, 35, and her children, Taye, 13, Ryan, 12, Ayre, 10, and Kayden, 8. The grandfather, Peter Miles, was the shooter.

What Went Wrong with Grandad?

As news of the tragedy spread around the community, people were left dumb-founded that Peter Miles could have done such a horrendous thing. According to those who knew him, he was a hardworking man with a lovely nature. Others who didn't know him so well thought of him as a quiet man.

For over two decades, Miles had worked at the farm school which was part of the Margaret River Senior High School. He taught children how to drive tractors, take care of livestock and how to work farm equipment safely. The purpose of teaching the students practical knowledge was because it was a rural area, and many would end up working on farms.

On the family farm was a shed that Miles had converted into a living area after his daughter Katrina separated from her partner, Aaron Cockman, the father of her children. Katrina and the four children moved into the converted shed.

All four of the children had been diagnosed with autism spectrum disorder, which made caring for them challenging. They had attended the local school for a while, but because of their difficulties, they ended up being home-schooled by Katrina.

Neighbors who were close to the family were aware that Miles had been dealing with depression for quite some time. Some believed he was on medication for the depression, but that wasn't confirmed. His wife Cynda had told friends that her husband's mental state was deteriorating in the days leading up to the tragedy. A member of the community who had visited the farm that week to return a borrowed tool thought that Miles was 'in a bad way' mentally.

A Grieving Father Speaks

According to the children's father, Aaron Cockman, Miles had been struggling with depression for many years, after one of his sons had committed suicide. Then recently, one of the grandchildren had developed kidney problems and had been seriously ill, and Cockman felt that this may have been the final straw for Miles.

Cockman stated, "Peter has been just trying to hold it together for a long time. I thought, 'There's no way possible he could lose another son, he'll kill himself'. But I thought, 'No, he won't do that either because he's so close to my kids that he would not leave the kids upset for the rest of their lives about it'."

Cockman thought that Miles may have considered that by killing the family it would fix his own pain and mental turmoil. He believed Miles had carefully thought the idea of killing them all, rather than it being a case of him doing it on the spur of the moment.

<u>Family Massacre in Texas</u>

On May 16, a man entered the home of his ex-wife and opened fire on the people in the house, in Ponder, North Texas. The massacre took the lives of three children, an adult male, and finally the shooter himself.

The Day of the Massacre

At around 8:30am, the Volunteer Fire Department received a call to attend a home on Lone Star Park Lane. Just before they arrived, they were notified that there were multiple victims at the address and a request had been made for several ambulances to attend the scene.

Inside the home, the Denton County Sheriff's Department found five deceased victims. The identities of the victims were Seth Richardson, Drake Painter, 4, Caydence Painter, 6, Odin Painter, 8, and Justin Painter, 39. The mother of the children, Amanda Simpson, 29, had also been shot but she was still alive. She was quickly transported to the hospital with a gunshot wound to the shoulder.

Breakdown of a Marriage

Court documents showed that the marriage between Justin Painter and Amanda Simpson had ended last year in divorce. The children had been living with their father for most of the time, and although Painter had tried to get a temporary restraining order against Simpson, the custody was shared between the two parents. According to Simpson, Painter had threatened to shoot himself a year earlier, and she had remained frightened of him ever since. At the time when he was threatening suicide, she took his gun and hid in insider her car so he wouldn't have access to it.

When she left Painter, she gave the gun to his stepfather, who assured Simpson he wouldn't give it to Painter. However, he didn't go through with his assurances and the gun was given back to Painter.

Simpson claims that she had informed the court during the divorce proceedings that Painter was mentally unwell. According to the judge involved in the case, this was never actually mentioned, and there are no records stating Painter had mental health issues or was a danger to anyone.

Who Was Seth Richardson?

Seth Richardson had been involved in a long distance relationship with Simpson following her divorce from Painter. Both Simpson and Painter had met Richardson more than a decade earlier through online video games, but, In December 2017, the relationship between Richardson and Simpson progressed to a romantic relationship.

At that time in December, both Richardson and Simpson were going through divorces, and they both had children, so they bonded over their experiences. Once their divorces were finalized, they celebrated, and looked forward to their future together.

According to Richardson's mother, he had said he was ready to make the move from South Carolina to Texas to be with Simpson and her children. He was full of life and looking forward to creating a family with Simpson.

Tragically, he had only arrived in Texas a few hours before his life was taken by Painter. When police found the bodies, both Richardson and Painter were dead in the bedroom.

Hollywood Indictment - Harvey Weinstein

Weinstein went from being a highly successful film producer to a despised, alleged sexual predator almost overnight. Allegations of sexual abuse started to appear in October 2017, and from there, more and more victims have come forward, leading to Weinstein's indictment in May.

Background of Harvey Weinstein

Born in 1952, Weinstein and his brother Bob later co-founded Miramax, a major entertainment company. They produced multiple successful films, such as, Sex, Lies, and Videotape (1989), The Crying Game (1992), Pulp Fiction (1994), Heavenly Creatures (1994), Flirting with Disaster (1996), and Shakespeare in Love (1998). For Shakespeare in Love, Weinstein won an Academy award. He also won seven Tony Awards for plays and musicals, including The Producers, Billy Elliot the Musical, and August: Osage County.

Weinstein and his brother left Miramax and created a new company called The Weinstein Company, which became a small to major film studio. From 2005 to 2017, the brothers chaired the company together.

When the sexual abuse allegations were brought to light in October 2017, Weinstein was fired from his own company and was expelled from the

Academy of Motion Picture Arts and Sciences, the British Academy of Film and Television Arts, and he resigned from the Directors Guild of America. By the end of October, more than 80 women had made sexual abuse allegations against Weinstein. The situation lead to a social media campaign, '#MeToo', and from that came allegations against other powerful men from all over the world. This was ultimately called 'The Weinstein Effect'.

Allegations against Weinstein

It was reported in October 2017 that over a dozen women had made a variety of sexual allegations against Weinstein. These included rape, sexual assault and sexual harassment. A lot of other women from the film industry also came forward with similar allegations, but Weinstein denied he had ever been involved in nonconsensual sex.

After headlines broke of the allegations, Weinstein's wife Georgina Chapman left him. Political figures that Weinstein had publicly supported denounced him, and the Los Angeles Police, New York Police and London Police, opened investigations into the allegations against Weinstein.

According to The New Yorker, a British-Israeli private intelligence company Black Cube was hired by Weinstein to block the publication of any allegations that had been made against him. Black Cube investigators, using false identities, tracked down actresses who had accused Weinstein, and journalists, and gathered information. The type of information he wanted was the psychological profiles of each person, particularly focusing on any personal history or sexual histories.

The purpose of gathering the information against his accusers and the journalists was so he could find a way to make them look worse than he did. If he had information that was not so golden about them, then he could create the belief in the public that they were not being honest about the allegations. One such target was actress Rose McGowan, who had accused Weinstein of raping her.

The Accusers

A group of victims lead by Asia Argento, the Italian actress, released a list of more than 100 allegations of sexual abuse committed by Weinstein. These alleged instances spanned decades, from 1980 to 2015, and among them were 18 allegations that they had been raped by Weinstein.

The reports explained the modus operandi of Weinstein. He would allegedly invite models or young actresses to his office or hotel room, pretending that they would be discussing their career. He would then demand they massage him or have sex with him. The women were told by Weinstein that if they complied, he would help their careers. He claimed to have had sex with actress Gwyneth Paltrow, and then catapulting her acting career as a reward.

Some of Weinstein's former colleagues made statements to journalists that these sexual activities were actually enabled by associates, employees, lawyers and publicists, and agents. The agents were involved in setting up the meetings between Weinstein and the women. When complaints were made, the publicists and lawyers would suppress them by making threats or payments.

According to reports, Weinstein's brother Bob had also been involved in covering up at least three complaints with settlements, dating back to 1990.An executive at Miramax reported that Weinstein had harassed her after he had praised her work and she had been promoted. The executive and other employees at Miramax discovered that the HR department protected Weinstein much more than the other employees.

Charges and Arrest

On November 3, 2017, the NYPD announced they were preparing a warrant to arrest Weinstein. The investigation was on the alleged rape of Paz de la Huerta, which was still ongoing as of May 2018.

Weinstein was charged by prosecutors in New York on May 25, 2018, with rape, criminal sex act, sexual misconduct and sexual abuse. These charges related two incidents involving two women, and the cases had been under investigation for two months. Weinstein surrendered to police. He was released on $1 million bail the same day, and agreed to surrender his passport. He was also made to wear an ankle monitor which confined him to New York and Connecticut. According to his lawyer, Benjamin Brafman, Weinstein planned to plead not guilty.

Weinstein was indicted again in July 2018, for predatory sexual assault. Weinstein had allegedly forced a woman to perform oral sex in 2006. This charge carries a maximum sentence of life imprisonment if Weinstein is found guilty. In October, one of the sexual assault charges was dismissed, but there were enough charges to come that dismissing one wouldn't make too much difference when it came to sentencing.

From February 2018, 15 alleged sexual assaults committed by Weinstein were being investigated by London police. These accusations dated back to 1990, and the investigation has been named 'Operation Kaguyak'. The LAPD is also investigating allegations of rape from an actress who has remained unnamed.

Civil Lawsuits

Eric Schneiderman, the New York Attorney General, announced on October 23, 2017, that he was opening a civil rights investigation into The Weinstein Company. As part of the investigation, he issued a subpoena for all records from the company that pertained to sexual harassment and discrimination complaints.

Weinstein's former personal assistant, Sandeep Rehal, sued Weinstein and his brother, along with The Weinstein Company for harassment and discrimination, in January 2018. She claimed that the majority of her work involved working while Weinstein was naked, and, in her words, "catering to Harvey Weinstein's sexual appetites and activities".

Actress Ashley Judd sued Weinstein on April 30, 2018, for allegedly making false statements about her following her rejection of his sexual demands. Her lawsuit claims that by rejecting him, her career was damaged and she subsequently missed out on a role in the blockbuster movie Lord of the Rings.

Weinstein's Responses

Weinstein responded to the report published in the New York Times by saying, "I appreciate the way I've behaved with colleagues in the past has caused a lot of pain, and I sincerely apologize for it." He further stated that he was working with a therapist to deal with his issues, and he would be taking a sabbatical.

One of Weinstein's lawyers, Lisa Bloom, described Weinstein as 'an old dinosaur learning new ways'. She was criticized for the way she handled Weinstein's defense, and ultimately she ended her involvement with Weinstein as of October 7, 2017. Weinstein hired Strick and Company, a public relations company, to handle the crisis on October 9, 2017. They dropped him as a client in April, 2018. Attorney for Weinstein Charles Harder stated they would be suing the New York Times for their published reports, but since October 15, 2018, Harder has stopped working for Weinstein.

A spokesman for Weinstein stated in relation to The New Yorker report:

"Any allegations of non-consensual sex are unequivocally denied by Mr. Weinstein. Mr. Weinstein has further confirmed that there were never any acts of retaliation against any women for refusing his advances ... Mr. Weinstein has begun counseling, has listened to the community and is pursuing a better path. Mr. Weinstein is hoping that if he makes enough progress, he will be given a second chance.

Subsequent reports and accusations of rape were likewise met with the response that "any allegations of nonconsensual sex are unequivocally denied by Mr. Weinstein"

On January 30, 2018, an attorney for Weinstein made public private emails from actor Ben Affleck, and Rose McGowan's former manager Jill Messick. The emails contradicted the version of events as depicted by Rose McGowan. Then on February 7, Jill Messick tragically committed suicide, perhaps brought about by all the negative media and public attention she received following the release of the emails.

Lawyer Benjamin Brafman gave an interview to The Times of London in March 2018, stating:

"The casting couch in Hollywood was not invented by Harvey Weinstein."..."If a woman decides that she needs to have sex with a Hollywood producer to advance her career and actually does it and finds the whole thing offensive, that's not rape." Rhetorically addressing such a woman, Brafman said, "You made a conscious decision that you're willing to do something that is personally offensive in order to advance your career."

Timeline of Events Including Latest Information

Published by BBC News:

October 5, 2017

A story is published by The New York Times detailing decades of allegations of sexual harassment against Harvey Weinstein. Among the women who came forward are actresses Rose McGowan and Ashley Judd.

The accusations include that he had forced women to massage him and watch him while he was naked. He had promised to help advance their careers in return for sexual favors.

Weinstein issues an apology acknowledging he "has caused a lot of pain" - but denies the allegations he harassed female employees over a period of nearly three decades.

Weinstein's lawyer tells The Hollywood Reporter his client is preparing to sue the New York Times.

Weinstein says he is taking a 'leave of absence' from The Weinstein Company and is working with a therapist.

October 6, 2017

Brie Larson and Lena Dunham are among those to react to the allegations in the article, praising the bravery of those who have come forward.

The Weinstein Company says it takes the allegations 'extremely seriously' and is launching an inquiry.

October 7, 2017

Weinstein's lawyer Lisa Bloom announces her resignation, saying she understands that "Mr. Weinstein and his board are moving toward an agreement".

October 8, 2017

Harvey Weinstein has been sacked by the board of his company, effective immediately.

They say the decision was made "in light of new information about misconduct".

October 9, 2017

British actress Romola Garai tells the Guardian newspaper that she felt 'violated' when Weinstein auditioned her as an 18-year-old, saying that he had answered the door to his hotel room in a bathrobe.

Meryl Streep and Dame Judi Dench join the list of people reacting to the accusations, with George Clooney saying the alleged behavior is "indefensible".

October 10, 2017

Allegations from 13 more women are published in the New Yorker magazine, including three accusations of rape, which Weinstein strongly denies.

Actress Asia Argento and a former aspiring actress named Lucia Stoller say Weinstein forced himself on them sexually. A third woman withholds her name from the article, the result of a 10-month investigation by the magazine. Argento says the incident happened in 1997 in the south of France while Stoller, who now goes under the name Evans, says she was forced into a sexual act by the producer after going for a casting meeting in 2004.

Mira Sorvino, who starred in several of Weinstein's films, told the New Yorker that Weinstein sexually harassed her and tried to pressure her into a physical relationship.

Weinstein's spokeswoman Sallie Hofmeister tells the publication: "Any allegations of non-consensual sex are unequivocally denied by Mr. Weinstein."

Hollywood A-listers Gwyneth Paltrow and Angelina Jolie say they were harassed by Weinstein. Paltrow says she was propositioned as a 22-year-old, while Jolie refers to a "bad experience" in her youth.

Other figures to speak out against Weinstein include Barack Obama, Benedict Cumberbatch and Leonardo DiCaprio.

Weinstein's wife Georgina Chapman announces she is leaving him and that her priority is her young children.

October 11, 2017

Bafta says it is suspending Weinstein's membership, with immediate effect.

A number of senior Labor MPs call for Weinstein's honorary CBE to be taken away. Prime Minister Theresa May says a decision about the honour would not lie with Downing Street.

Cara Delevingne also says Weinstein made advances towards her.

A statement from the Cannes Film Festival says organizers are "dismayed" to learn of the allegations about Weinstein.

October 12, 2017

Overnight, police are called following a "family dispute" at the home of Weinstein's daughter. The Los Angeles Police Department (LAPD) confirms they were called to reports of a "disturbance" at the house but say no crime was committed. Weinstein was not there when officers arrived.

Police in New York tell the BBC they are looking to speak to an individual regarding an allegation against Weinstein dating from 2004. The NYPD does not provide further details.

The Academy of Motion Picture Arts and Sciences, the organization behind the Oscars, says it will meet on Saturday to discuss any course of action to be taken concerning Weinstein. It describes the allegations against Weinstein as "repugnant" and "abhorrent".

Family Guy creator Seth MacFarlane addresses a joke he made about Weinstein's sexual conduct at the 2013 Oscar nominations, saying he decided to speak out after a co-star had been harassed by the producer.

Police in the US and UK say they are investigating specific allegations from 2004 and the 1980s. No charges have been brought.

Rose McGowan says on Twitter that Weinstein raped her. Weinstein has "unequivocally denied" any allegations of non-consensual sex in a statement released through his publicist.

Amazon Studio chief Roy Price is put on a "leave of absence". McGowan has accused Price of having ignored her when she previously made an allegation about Weinstein. And Price has himself been accused of sexually harassing a female producer, it emerges. In addition, Amazon says it is reviewing projects it has with The Weinstein Company.

October 13, 2017

Weinstein's former office assistant Lisa Rose says the film mogul tried to invite her to another room, mentioning a massage.

The Late, Late Show presenter James Corden makes jokes about Weinstein's alleged sexual assaults at a charity gala in Los Angeles. He later apologized on Twitter, saying he "was not trying to make light of Harvey's inexcusable behavior, but to shame him, the abuser, not his victims".

October 14, 2017

The organization behind the Oscars votes to expel Weinstein following the allegations. In a statement, The Academy of Motion Picture Arts and Sciences says: "What's at issue here is a deeply troubling problem that has no place in our society."

Actress Alice Evans tells Radio 5 Live that Weinstein made lewd comments towards her.

Kate Winslet reveals she deliberately did not thank Weinstein when she won her Oscar for The Reader in 2009. "I remember being told, 'Make sure you thank Harvey if you win'," the actress tells the Los Angeles Times. "And I remember turning around and saying, 'No I won't'."

October 15, 2017

British actress Lysette Anthony says Weinstein raped her at her London home in the late 1980s while another, unidentified woman says she was raped in 1992.

Woody Allen says he is "sad" for Harvey Weinstein as the producer faces numerous allegations of sexual assault. "The whole Harvey Weinstein thing is very sad for everybody involved. Tragic for the poor women that were involved, sad for Harvey that [his] life is so messed up." He later clarifies his comments in a statement to Variety: "When I said I felt sad for Harvey Weinstein I thought it was clear the meaning was because he is a sad, sick man. I was surprised it was treated differently. Lest there be any ambiguity, this statement clarifies my intention and feelings."

The BBC understands that UK police are investigating a number of sexual assault allegations involving Harvey Weinstein. The Metropolitan Police says he is accused of assaulting three women in separate incidents in London in the late 1980s, 1992, 2010, 2011 and 2015. The Hollywood film producer has "unequivocally denied" any allegations of non-consensual sex.

The Academy of Motion Picture Arts and Sciences votes to expel Weinstein, saying its board "voted well in excess of the required two-thirds majority" to expel him.

Actress Alice Evans thought her Weinstein encounter had ruined her boyfriend's career because she shunned his advances

October 16, 2017

The board of the Producers Guild of America vote to terminate Weinstein's membership. In a statement, the guild says he will be given the opportunity to respond before it makes its final decision on 6 November.

Jeffrey Katzenberg, chairman of the DreamWorks film studio, describes Weinstein as "a monster" at a conference organised by the Wall Street Journal.

Screenwriter Scott Rosenberg writes about his early days at Miramax Films, Weinstein's former company. In a Facebook post, he says that while he never heard of any rape allegations, he and many others were aware of Weinstein's "dreadful" behavior.

Actress Lauren Holly tells a Canadian talk show about a hotel room encounter with Weinstein in the late 1990s. She says the producer showered and used the toilet in front of her before approaching her naked and requesting a massage.

In an interview on French television, Weinstein's chauffeur, Mickael Chemloul, reveals he had to drive around "tearful aspiring actresses" for the producer and that he would often console them after their encounters with him.

October 17, 2017

Actress Lena Headey accuses Weinstein of sexual harassing her in Los Angeles. In a series of Twitter posts, the Game of Thrones star says the mogul was "furious" after she resisted his advances and told her not to say anything about their encounter to her manager or agent.

Harvey Weinstein resigns from the board of the company that bears his name, according to multiple reports. According to Variety, Weinstein still owns 22% of his company's stock.

Television producer Amanda Segel accuses Harvey Weinstein's younger brother Bob of sexual harassment. Ms. Segel says he made repeated romantic overtures and requests to join him for private dinners over a three-month period, which Mr. Weinstein has denied.

Roy Price, head of Amazon Studios, resigns over allegations of sexual harassment.

October 18, 2017

Star Wars director JJ Abrams tells the Today program he had never heard of any sexual allegations made against Weinstein but doubts he was "a lone operator".

Actor Channing Tatum says he is halting the development of a film about child sexual abuse that he had been making with Harvey Weinstein's company.

Robert Lindsay says his Hollywood film career was halted after a run-in with Weinstein, which he says led to him losing a role in Shakespeare in Love.

Harvard University announces it is stripping Weinstein of the Du Bois medal it gave him in 2014 for his contributions to African-American culture.

October 19, 2017

Quentin Tarantino reveals he knew about Harvey Weinstein's alleged misconduct toward women for years. "I knew enough to do more than I did," the film director tells the New York Times.

Actor Tom Hanks says there can be no way back for Weinstein. "His last name... will become an identifying moniker for a state of being for which there was a before and an after," he tells the BBC.

Actress Lupita Nyong'o accuses Weinstein of harassment. Writing in the New York Times, she says she was lured to his bedroom under false pretenses, when she was a drama student.

Police in Los Angeles confirm they have interviewed a woman who was allegedly sexually assaulted by Harvey Weinstein in 2013.

The British Film Institute announces it is withdrawing the BFI Fellowship it awarded Weinstein in 2002.

A group of Weinstein Company employees write an open letter asking their employer to release them from the NDAs (non-disclosure agreements) that stop them speaking publicly about what they have experienced and witnessed.

October 23, 2017

Zelda Perkins, a British former assistant of Weinstein, tells the Financial Times she was paid £125,000 ($165,200) to keep quiet after accusing the movie mogul of sexual harassment. She said he asked her to give him massages and tried to pull her into bed, but she "was made to feel ashamed for disclosing his behavior".

The producer of Paddington 2 says he's exploring all options to cut ties with The Weinstein Company, which has distribution rights of the film. David Heyman told Deadline that he hoped, ultimately, "The Weinstein Company name is nowhere near Paddington 2".

October 24, 2017

George Clooney and Matt Damon speak out over Weinstein, saying it is time for Hollywood to change and it is now "the moment to believe women".

Actress Brit Marling writes in The Atlantic about her experience with Harvey Weinstein in a hotel room, where he suggested they take a shower together. The OA co-creator describes being sat "paralyzed by mounting fear", but says she managed to escape.

October 25, 2017

A former production worker, Mimi Haleyi, alleges that she was raped by Weinstein when he forcibly performed oral sex on her in 2006.

The removal of Weinstein's CBE is believed to be being "actively considered" by the government's Honours Forfeiture Committee.

Actress Dominique Huett, who also alleges she was raped by Weinstein when he performed oral sex on her without her consent, files a negligence case against The Weinstein Company.

October 26, 2017

Norwegian actress Natassia Malthe accuses Weinstein of raping her in a London hotel after the 2008 Bafta awards.

October 27, 2017

Weinstein takes legal action against his former company after his lawyer alleges, The Weinstein Company has denied requests for documents to defend himself from allegations.

The Sopranos actress Annabella Sciorra accuses Weinstein of forcing himself into her apartment and raping her in 1992.

Actress Daryl Hannah also comes forward and alleges that Weinstein tried to force himself into her hotel room and repeatedly sexually harassed her during promotion of Kill Bill and its sequel.

October 28, 2017

Actress Rose McGowan claims she turned down a $1m (£760,000) offer from Harvey Weinstein in exchange for her silence.

The New York Times reports on new allegations made against Weinstein dating from the 1970s when he was a concert promoter in Buffalo, New York.

Environment secretary Michael Gove apologizes "unreservedly" after making a joke about Weinstein on BBC Radio 4's Today program.

October 30, 2017

The Producers Guild of America bans Weinstein for life. It says the "unprecedented" step reflects the seriousness with which it regards reports of his "reprehensible" conduct".

November 1, 2017

A Canadian actress sues Weinstein for two alleged sexual assaults in 2000 in Toronto. She also sues Miramax, The Walt Disney Company and Barbara Schneeweiss, who worked for Weinstein. The anonymous actress, identified as "Jane Doe", seeks a total of 14 million Canadian dollars (£8.34m).

November 2, 2017

Speaking to Vanity Fair, Boardwalk Empire actress Paz de la Huerta claims Weinstein raped her twice in New York in 2010.

November 3, 2017

Police in New York say they have "an actual case" against Weinstein, citing the "credible and detailed narrative" an unidentified woman - believed to be Paz de la Huerta - has given them.

November 7, 2017

The New Yorker claims Weinstein used private investigators to cover up sexual abuse claims. Asia Argento, one of his accusers, describes the report as "terrifying".

The Television Academy expels Weinstein from its organization.

November 8, 2017

Weinstein's representatives say they "do not believe" an indictment is imminent from the New York Police Department. "We strongly believe we will demonstrate that no criminal charges are warranted," the statement continues.

The BBC learns that talks over the possible sale of The Weinstein Company have fallen through.

November 9, 2017

Actor Robert Lindsay claims he lost out on a role in the film Shakespeare in Love because Harvey Weinstein held a grudge against him.

November 10, 2017

Speaking to the BBC, actress Hayley Atwell says Weinstein is "a predator" and "should be punished in the highest way the law offers".

November 16, 2017

Warner Bros severs ties to Weinstein by buying the rights to the film Paddington 2.

The film's British producer David Heyman said he was trying to "break Paddington out of prison" by ensuring The Weinstein Company did not distribute the film in North America.

November 19, 2017

It is reported that businesswoman Maria Contreras-Sweet is behind a $275m (£206.3m) bid for The Weinstein Company.

November 20, 2017

Singer Morrissey is criticized for expressing skepticism over women accusing Harvey Weinstein of assault.

November 21, 2017

Jennifer Lawrence says Harvey Weinstein was never inappropriate with her but admits she had heard rumors he was "a dog".

November 23, 2017

Kill Bill actress Uma Thurman sends out a Thanksgiving message in which she vents anger at Weinstein "and all [his] wicked conspirators".

November 27, 2017

A woman who wishes to remain anonymous alleges a series of sexual assaults by Harvey Weinstein in the first UK civil claim against the producer. The woman seeks damages for personal injury, expenses and consequential loss that are expected to exceed £300,000.

November 28, 2017

The first UK civil claim against Harvey Weinstein is issued in the High Court. A woman, who worked in the film industry and wishes to remain anonymous, alleges a series of sexual assaults by the film producer.

December 1, 2017

Actress Kadian Noble accuses Weinstein of luring her into a hotel room in Cannes and assaulting her in 2014. In a civil action filed in New York, she accuses Weinstein, his brother Bob and The Weinstein Company of violating US federal sex trafficking laws.

December 14, 2017

Frida actress Salma Hayek claims that Weinstein sexually harassed and threatened her. Writing in the New York Times, she says she repeatedly refused sexual advances. In response, a spokeswoman for Weinstein disputes the account and says "all of the sexual allegations as portrayed by Salma are not accurate".

December 16, 2017

Lord of the Rings director Peter Jackson claims he was fed "false information" about Mira Sorvino and Ashley Judd by Weinstein's former company Miramax. Both actresses have claimed the media mogul sexually harassed them. Weinstein denies allegations of misconduct, and of blacklisting the actresses.

December 18, 2017

The BBC announces plans to make a "definitive documentary" about the Harvey Weinstein scandal. The makers of the feature-length BBC Two film promise to interview "the many actresses who have been brave enough to tell their stories", plus reporters and other Hollywood insiders.

December 19, 2017

A former assistant to Harvey Weinstein says she left after a co-worker said he had tried to rape her, which he denied. Zelda Perkins claims she tried to expose his behavior but was told by lawyers she "didn't have a chance".

Meryl Streep defends herself against criticism from Harvey Weinstein accuser Rose McGowan after she says her "silence is the problem". Streep responds by saying she did not know about Weinstein's alleged behavior when she worked with him.

January 15, 2018

In an interview with the BBC's Hardtalk program, Ashley Judd says she was "not frightened" of Harvey Weinstein and ascribes that as the reason why the producer "sabotaged" her career.

February 2, 2018

Bafta announces it has formally terminated Harvey Weinstein's membership.

February 3, 2018

Actress Uma Thurman details long hinted-at allegations against Weinstein. In a New York Times article, she says Weinstein pushed her down and "tried to expose himself" at the producer's hotel room in London during the 1990s, before she managed to "wriggle away". Harvey Weinstein's spokeswoman said the claims about an assault "are untrue".

UK police investigating Weinstein say they are looking at allegations of sexual assault against two more women. The alleged offences, reported to police in October and November, took place in the Republic of Ireland in 1991, Westminster in 2011 and abroad in 2010, the Metropolitan Police say. These bring the number of women making accusations to the Met to nine.

February 11, 2018

After a four-month investigation, New York state prosecutors announce they have filed a lawsuit against the Weinstein Company on the basis the studio failed to protect employees from his alleged harassment and abuse.

The lawsuit alleges that Weinstein sexually harassed and abused female employees at the studio for years, including making verbal threats against their lives and employing female staff as "wing women" to facilitate sexual conquests.

His lawyer concedes Weinstein's behavior is "not without fault" but says there was "no criminality"

February 20, 2018

The producer of Golden Globe-winning film My Week With Marilyn accuses Weinstein of physically attacking him. David Parfitt says Weinstein was "in a fury" about a test screening of the film doing so well with the audience as he wasn't happy with the final cut.

February 28, 2018

A 10th woman reports Weinstein to British police for alleged sexual assault. The woman, who has not been named, went to the police on 8 February to accuse the movie mogul of assaulting her in central London in the mid-1990s.

March 20, 2018

Weinstein's former company files for bankruptcy, months after the Oscar-winning producer was accused of multiple sexual assaults.

March 28, 2018

An ex-assistant of Weinstein says she was pressured into signing a non-disclosure agreement [NDA] that was "morally lacking on every level".

"There cannot be a legal document that protects criminal behavior," Zelda Perkins tells MPs on the Women and Equalities Committee. She says she left Weinstein's company Miramax after a colleague accused him of trying to rape her.

May 1, 2018

Actress Ashley Judd sues Weinstein claiming he damaged her career in retaliation for her rejecting his sexual advances.

May 10, 2018

Weinstein's estranged wife gives her first interview since he was engulfed in scandal, saying she was "never" suspicious about his behavior. Georgina Chapman admits she had been "so naive", and was "so humiliated and so broken" when the scandal unfolded.

Weinstein's lawyer tells BBC Radio 5 live he believes the allegations are "legally defective or factually not supported". In his first broadcast interview in the UK, Benjamin Brafman accuses "some of the more vocal critics of Harvey Weinstein" of "just not telling the truth".

May 25, 2018

Weinstein turned himself in to New York police on sexual misconduct charges.

He was charged with rape and several other counts of sexual abuse against two women.

May 26, 2018

Weinstein released on $1m bail over rape and abuse charges.

He also agreed to wear a GPS tracker and to surrender his passport after turning himself in to police.

Rose McGowan, who accused Mr. Weinstein of rape, told the BBC it was an "amazing day for his survivors".

May 31, 2018

A grand jury in New York indicts Weinstein on charges of rape and a criminal sexual act, moving the case towards a trial.

The offences relate to an alleged attack on a woman in 2013 and another woman in 2004. Neither woman was named.

The mogul could face up to 25 years in prison if convicted of either offence.

June 5, 2018

Weinstein formally pleads not guilty to rape and sexual assault charges in the New York Supreme Court.

The identity of one of the women whose accusations prompted the charges has been confirmed by her lawyer. Lucia Evans, a former actress, had already publicly accused Mr. Weinstein of carrying out a sexual assault in 2004.

July 2, 2018

Weinstein faces fresh sexual assault charges in New York from a third woman, in a case dating back to 2006.

This is in addition to other investigations in Los Angeles, London, and by the US federal government.

July 9, 2018

Weinstein pleads not guilty in third sex assault case, after previous not guilty pleas in June.

The new charges - which he denied at the State Supreme Court - include two counts of predatory sexual assault for allegedly forcing a woman into oral sex.

Speaking outside the courthouse, lawyer Benjamin Brafman said: "Mr. Weinstein is not a predator; he is not a rapist and I believe that when this case is over we will ultimately see him be exonerated."

August 3, 2018

Weinstein seeks to dismiss criminal case based on accuser's emails.

His lawyers file a defence motion citing dozens of "warm" emails they say Mr. Weinstein received from one of his accusers after an alleged rape.

Other objections included a lack of detail on the timeline of an alleged assault in 2004, and the lack of advance warning from the District Attorney's office about the presentation of more serious charges.

August 22, 2018

German actress Emma Loman sues Weinstein for alleged rape.

Loman - understood to be a pseudonym - says in a complaint that Weinstein invited her to Cannes to discuss her career in 2006.

She says she was constantly called by his assistant, up to 30 times a day, until she accepted his invitation.

Mr. Weinstein's lawyer says the claims were "untrue", adding they were seeking to have the lawsuit dismissed.

September 18, 2018

The Metropolitan police say it has received a further allegation of sexual assault in connection with Harvey Weinstein after an 11th woman came forward.

Scotland Yard said the latest allegation was received on 16 August after a woman alleged she was assaulted at an "unknown location in the early 1990s".

List of Accusers So Far

1. Amber Anderson, an actress known for The Riot Club, posted to Instagram on October 16 that Weinstein "coerced" her into a private

meeting. "He behaved inappropriately and propositioned a 'personal' relationship to further my career whilst bragging about other actresses he had 'helped' in a similar way," she wrote. "He tried to take my hand and put it in his lap which is when I managed to leave the room."

2. Lysette Anthony, an English model and actress of Husbands and Wives, told 'The Sunday Times' on October 15 that Weinstein raped her in her home in the late 1980s.

3. Asia Argento, an Italian actress, model and director, told The New Yorker that in 1997 when she was 21, Weinstein asked for a massage and forcibly performed oral sex on her at a hotel in France.

4. Rosanna Arquette, 58, told The New Yorker she rebuffed an early 1990s advance from Weinstein, saying he asked for a massage while wearing only a bathrobe. She says the producer told her she was making a "big mistake" by rejecting him and claims he has made things "very difficult for (her) for years." Arquette is an actress, director and producer known for her work in Pulp Fiction and The Executioner's Song.

5. Jessica Barth, the 37-year-old actress from the Ted films, told The New Yorker Weinstein invited her to a business meeting at his Beverly Hills hotel room after the 2011 Golden Globes. Barth later recalls he had champagne waiting, and alternated between offering to cast her in a film and demanding a naked massage. She claims that when she moved toward the door to leave, Weinstein lashed out, saying that she needs to lose weight "to compete with Mila Kunis."

6. Ambra Battilana Gutierrez, an Italian model, can be heard being pressured by Weinstein in audiotapes from a New York Police Department sting in 2015. In the tapes, he seemingly admits to groping the model on the previous day. Weinstein reaches a settlement with Gutierrez, according to the Times.

7. Kate Beckinsale, 44, posted to Instagram on October 12, accusing Weinstein of offering her alcohol during their first meeting when she was

just 17. "I assumed it would be in a conference room which was very common," she wrote. "When I arrived, reception told me to go to his room. He opened the door in his bathrobe." Beckinsale is an English actress who has starred in Much Ado About Nothing and Pearl Harbor.

8. Juls Bindi, a massage therapist, alleged in a 20/20 interview that Weinstein masturbated in front of her while he groped her chest in 2010. She was 29 years-old at the time and says that Weinstein discussed a possible book deal with her before the incident happened.

9. Zoe Brock, a New Zealand model, told The Guardian and wrote in a 2,700-word post on Medium that Weinstein cornered her in a hotel room during the Cannes Film Festival in 1997, asking her for a massage while he was naked. The model, who was 23 at the time, says she locked herself in a bathroom to escape.

10. Cynthia Burr, now 62, told the New York Times in an interview published October 30 that as a young actress in New York, she met Weinstein in a hotel lobby and he unzipped his fly and forced her to perform oral sex on him in a hallway. "It was just him and me alone," she said. "I was fearful I didn't have the wherewithal to get away."

11. Liza Campbell, a Scottish artist and writer, told The Sunday Times that Weinstein invited her to take a bath with him after meeting with him in his hotel room in 1995.

12. Marisa Coughlan, a 43-year-old actress who starred in Super Troopers, told The Hollywood Reporter on October 18 that Weinstein asked her to meet at a hotel in 1999 to discuss a film role, alleging that, once she was there, he requested a massage from her.

13. Hope Exiner d'Amore worked for Weinstein's concert promotion company, Harvey and Corky Productions, in the late '70s, she told the Times. On a business trip to New York City, she says Weinstein claimed there was a mistake at the hotel and only one room was available. In the

middle of the night, Exiner d'Amore, now 62, says Weinstein forcibly performed oral sex and intercourse on her.

14. Florence Darel, a 49-year-old French actress, told People on October 12 that Weinstein pursued her in the mid '90s and then propositioned her in a hotel room while his wife at the time, Eve Chilton, was in the room next door. Darcel starred in The Stolen Children and Uranus.

15. Emma de Caunes, a French actress, told The New Yorker that Weinstein invited her to his hotel room in Cannes in 2010. While she takes a call from a friend, he goes into his bathroom, where she hears the shower being turned on. She later says that he came out with an erection and demanded she lie on the bed. "It was like a hunter with a wild animal," she said. "The fear turns him on." De Caunes starred in The Science of Sleep and Mr. Bean's Holiday.

16. Juliana De Paula, a former model, told the Los Angeles Times that Weinstein groped her and forced her to kiss other models in New York a decade ago. She added that when she tried to leave, he chased her around naked, and she had to fight him off with broken glass.

17. Cara Delevingne, the 25-year-old English actress and model shared in an Instagram post on October 11 and in a statement to New York Magazine and Huffington Post that the movie producer attempted to kiss her in a hotel room. "As soon as we were alone he began to brag about all the actresses he had slept with and how he had made their careers and spoke about other inappropriate things of a sexual nature," she wrote. Delevingne stars in Valerian and Tulip Fever.

18. Sophie Dix, an English actress known for her role in The Advocate, told The Guardian on October 13 that she was sexually assaulted by Weinstein in the Savoy hotel in London in the '90s.

19. Lacey Dorn, a recently-graduated documentary filmmaker, told the Times she ran into Weinstein at a Halloween party at the Gramercy Park

Hotel in 2011, where he grabbed between her legs, touching her buttocks and crotch through her clothes.

20. Dawn Dunning, a waitress and aspiring actress, told the Times that in 2003 Weinstein lured her to his hotel, where he waited in a bathrobe in front of what he said were contracts for his next three films -- but she could only sign them on a condition: She would have to have three-way sex with him. Dunning laughed, assuming he was joking. Weinstein grew angry, she recalls. "You'll never make it in this business," she said he told her. "This is how the business works." Dunning fled.

21. Lisa Esco, the 32-year-old S.W.A.T. actress and director, told the Washington Post and later People that Weinstein propositioned her with a kiss, and when she brushed him off, he threatened her career.

22. Alice Evans, a British actress, wrote in The Telegraph on October 14 that Weinstein tried to touch and kiss her during the 2002 Cannes Film Festival. In the essay, she also claims that her rejection of Weinstein negatively impacted her and her husband's careers. Evans starred in The Christmas Card and The Vampire Diaries.

23. Lucia Evans (formally Lucia Stoller), told The New Yorker that she was approached by Weinstein at a New York club and invited to a meeting in 2004. Upon arrival, she was escorted to an office, where he both flattered her and recommended she lose weight to be on his reality show, Project Runway. "After that is when he assaulted me," Evans told the newspaper. "He forced me to perform oral sex on him. I said, over and over, 'I don't want to do this, stop, don't.' " In the end, she said, "He's a big guy. He overpowered me."

24. Angie Everhart, an actress (Take Me Home Tonight) and former model came forward on the KLOS morning show alleging Weinstein masturbated in front of her while on a boat during the Venice Film Festival. The former model and actress claims Weinstein told her, "You're a really nice girl, you shouldn't tell anybody about this."

25. Claire Forlani, an English actress (Meet Joe Black and Boys and Girls), took to Twitter on October 12 to claim she dodged five different advances from Weinstein over the years.

26. Romola Garai, an English actress, told The Guardian that in 2004 during the audition process for Havana Nights, she was told to arrive at Weinstein's hotel room, alone. "He answered the door in his bathrobe," she said. "I was only 18. I felt violated by it; it has stayed very clearly in my memory."

27. Louisette Geiss, a former actress and screenwriter, said at a press conference on October 10 that at the Sundance Film Festival in 2008, Weinstein invited her to his room to discuss her script, but after about 30 minutes, he returned from the bathroom in nothing but a robe with the front open. Weinstein proceeded to get in the bathtub and "just kept asking me to watch him masturbate," she said. Geiss says she moved to leave his hotel room, and Weinstein trailed her to the door, promising to introduce her to his brother, Bob, greenlight her script and give her a three-picture deal. But she had to watch him masturbate first.

28. Louise Godbold, a co-executive director of the non-profit Echo Parenting & Education, wrote in a blog post published on October 9 that in the early '90s she was also a victim of Weinstein. She describes being trapped in an empty meeting room, being propositioned for a massage and being touched on her shoulders.

29. Judith Godreche. At 24-years-old, the French actress (The Man in the Iron Mask) was invited to breakfast with Weinstein during the Cannes Film Festival in 1996, she tells the Times. Afterward, the mogul, who had just acquired her film Ridicule, allegedly lured her to his room, promising to talk about planning an Oscar campaign. Then he asked to give her a massage. She said no. "The next thing I know, he's pressing against me and pulling off my sweater," she recalls. She pulls away and leaves the suite.

30. Trish Goff, a former model and actress, told the Times that Weinstein allegedly groped her during a lunch meeting in 2003. "When we finally stood up to go, he really started groping me, grabbing my breasts, grabbing my face and trying to kiss me," she said.

31. Heather Graham, an actress known for her role in The Hangover films, wrote an essay for Variety on October 10 describing a time in the early 2000s when Weinstein allegedly insinuated that she would need to have sex with him in order to get a role in one of his upcoming films. She was never hired for one of his films.

32. Eva Green, an actress known for Casino Royale and Weinstein Company's Sin City, told Variety that she had to push Weinstein off of her during a business meeting in Paris.

33. Larissa Gomes, an actress known for Saw VI, told the Los Angeles Times that Weinstein asked her to bare her chest while working on the Toronto set of the Miramax-produced film Get Over It about 17 years ago. In a class-action lawsuit filed on June 1, she detailed how Weinstein tried to kiss her, forcibly massaged her shoulders and threatened her, saying "Ashley Judd had no problem" sleeping with him. She was 21 at the time.

34. Mimi Haleyi, a former production assistant, said she met Weinstein at the 2004 premiere of The Aviator, and again at the Cannes Film Festival in 2006, where she offered to help on his productions in New York. He told her to come by his hotel. When she did, he suggested she massage him. "I felt the meeting was going nowhere and I left," Haleyi said with lawyer Gloria Allred at a press conference October 24. Later in New York, Weinstein orally forced himself on her while she was on her period, she said.

35. Daryl Hannah, an actress known for Steel Magnolias and the Kill Bill films, told The New Yorker on October 27 that Weinstein sexually harassed her on two different occasions in the past decade.

36. Salma Hayek accused Weinstein of sexually harassing her while working together on the 2002 film Frida, in a column for The New York Times

December 13. She claims the list of unwanted advances from the producer included showers, oral sex, massages and more. She also alleges he threatened to kill her following one of her refusals, and verbally insulted her on set.

37. Lena Headey, 44, who plays Cersei on Game of Thrones, shared a series of tweets on October 17 describing an incident in 2005 involving "some suggestive comment, a gesture" from Weinstein. Years later, she said she also experienced him asking her personal questions about her love life before asking her up to his hotel room.

38. Natasha Henstridge, 43, appeared on Megyn Kelly Today on November 15 detailing an accusation of sexual assault against producer Brett Ratner. But she also accused Weinstein of inappropriate behavior. Henstridge says she was at a meeting with Weinstein in a Sundance hotel when "suddenly, it became not anything about the job that he was trying to offer me or put me up for anymore and it became all about flirtation," she told Kelly, adding he "came on to me repeatedly." While the actress says she was able "to avoid an actual physical attack" by Weinstein she alleged "He pleasured himself in front of me."

39. Lauren Holly said on the Canadian talk show The Social on October 16 that Weinstein, who she met while working on the 1996 film Beautiful Girls, acted inappropriately towards her during a meeting in his hotel room. After what appeared to be a normal business meeting, she claims Weinstein left the room before returning in a bathrobe and asking her to follow him into the bedroom. She says he then dropped the robe and took a shower. Once out of the shower he approached her naked before she fled the room.

40. Paz de la Huerta, 33, a model and actress best known for roles in Boardwalk Empire and A Walk to Remember, accused Weinstein of raping her on two separate occasions. In an interview with Vanity Fair published November 2, the actress said the first alleged assault happened in October 2010 when she was 26; the second in December 2010. "I laid there feeling sick," de la Huerta told Vanity Fair. "He looked at me and said, 'I'll put you

in a play.' He left and I never heard from him again." Weinstein spokeswoman Holly Baird told USA TODAY in a statement, "Any allegations of non-consensual sex are unequivocally denied by Mr. Weinstein."

41. Dominique Huett, 35, a New York-based actress, filed a lawsuit in Los Angeles October 24 against The Weinstein Company, alleging that Harvey Weinstein pressured her into sex at the Peninsula Hotel in Beverly Hills in 2010 and that his company knew about multiple allegations of sexual misconduct against him dating back to the '90s.

42. Angelina Jolie, a 42-year-old actress, filmmaker and humanitarian, told the Times that during the release of Playing By Heart, she rejected advances by Weinstein in a hotel room. She was 23 at the time. "I had a bad experience with Harvey Weinstein in my youth, and as a result, chose never to work with him again and warn others when they did," Jolie explained in an email to the newspaper.

43. Ashley Judd, 49, told the Times that during a 1997 breakfast meeting at Weinstein's hotel room in Beverly Hills, the producer propositioned her, saying he could give her a massage or she could watch him shower. She was starring in Miramax's Kiss the Girls at the time.

44. Katherine Kendall, a 48-year-old actress from Swingers, told the Times that Weinstein convinced her to stop by his apartment in 1993 when she was 23 years old. Once there, he came out of his bathroom in a robe, asking for a massage. She refused; he left the room and returned nude, she says. "He literally chased me," she told the newspaper. "He wouldn't let me pass him to get to the door."

45. Minka Kelly, a 37-year-old actress from Friday Night Lights, took to Instagram on October 13, describing how Weinstein allegedly propositioned her to be his girlfriend at a meeting.

46. Heather Kerr, a 56-year-old former actress, read a statement on October 20 at a press conference with attorney Gloria Allred, describing a 1989 encounter with Weinstein where he exposed himself to her and told

her she had to sleep with him and other Hollywood producers in order to succeed in the industry.

47. Mia Kirshner, a 42-year-old Canadian actress (The L Word), wrote an op-ed for The Globe and Mail on October 13 that alleged Weinstein harassed her in a hotel room.

48. Myleene Klass, a British singer-turned-TV-host, was propositioned by Weinstein during a film festival lunch at Cannes in 2010, according to UK's The Sun. The report claims she immediately declined his offer, telling him to "(expletive) off," and left the meeting "disgusted and angry." She was 32 at the time.

49. Liz Kouri, an actress, told USA TODAY Weinstein put his fingers inside her and moved her hand to help him masturbate after they met at an opening party for an off-Broadway show in 1999. "I couldn't react," she said. "I didn't want to make him mad... I didn't want to ruin any chances that I might have had at all to audition for him. Or my career."

50. Ivana Lowell, a former Miramax employee and former girlfriend of Bob Weinstein, wrote in her 2010 memoir 'Why Not Say What Happened?' that Harvey Weinstein showed up at her apartment, lay naked on her bed and asked for a massage. In an article for The Daily Mail, she recounted her experience with the movie mogul and revealed he threatened to sue her after the memoir was released.

51. Laura Madden, a London-based assistant, told the Times that Weinstein asked her for massages at hotels in Dublin and London in 1991, adding he had a way of making anyone who objected feel like an outlier. "It was so manipulative," she recalled, two decades after the original incident.

52. Natassia Malthe, 43, said Weinstein barged into her London hotel room and raped her in 2008 after she met him at the BAFTA Awards. After the rape, he masturbated in front of her, the Norwegian-born actress said in her statement at a press conference with attorney Gloria Allred on October 25.

53. Brit Marling, the OA actress/writer shared in an essay for The Atlantic that Weinstein pulled the hotel room-massage act on her in 2014. "I, too, was asked if I wanted a massage, champagne, strawberries. I, too, sat in that chair paralyzed by mounting fear when he suggested we shower together," she wrote.

54. Sarah Ann Masse, a writer and actress (Awkward Exes), told Variety on October 11 that Weinstein hugged her in his underwear and told her he loved her during an interview for a nanny job in 2008.

55. Ashley Matthau, a dancer who worked on Dirty Dancing: Havana Nights, which was produced by Weinstein's company, told the Times that Weinstein began hitting on her on set. He asked her to get in his car and took her to a hotel room, where she says she refused his sexual advances but he pushed her onto the bed and fondled her breasts before stripping, straddling her and masturbating on top of her. She hired an attorney from Gloria Allred's firm, but says Weinstein and his lawyer threatened to drag her through the mud if she went public, so she took a settlement.

56. Rose McGowan, 44-year-old Charmed actress, reached a previously undisclosed settlement with Weinstein in 2007 after an episode in a hotel room during the Sundance Film Festival, the Times reported in early October. In 2016, she tweeted that she was raped by a studio head in 2007, but didn't identify Weinstein at the time.

57. Katya Mtsitouridze, a Russian TV host, told The Hollywood Reporter on October 19 that she was harassed by Weinstein, alleging he arranged a private meeting in 2004 during the Venice Film Festival where he greeted her in a bathrobe and suggested she give him a massage.

58. Emily Nestor, who had worked just one day as a temporary employee for the Weinstein Company in 2014, was invited to a hotel room and propositioned by Weinstein, according to the Times and New Yorker.

59. Connie Nielsen, a 52-year-old Danish actress (The Devil's Advocate), wrote a guest column for Variety on October 24, adding her name to the

list of women allegedly harassed by Weinstein, who produced her 2005 film The Great Raid. The actress claims the producer put his hand on her thigh during the opening night of the film.

60. Kadian Noble, 31, filed a civil suit on November 27 in New York alleging that Harvey Weinstein summoned her to his hotel room at Cannes Film Festival in 2014 to talk about a role. He began massaging her shoulders and told the British actress to "relax." According to her civil suit, which alleges Weinstein and his company engaged in sex trafficking, the producer groped her, pulled her into a bathroom, and forced her to fondle him.

61. Lupita Nyong'o, a 34-year-old Academy Award-winning actress, penned a lengthy column in the Times on October 19 recounting her experience with Weinstein. "Harvey led me into a bedroom — his bedroom — and announced that he wanted to give me a massage. I thought he was joking at first. He was not," Nyong'o wrote. She said Weinstein's advances continued later during a dinner in New York. Weinstein issued a written response via Variety the following day. "Mr. Weinstein has a different recollection of the events, but believes Lupita is a brilliant actress and a major force for the industry," the statement read.

62. Gwyneth Paltrow, 45, told the Times that before shooting Emma when she was 22, Weinstein summoned her to his suite at the Peninsula Beverly Hills hotel for a work meeting which ended with Weinstein placing his hands on her and suggesting they head to the bedroom for massages. "I was a kid, I was signed up, I was petrified," she said.

63. Samantha Panagrosso, a model, told Variety that Weinstein made unwanted sexual advances toward her during the Cannes Film Festival in 2003 while on a friend's yacht, and groped her underwater at a nearby hotel pool.

64. Zelda Perkins, a former assistant to Weinstein, broke her NDA for an interview with the Financial Times, saying she confronted the producer after being subjected to harassment on a near daily basis during the time

she worked for him. At the Venice Film Festival in 1998, she told the Times, he assaulted a colleague, and the women entered a settlement agreement for approximately $330,000.

65. Vu Thu Phuong, a Vietnamese actress, came forward in a Facebook post on October 12 claiming Weinstein made sexual advances towards her during a hotel room meeting in 2008, attempting to teach her how to perform in a sex scene, Vulture and The Huffington Post reported.

66. Tomi-Ann Roberts. In 1984, the then 20-year-old college junior and waitress was hoping to start an acting career. She says Weinstein, a customer, sent her scripts and asked her to meet to discuss the film. When she arrived, he was nude in the bathtub, she told The New York Times. According to the newspaper's account, he suggested she get naked as part of her audition because the character she might play would have a topless scene. Roberts recalls apologizing, excusing herself as prudish, and leaving.

67. Lisa Rose, a then-aspiring actress who worked for Miramax in London when she was 22, told BBC News that Weinstein harassed her in 1988 at the Savoy hotel. She claims Weinstein asked her for a massage and, when she declined, said "nasty things" to her. She later resigned.

68. Erika Rosenbaum, a Canadian actress (The Last Kiss), said in an interview with CBC (Canadian Broadcasting Corporation) that Weinstein held her by the back of her neck and masturbated in front of her in a hotel room during the Toronto International Film Festival in the mid-2000s.

69. Melissa Sagemiller told The Huffington Post that Weinstein harassed her when she was 24-years-old while she worked on Get Over It, which was distributed by Weinstein's Miramax. During a meeting in his hotel room, the producer allegedly refused to let her leave until she kissed him.

70. Annabella Sciorra, an actress known for her work in Reversal of Fortune and The Hand That Rocks the Cradle, told The New Yorker on October 27 that Weinstein violently raped her in the early 1990s and repeatedly sexually harassed her over the next several years.

71. Léa Seydoux, 32-year-old French actress of Blue is the Warmest Colour, wrote an op-ed for The Guardian on October 11 describing an interaction she had with Weinstein, which involved him inviting her to his hotel room for a drink and later lunging at her and attempting to kiss her.

72. Lauren Sivan, a New York TV reporter, says she was cornered by Weinstein in the kitchen of a restaurant in which he is an investor in 2007, according to The Huffington Post. When she avoids his kiss, he reportedly tells her to "stand there and shut up" while he masturbates and ejaculates into a nearby potted plant.

73. Chelsea Skidmore, an actress known for Leah & Chelsea Have a Sleepover, told the Washington Post that Weinstein asked her for a massage after a meeting at the Peninsula Hotel in 2013. After declining, she claims he masturbated in front of her.

74. Mira Sorvino, 50, told The New Yorker that while promoting Mighty Aphrodite at the 1995 Toronto International Film Festival, Weinstein "started massaging my shoulders, which made me very uncomfortable, and then tried to get more physical, sort of chasing me around." Weeks later, she says he evaded her doorman and showed up at the door of her New York apartment, but was able to scare him off on both occasions.

75. Tara Subkoff, a 44-year-old actress (The Cell), told Variety that Weinstein sexually harassed her in the 1990s, recounting a time when he "grabbed" her to sit on his lap. "I could feel that he had an erection," she recalled.

76. Paula Wachowiak, 62, told The Buffalo News that Weinstein exposed himself to her when she was a 24-year-old production assistant on his first film, The Burning, in 1980. Wachowiak says she left the room in tears. Later, she says, he asked, "Was seeing me naked the highlight of your internship?"

77. Paula Williams, a then-model trying to break into the movie business, told ABC 20/20 Weinstein invited her to a party in 1990 when she was 20.

Once she arrived, she said he was alone and started touching her neck before quickly exposing himself to her. She says she escaped before anything else happened.

78. Sean Young, a 57-year-old actress (Blade Runner), said Weinstein exposed himself to her while on the set of the 1992 Miramax film Love Crimes, during an interview October 20 on KLBJ's Dudley and Bob With Matt Show Daily Podcast. She says she "personally experienced him pulling his you-know-what out of his pants."

79. Caitlin Dulany told The Wrap that in 1996 Weinstein used his influence to talk his way into her apartment, where he stripped down naked. In June, a lawsuit revealed he allegedly also forcibly performed oral sex on her during the Cannes Film Festival the same year.

80. Melissa Thompson, a Columbia MBA grad, joined the lawsuit on June 1. She says in 2011, while pitching him on her technology startup he put his hands up her skirt, and later, under the guise of a business meeting, led her to a hotel suite above his office and raped her. Years later, she alleges she was tricked by Weinstein's lawyer, Benjamin Brafman, into sharing evidence of her assault, believing he was representing victims of the mogul.

Anonymous accusers:

81. An unidentified woman, who worked for Weinstein and told the New Yorker she was too afraid to use her name for fear of legal retaliation, said Weinstein brought her to a hotel room under professional pretext, then changed into a bathrobe and forced himself on her sexually.

82. An unnamed 38-year-old Italian actress whose accusation that Weinstein raped her in 2013 is now being investigated by Los Angeles police.

83. A former Miramax employee going by the alias Sarah Smith told The Daily Mail that Weinstein raped her in the basement of his London office in 1992. "He grabbed me and he was so big and powerful. He just ripped my clothes away and pushed me, threw me down," she said.

84. The Washington Post reported an account from 1984 on October 14, in which a young crew member on Weinstein's film Playing for Keeps was reportedly asked to visit Weinstein's hotel room where he attempted to perform oral sex on her.

85. An unnamed Canadian actress from Toronto is launching a lawsuit against Weinstein, alleging the movie mogul sexually assaulted her while filming a movie in Toronto in 2000, according to the Toronto Sun and CBC News. Once alone with the actress in his suite at the Sutton Place Hotel, Weinstein allegedly asked her if she liked massages, exposed himself to her and performed oral sex on her without her consent. Once she was able to free herself, she left the hotel and told her agent. The lawsuit claims the Jane Doe returned to Weinstein's suite after he insisted there had been a misunderstanding, and once back in his room, "he threw his weight onto her and tried to stick his tongue down her throat." She was in her 20s at the time.

86. An unnamed actress filed a lawsuit against the mogul in Beverly Hills on November 14, according to the Associated Press. Known only as "Jane Doe," the woman alleges Weinstein held her against her will while he masturbated in a Beverly Hills hotel room in 2015. A year later, she says, he threw her on his bed in a hotel room, started performing oral sex on her and then held her down while he masturbated on her. The suit says the woman was able to break free and flee the room.

87. An unnamed former employee filed the first civil claim in the U.K. on November 23 against Weinstein and the Weinstein Co. for a series of sexual assaults. Her lawyer, Jill Greenfield, said the woman has not filed a complaint with police about the alleged incidents that occurred after the year 2000 but believes she will do so.

Terrorist Attacks in Short for May

May 1

Bangui, Central African Republic: Gunmen equipped with grenades attacked the Notre-Dame de Fatima church in Bangui, the capital of the Central African Republic, during mass, killing 26 people, including a priest, and injuring 170 others.

Ménaka Region, Mali: Extremists linked to the Islamic state group killed at least 17 people, including elderly persons, who were burned alive in their homes, in Tindinbawen and Taylalene in the Ménaka region of Mali.

Mubi, Nigeria: At least 86 people were killed in two suicide attacks at a mosque and a market in Mubi, a town in the state of Adamawa in northeastern Nigeria. 58 others were injured in the bombings.

Al Tarmia, Iraq : Islamic state militants dressed in Iraqi military uniforms attacked Al Tarmia north of Baghdad, killing 21 members of a local tribe that was a vocal opponent of the extremists and injuring 13 others.

May 2

Tripoli, Libya: Suicide bombers attacked the head offices of Libya's electoral commission in Tripoli, killing at least 16 people, injuring 20 and setting fire to the building.

May 5

Far North Region, Cameroon: At least 12 people were killed, and 20 others were injured when two suicide bombers detonated their explosives at a mosque in Mabanda in the Far North region of Cameroon.

May 6

Khost Province, Afghanistan: 21 people were killed and 33 others injured when a bomb exploded in a mosque that was used as a voter registration center in Khost province.

Dhobley, Somalia: Nine Kenyan soldiers were killed after a military vehicle ran over an improvised explosive device in the Somali city of Dhobley

May 8

Guasipati, Venezuela: At least 20 miners and co-workers were killed during an encounter in Guasipati, Roscio Municipality, Bolivar state. Others were injured during the attack.

May 9

Kabul, Afghanistan: Suicide bombers attacked two police stations in the Afghan capital Kabul, killing at least ten people, including two police officers, and wounding 23 others. Eight terrorists also died in the attacks.

Wanlaweyn, Somalia: A suicide bomber killed at least 14 people and wounded 15 more at a market in the town of Wanlaweyn in the Lower Shabelle region of Somalia.

May 10

Farah Province, Afghanistan: At least 43 Afghan security soldiers were killed and ten others injured in Taliban attacks on two checkpoints in the Farah province of Afghanistan.

May 11

Argahandab District, Afghanistan: Taliban insurgents attacked security checkpoints in the Argahandab district of Zabul province in Afghanistan, killing 22 police officers and wounding 12 others.

Commune of Buganda, Burundi: At least 26 people were killed and eight others seriously injured in an attack in a village in the commune of Buganda in the province of Cibitoke in northwest Burundi.

May 12

Muse, Myanmar: At least 19 people were killed and 32 others injured in three attacks in the town of Muse in Shan State, Myanmar.

Idlib, Syria: At least 28 people, including civilians and jihadists, were killed in a car bomb attack in the northwestern Syrian city of Idlib. About 25 others were injured in the bombing.

Kirkuk Governorate, Iraq: At least six people were killed and three others injured in an attack on a security checkpoint in the northern province of Kirkuk in Iraq. In another attack, three men were killed by a bomb attached to their car.

Archi District, Afghanistan: Eight Afghan National Army troops and one local policeman were killed and five others injured in a Taliban attack in Archi district in the northern Afghan province of Kunduz.

May 13

Jalalabad, Afghanistan: At least 15 people were killed and 42 others injured when terrorists attacked a provincial government building in the eastern Afghan city of Jalalabad. Security forces killed six of the attackers after two of them carried out suicide attacks near the entrance of the building.

Patikul, Philippines: Eleven Abu Sayyaf terrorists and three soldiers were killed and 17 others injured in several shootouts in Patikul in the Philippine province of Sulu.

Surabaya and Sidoarjo, Indonesia: A series of terrorist attacks occurred in Surabaya and Sidoarjo in Indonesia. The attacks killed 15 civilians, mostly churchgoers, and injured 57 others. 13 perpetrators also died as a result of the bombings.

May 15

Zana Khan District and Jaghatū District, Afghanistan : 22 security force members were killed in shootouts with Taliban militants in the districts of Zana Khan and Jaghatū in the central Afghan province of Ghazni.

Shirin Tagab District, Afghanistan: At least nine members of an anti-Taliban militia were killed in a firefight with Taliban insurgents in Shirin Tagab district in the northwestern Afghan province of Faryab.

May 16

Al Tarmia, Iraq : At least eight people were killed and 31 injured in a suicide bombing which targeted a funeral in the town of Al Tarmia in the Saladin province, north of Baghdad.

May 18

Jalalabad, Afghanistan: Ten people were killed and 57 others injured by several explosions at a sports stadium in the eastern Afghan city of Jalalabad.

May 21

Beni Territory, Democratic Republic of Congo: At least ten civilians were killed and two others were seriously injured during an armed attack staged for Ugandan rebels, in Mbau village, Beni Territory.

Dih Yak District and Jaghatū District, Afghanistan: Taliban militants launched a wave of attacks in the districts of Dih Yak and Jaghatū in the eastern Afghan province of Ghazni, killing at least 20 police officers, including a district police chief and a reserve unit's commander, and injuring 12 others.

May 22

Kandahar, Afghanistan: At least 21 people were killed and 41 injured when a car packed with explosives blew up as members of the security forces tried to defuse it in the city of Kandahar in southern Afghanistan.

Tadmur District, Syria: At least 30 Syrian army troops and Iranian-backed militiamen were killed and an unknown number of others wounded when Islamic state militants attacked a military outpost near Palmyra in eastern Syria. The attack began with a suicide bomber detonating his vehicle, and later a gunfight occurred.

May 23

Mayadin District, Syria: At least 26 Syrian regime forces and nine Russian fighters were killed and an unknown number of others injured in an attack by Islamic State militants near the town of Mayadin in the province of Deir ez-Zor.

May 24

Shirin Tagab District, Afghanistan: Taliban militants attacked security forces in the Shirin Tagab district of the Afghan province of Faryab, killing twelve soldiers, injuring four others and kidnapping eight.

May 26

Talataye, Mali: Gunmen in vehicles and on motorcycles attacked a checkpoint in Talataye in the Gao region of Mali close to the Niger border that was manned by fighters of the Movement for the Salvation of Azawad, killing at least 20 people and injuring two others.

May 27

Palma District, Mozambique: Ten people, including some children, were beheaded in Monjane, a village near the border with Tanzania and not far from the town of Palma in northern Mozambique, in an attack by Islamists.

Chapter 6:
JUNE

Shooting at the Capital Gazette

A mass shooting took place on June 28 at the offices of the Capital Gazette newspaper, in Maryland. Five employees of the newspaper were killed and two others were injured while they were trying to flee.

The Incident

At around 2:34pm, a gunman shot out the glass door of the office and started shooting at the employees inside. The rear exit of the office had been barricaded by the gunman to prevent employees from escaping out the back door. A reporter, Phil Davis, was there when the shooting took place, and posted updates on Twitter as the incident unfolded. He claimed to see just one gunman carrying what looked like a long gun. It was later determined to be a 12-gauge pump-action shotgun.

During a pause while the gunman was reloading, some of the survivors sought refuge between the filing cabinets. Some of the witnesses saw Wendi Winters confront the gunman, charging at him with a trash can and recycling bin, effectively distracting the gunman so the others could escape. As a result, she lost her life.

The police evacuated the building, which contained 170 people, and conducted quick interviews with survivors to get more information on the gunman. When they entered the building, they located the gunman hiding beneath a desk. He was promptly disarmed and arrested, while the injured victims were transported to hospital for treatment.

The Victims

Those who were killed during the shooting rampage were:

- Gerald Fischman, 61 - editorial page editor and columnist
- Rob Hiaasen, 59 - weekend columnist and assistant editor
- John McNamara, 56 - sports reporter for The Capital and primary reporter and editor of The Bowie Blade News
- Rebecca Smith, 34 - sales assistant of Capital Gazette Communications
- Wendi Winters, 65 - community beat reporter

The Suspect - Jarrod Ramos

Ramos, 38, refused to identify himself when he was arrested at the scene by police. There was a problem with the finger print machine which further delayed identification. When he was arrested, he was carrying a backpack that contained flashbang devices, smoke bombs and grenades. It was determined that the attack by Ramos had been targeted at Capital Gazette Communications.

According to court filings, Ramos had been seen by five mental health professionals prior to the shooting, with a total of 75 appointments. Despite him issuing a pattern of threats, he never gave any indication to the mental health professionals that he would carry out any of the threats.

Ramos was described by those around him as a calculated and manipulative loner. He often became angry if things didn't go his way, and many believed that one day he would hurt somebody. When his family was contacted, many relatives stated they hadn't had any contact for several years with Ramos.

Charges Laid Against Ramos

Ramos was charged with five counts of first degree murder. He was held without ball because he was deemed to be a flight risk as well as a danger to the public. By July 2018, he was further charged with attempted first degree murder of the survivors. While in custody, Ramos was placed on suicide watch in case he tried to kill himself.

Throughout his bail hearing, Ramos didn't speak a word. He appeared in court again on August 20, at which time he plead not guilty to all charges. His lawyers were given a deadline of October 24 for them to enter a revised plea of not criminally responsible. The date for the trial has been set for June 3, 2019.

Previous Disputes with Newspaper

Ramos filed a lawsuit against The Capital in 2012, claiming defamation over an article they had published about him pleading guilty to a case of criminal harassment. The case was eventually dismissed in 2015, after Ramos had lodged a number of appeals. The court rules in favour of The Capital as they had reported on publicly available records. Also, Ramos had not provided any evidence that the article was false.

Thomas Marquardt, former editor and publisher of The Capital, stated that after the article was published, Ramos began to harass the staff of the newspaper. Marquardt contacted the police in 2013 regarding the harassment and behavior of Ramos, but the police didn't follow up on the complaint. As a result, Marquardt asked the newspaper's attorneys if they could file a restraining order against Ramos. He actually told them, "This is a guy who is going to come in and shoot us."

Ramos set up a Twitter account after the failure of his lawsuit, and began to attack the newspaper, the staff and the owners of the publication. He also sent threatening letters to the former attorney of the newspaper, and to the Maryland Court of Special Appeals, and to the appellate judge, Charles Moylan Jr, who had ruled against him in the defamation lawsuit.

Rapper Gunned Down

American rapper XXXTentacion was shot and killed during an alleged robbery on June 18. The shooting took place outside a store in Deerfield Beach, Florida, that specialized in selling boats and motorcycles.

The Day of the Shooting

XXXTentacion, real name Jahseh Dwayne Ricardo Onfroy, had gone to the bank on June 18 to withdraw some money. He then headed to RIVA Motorsports in Deerfield Beach. He was apparently unaware that he was being followed from the bank by a dark-colored Dodge Journey SUV. Inside the vehicle were Dedrick Williams, Michael Boatwright, Robert Allen and Trayvon Newsome.

Onfroy arrived at the store at 3:30pm, and entered with his friend who had accompanied him. To confirm that it was Onfroy they had seen in the BMW they had been following, Robert Allen entered the store to check. A few minutes later, Boatwright and Newsome also entered the store.

About 30 minutes later, Onfroy left the store and got back into his black BMW. As he started to drive away, the SUV drove in front and blocked his car. Boatwright and Newsome got out and demanded Onfroy hand over his property to them. A struggle took place, during which Onfroy was shot in the neck, allegedly by Boatwright.

Witnesses to the robbery saw Boatwright and Newsome remove a Louis Vuitton bag from Onfroy's vehicle before getting back into the SUV and fleeing the scene. Onfroy's friend, who had been in the BMW throughout the robbery, quickly got out of the car and fled.

The Broward County Fire Department was called to the scene and provided medical care before Onfroy was rushed to Broward Health North, nearby. Initially it was reported that Onfroy was in a critical condition, but he later succumbed to his injuries and died at 5:30pm.

The Investigation

Within a short time of Onfroy's death, the Broward County Sheriff's Office announced a bounty of $3,000 for information leading to the arrest of the suspects. Initially, fans of Onfroy's, local residents, and many internet users, suspected that the shooting and robbery may have been carried out by rappers Soldier Kidd and Soldier Jojo. The two rappers had allegedly posted suspicious comments on Instagram that seemed to repeat the details that had been given by witnesses at the scene.

Dedrick Williams, 22, was arrested on June 20. Police had attempted to perform a traffic stop on Williams as he was driving his silver 2004 Honda, and a police chase ensured. He was eventually captured, and was identified as being involved in the murder of Onfroy through clothing he had been wearing.

When police looked at pictures from Williams' Instagram, they noted that the clothing in the pictures matched the security footage taken on the day of the shooting. In particular, he had been wearing a bright orange pair of sandals. Employees from RIVA Motorsports also identified Williams as the man who had come in and purchased masks just before the shooting.

Robert Allen, 22, was first declared a person of interest on June 27, but he wasn't arrested until July 26. On July 5, Michael Boatwright, 22, was arrested, originally on charges relating to drugs. But, on July 10, a warrant was issued for his arrest in relation to the murder of Onfroy. From the investigation, police were convinced that Boatwright was the man who pulled the trigger.

Trayvon Newsome, 20, was finally arrested on August 7 for his participation in the murder. Some believe Newsome may have been the shooter, not Boatwright.

All four suspects have been charged with first degree murder and armed robbery with a firearm.

The Aftermath

Fans and local residents created a makeshift memorial following the announcement of Onfroy's death. It consisted of lyrics from Onfroy's music and words of remembrance written in chalk over the distance of 100 yards.

A vigil was organized by the owner of RIVA Motorsports and held on June 19, with hundreds gathered to pay their respects. There were so many people there that the police had to close down the street. A walk was organized, Onfroy's new home that was still being built was memorialized by fans in Parkland, Florida. A statement was then released by Onfroy's team that a proper memorial service would take place.

Adam Grandmaison, an internet personality known as Adam22, held a memorial the day following Onfroy's death. Grandmaison had given Onfroy his first professional interview on his podcast No Jumper. The memorial took place inform of Grandmaison's BMX store, OnSomeShit on Melrose Avenue, Los Angeles. Initially 300 people turned up, but it soon grew to over 1,000, so police in riot gear eventually had to disperse the crowd. Reports say the police used tear gas and rubber bullets to clear the crowds.

Onfroy's Funeral

The funeral service for Onfroy took place on June 27, at BB&T Center in Sunrise, Florida. It was an open casket service, and fans were let in to pay their respects. The family then held a private funeral the following day. During the private service, rappers Lil Uzi Vert, Lil Yachty, Denzel Curry and singer Erykah Badu attended. Onfroy was laid to rest in a grey colored mausoleum at the Gardens of Boca Raton Memorial Park.

The Commercial Impact of Onfroy's Death

The day following Onfroy's death, his single 'Sad!' broke the single-day streaming record on Billboard previously held by Taylor Swift's single 'Look What You Made Me Do'. Onfroy's track received 10.4 million streams, whereas Swift's single had 10.1 million streams. Following this was a 16-

fold sales increase across all download and streaming platforms. On Amazon.com there was a 7000-fold sales increase on Onfroy's CD.

In the week of his death, Onfroy's album reached number three with 90,000 album-equivalent units sold. The previous week, before his death, it had reached 19,000. Also in the week following his death, his single 'Sad!" went from 52nd place on the Billboard Hot 100 to 1st place. He was the first artist since The Notorious B.I.G. to reach number 1 posthumously.

Onfroy's management team released the music video for 'Sad!' after his death and the video has received over 90 million views, and the audio for the video has received more than 520 million views.

Nerve Agent Poisonings in Amesbury

Two people were admitted to the Salisbury District Hospital in Wiltshire, England, on June 30. It was later determined they had been poisoned by the same Novichok nerve agent that had been used to poison Sergei and Yulia Skripal in Salisbury, 8 miles away. Police then had the task of trying to work out what the connection was between the Skripals and the British Nationals who had now been the victims of poisoning.

Hospital Admissions and Death

An ambulance had been called to an address in Amesbury at 10:15am, June 30.On arrival they encountered Dawn Sturgess, 44, who had collapsed. They transported her to hospital, where she was admitted. A few hours later, the emergency services were called back to the same address, and this time the patient was Charlie Rowley, 45, who had fallen ill. He was also taken to the hospital, and due to the nature of the two admissions from the same address, the police were notified.

A friend of both victims stated that when Sturgess collapsed it seemed she had a seizure and was foaming at the mouth. When Rowley fell ill, he was dribbling and sweating profusely, and his eyes were red with pin-prick pupils. Police stated that at first they thought both patients had been using contaminated heroin or crack cocaine. Once tests were performed at the hospital, and further tests undertaken at the UK's Military research laboratory, it was discovered they had been exposed to the Novichok nerve agent.

On July 8, after doctors had decided to turn off life support, Dawn Sturgess died. Two days later, Rowley regained consciousness, and it was reported that he had made a small improvement in his condition. The following day he was downgraded from critical to serious but stable. It was then that investigators were finally able to speak to Rowley about the circumstances surrounding the poisoning.

Rowley told his brother that they had found a perfume or aftershave bottle in a park several days before the poisoning. It wasn't until the day they fell ill that they had both sprayed themselves with it. As a result, police closed Queen Elizabeth Gardens, where Rowley said they had found the bottle, and they searched it thoroughly.

The funeral for Sturgess took place on July 30, at the Salisbury Crematorium. Ten days earlier, Rowley was discharged home from hospital. Unfortunately, he was readmitted August 18 with vision problems, and on September 4, he reportedly had meningitis and was back in hospital but was expected to be discharged in a month or so.

The Investigation

Because of the seriousness and circumstances of the poisoning, the Specialist Operations Directorate of the Metropolitan Police conducted the investigation, along with assistance from the National Counter Terrorism Policing Network. The investigation concurred there was nothing in the background of either Sturgess or Rowley that would suggest they had been specifically targeted.

There were no further reports of anyone else in the area falling ill. Sturgess and Rowley had apparently been near the area where the roads were blocked off during the Skripal poisoning investigation, but this didn't raise any major concerns regarding them being specific targets or being poisoned from a distance.

It was believed the couple was most likely poisoned by a contaminated object, and the people behind the Skripal poisoning apparently hadn't disposed of the poison with care. As Rowley was known to scavenge through recycling bins for anything he could possibly sell, it was possible he had picked up an item and taken it back to the house.

Areas in Amesbury and Salisbury where Sturgess and Rowley had visited prior to the poisoning were cordoned off so they could be searched and to prevent any further poisoning from contamination. These areas included the Boots Pharmacy, Muggleton Road, Baptist Centre and the Queen Elizabeth Gardens.

Police announced on July 6 that they had located several key witnesses and had spoken to them. They had also amassed 1,300 hours of CCTV footage that needed to be viewed. On July 13, part of Rollestone Street, Salisbury, was cordoned off by police so they could search a hostel where Sturgess had lived. The cordon wasn't lifted until July 24, when it was clear there was no contamination there.

The small bottle Rowley had told his brother about was located inside his house and sent for analysis. On July 13, police made an announcement that the bottle was the source of the Novichok nerve agent. At the same time, the Organization for the Prohibition of Chemical Weapons was requested to provide technical assistance in investigating the incident.

The OPCW announced on September 4 that the nerve agent that poisoned Sturgess and Rowley was the same as the one used to poison the Skripals, but they could not confirm if it had come from the same batch.

Assistant Commissioner Neil Basu stated on September 5 that they were convinced the two poisonings were linked. He stated, "We do not believe Dawn and Charlie were deliberately targeted, but became victims as a result of the recklessness in which such a toxic nerve agent was disposed of."

Rowley Interview

On July 24 Rowley gave an interview to ITV News, during which he told how he had found a sealed box of perfume, from a recognizable brand, and had given it to Sturgess. Within about 15 minutes of her spraying what they thought was perfume on to her wrists and rubbing them together, she became sick. The 'perfume' was more like an oily substance rather than the fine liquid usually associated with perfume.

He explained that he came into contact with the contents of the bottle when some spilled on to his hands while he was attaching the spray dispenser on to the bottle. Even though he washed his hands shortly after, it was too late.

Ongoing Investigation

The investigation into the poisoning of the Skripals and Sturgess and Rowley is ongoing, and although some suspects have been identified, they are yet to be arrested.

The Killing of Antwon Rose Jr.

On June 19, Antwon Rose was shot and killed following a police traffic stop. There had been a drive-by shooting shortly beforehand, and police had stopped the vehicle because it showed evidence of bullet holes. People were confused at how a 17-year-old honor roll student and community volunteer, could have been involved in any type of criminal activity. There were many factors in how the shooting happened, who was involved, and what the outcome, both legally and publicly, would be.

The Night of the Shooting

At around 8:20pm, a drive-by shooting occurred in North Braddock, Pennsylvania and police were given a description of the car involved. Twenty minutes later, police officers saw a silver Chevrolet Cruze matching the description given in a nearby area. They stopped the car and noticed there were clear bullet holes and damage to the vehicle, indicating it was the vehicle involved in the drive-by shooting.

According to a video recording filmed by a bystander, police ordered the driver of the silver Chevrolet to get out of the vehicle. As he was being handcuffed, the two passengers in the car, including Rose, took off on foot. Police officer Michael Rosfield fired at the two fleeing men, striking Rose three times. The first shot hit Rose on the right-hand side of his face, and the bullet exited through his nasal cavity. The second shot hit Rose on the back of his right elbow. The last shot, which was the fatal wound, hit Rose in the middle of his back, and the bullet lodged in his chest.

Rose was transported to the hospital, where he later died. The second man who had tried to run away was later arrested. Police reported that Rose did not have a weapon when he was shot. Later that evening, the driver of the car was released, as there was no evidence that would enable them to charge him.

Police stated the vehicle the men were in may have been what is called a 'jitney', a low-cost private vehicle that picks up passengers. At first they didn't know if Rose had been in the vehicle during the drive-by shooting, or if he had gotten into the car later. However, the Allegheny County District Attorney Stephen Zappala stated there had been an empty 9-millimeter handgun magazine in Rose's pocket. There were also two guns in the car - a .40-caliber handgun and a 9-millimeter caliber handgun.

Indictment of a Police Officer

The police officer who fired the fatal shots, Rosfeld, was immediately put on leave as the Allegheny County Police Department undertook an investigation into the incident. After the autopsy on Rose's body, the medical examiner classified the death as a homicide. Rose had died from the gunshot wound to his torso.

On June 25, Rosfeld, 30, was placed under arrest and charged with criminal homicide. Detectives investigating the shooting found inconsistencies in the testimony provided by Rosfeld. Originally, Rosfeld had said he saw Rose pointing something dark colored at him which he thought was a gun, which was why he made the decision to shoot at Rose.

However, when he was asked to go over the event again, Rosfeld said he didn't see a gun in Rose's hand as he ran from the scene. The next time he was asked, he changed the story again. When challenged about the changes to his story, Rosfeld said he saw something in Rose's hand but he didn't know what it was. He also stated that he wasn't sure if Rose was still pointing towards him when he started shooting at Rose.

The district attorney stated at a news conference that the decision to charge Rosfeld was not influenced by the protests that were occurring in the area, but that the evidence in the case supported the homicide charge. He further said, "Taking a human life is one of the most important issues in this community, dealing with those types of tragedies," Zappala told reporters. "You do not shoot somebody in the back if they are not a threat to you."

A criminal homicide charge under Pennsylvania law can include first, second or third degree murder, and Zappala felt the case and the evidence meant that the most serious charge, first degree, was appropriate. If found guilty, Rosfeld could be incarcerated for life. Zappala said, "We think we should have the right to argue murder in the first degree," he said. "It's an intentional act, and there is no justification for it."

On June 26, the other passenger in the vehicle who fled was located and arrested and was sent to the Shuman Juvenile Detention Center, as he was a juvenile. He had been on probation at the time of the incident, and had cut off his ankle bracelet. The investigation into the drive-by shooting indicated that it was this passenger who had opened fire in the drive-by. He was therefore charged with criminal homicide and aggravated assault.

Because of the media attention and public response to the shooting of Rose, the defense team of Rosfeld filed a motion to have the case heard by a jury from outside of Allegheny County, for fear of bias.

Officer's Troubled Past

Rosfeld had only been sworn in as an officer in Allegheny County a few hours prior to the shooting of Rose. He had previously worked in East Pittsburgh, and had a total of seven years of experience working with other police departments. He had also been sued in civil court for making a false police report in 2017 while working as an officer at the University of Pittsburgh.

The attorney for the family of Rose stated that he was 'disturbed' that Rosfeld was hired at East Pittsburgh after his 'history of brutality and a history of falsifying reports'. Zappala also said he was concerned about the reports on Rosfeld's policing history, but he was unable to comment further.

Rose family attorney Merritt commented that he was in the process of requesting the official personnel file on Rosfeld from the University of Pittsburgh police. He said, "We believe that will reveal significant history of abuse of authority and a pattern that should have signaled East Pittsburgh not to hire this officer. He should have never been sworn in the day he killed Antwon Rose."

Multiple Protests - A Community Outraged

The first protests occurred on June 20 and 21, where hundreds of people gathered outside the Allegheny County Courthouse. Then, on the evening of June 22, protestors slowed traffic on the Parkway East freeway for miles as they marched. Further protests took place near PNC Park, located on the North Shore, and in the neighborhood of Pittsburgh's South Side.

The protests continued into July, and the preliminary hearing for Rosfeld had to be shifted to the Allegheny County Courthouse amid fears of security in the city. On July 8, while protestors were on Route 30 in North Versailles, a car drove through the group and struck four of the protestors. One person was taken to hospital and another was arrested.

A new protest policy was issued on July 26 because of the continuous disruption by the ongoing protests to the bridges and roadways in the city. Although the police don't prohibit protests, it does prohibit protestors who are unpermitted to block the traffic or cause the shutdown of high traffic times in red and yellow zones.

The Public Safety Director and the Police Chief were confronted by protestors at the corner of Grant Street and Forbes Avenue on July 27, regarding the new policy. One protestor, Nicky Jo Dawson, stated that the policy "put further restrictions on people who are peacefully protesting against an oppressive system."

The guidelines designate nine city intersections and nine roads and highways as 'Red Zones', which cannot be blocked at any time. These include I-279 and I-376, and routes 28, 51 and 65. This also includes any hospital entry and exit routes, special event entry and exit routes as well as all bridges and tunnels.

Eight other areas are designated as 'Yellow Zones', which can only be blocked by rallies and marches for 15 minutes only during non-rush hour periods. Among these are Grant Street, Liberty Avenue, Stanwix Street and all school zones.

Protesters violating the policy will be given three warnings to disperse before police action is taken. There is one exception whereby any acts of violence against persons or damaging of property shall result in immediate police action."

Terrorist Attacks in Short for June

June 1

Moqokori, Somalia: The Islamist group Al-Shabaab attacked the town of Moqokori in the Hiran region of Somalia. According to the militants, 72 soldiers were killed in the fighting.

June 2

Balad District, Iraq: A family of 12 was killed by Islamic state militants in the village of Al-Farahatiyah in the Balad district of the Iraqi Saladin governorate.

June 3

Wanna, Pakistan: At least ten activists of the Pashtun Tahafuz Movement were killed and 30 others sustained injuries when local Taliban militants shot at them in Wanna in South Waziristan, Pakistan.

June 4

Diffa, Niger: Three suicide bombers, two women and a man blew themselves up in Diffa in southeast Niger. The first explosion took place near a mosque, the second near a Koran school and the third not far from a business centre. Nine people were killed and 38 others injured in the attacks.

Kabul, Afghanistan: A suicide bomber detonated his explosives targeting a gathering of Afghanistan's top clerics in Kabul, killing at least 14 people and wounding 19. Shortly afterwards, a magnetic bomb attached to a police car exploded and as a result three people were wounded.

June 5

Middle Shabelle, Somalia: Two lawmakers from Somalia's semi-autonomous state of Hirshabelle were killed along with ten bodyguards in an ambush in the Middle Shabelle region near Somalia's capital Mogadishu.

June 6

Baghdad, Iraq: At least 20 people were killed and 110 wounded when two bombs exploded near an ammunition cache placed in a Shiite mosque in the Sadr City area of Iraq's capital Baghdad.

June 7

As-Suwayda Governorate, Syria: Islamic state militants killed 22 pro-regime fighters in an attack in the southern Syrian province of As-Suwayda.

June 8

Diamaré, Cameroon: At least 10 people were killed in attacks in villages in the department of Diamaré in the far north of Cameroon. Four Boko Haram terrorists were also killed.

Abu Kamal, Syria: 30 Syrian pro-regime fighters were killed when at least ten suicide bombers attacked the city of Abu Kamal in the Deir ez-Zor province.

Shah Wali Kot District, Qalay-I-Zal District and Shindand District, Afghanistan: Taliban insurgents killed as many as 65 government soldiers and police officers in attacks in the districts of Shah Wali Kot, Qalay-I-Zal and Shindand in three Afghan provinces. At least 17 security forces were injured in the incidents.

June 10

Oshnavieh, Iran: PDKI peshmergas claimed killed nine and injured 18 members of the Iranian Revolutionary Guards Corps in a clash on Friday near an Iran-Iraq border town.

June 11

Kabul, Afghanistan: At least 17 people were killed and 40 others seriously injured after a suicide bomber detonated his explosives at an Afghan ministry in Kabul.

Qalay-I-Zal District, Afghanistan: 15 members of the Afghan security forces were killed when Taliban fighters attacked their security post in Qalay-I-Zal district in the northern province of Kunduz.

June 12

Sayyad District, Afghanistan: The Taliban killed at least 14 members of Afghanistan's security forces in an attack in the Sayyad district of Sar-e Pol province. 25 others were wounded during the attack and four of the injured soldiers were taken hostage by the insurgents.

Kohistan District, Afghanistan : 13 security personnel, including the district administrative chief, were killed and 16 others injured when Taliban militants attacked the district center of the Kohistan district in the northwestern province of Faryab, Afghanistan.

Muqur District, Afghanistan: At least five policemen were killed and 26 others, including a governor and 18 policemen, were wounded by a suicide bomber using a military Humvee in the Muqur district of the eastern Afghan province of Ghazni.

June 13

Jurm District, Afghanistan: 20 soldiers were killed, at least three injured and six taken hostage in a Taliban attack on a military post in the Jurm district in the northern Afghan province of Badakhshan. Eight militants were also killed.

June 16

Rodat District, Afghanistan: A suicide bomber killed at least 36 people and injured 65 others at a gathering of Taliban and Afghan armed forces in the Rodat district of the eastern Afghan province of Nangarhar.

Damboa, Nigeria: At least 43 people were killed and 84 others injured when six female suicide bombers detonated their explosives in the Damboa local government area in the Nigerian state of Borno.

June 17

Jalalabad, Afghanistan: A suicide bomber detonated his explosives near the governor's compound in Afghanistan's eastern city of Jalalabad, killing at least 25 people and injuring 50 others.

June 18

Nganzai, Nigeria: Boko Haram militants killed nine soldiers and wounded two others when they attacked the town of Gajiram, headquarters of the local government of Nganzai in northeastern Nigeria.

June 20

Murghab District, Afghanistan: 30 soldiers of the Afghan army were killed after militants attacked two security checkpoints in the Murghab district in the Afghan province of Badghis. In the incident, also 16 Taliban fighters were killed and 15 wounded.

Farah Province, Afghanistan: At least 15 policemen were killed in two attacks in two different districts of the Afghan province of Farah.

June 22

Ab Kamari District, Afghanistan: Taliban militants killed at least 16 Afghan police officers and two civilians in the Ab Kamari district of the western Afghan province of Badghis.

June 27

Afrin, Syria: At least 10 civilians were killed and 20 more injured in two car bomb attacks in the northwestern Syrian city of Afrin.

Chah Ab District, Afghanistan : At least 16 members of the border police were killed in a Taliban attack in the Chah Ab district of the northeastern Afghan province of Takhar. Six other people were still missing.

Chapter 7:
JULY

Kid's Birthday Turns Violent

On June 30, an armed man walked into a child's birthday party in Idaho and began attacking people. The stabbing rampage resulted in the death of one young child, and caused injuries to nine other people, including six children.

The 3rd Birthday Party

The birthday was being held at the Wylie Street Station Apartments, and had been set up in an outdoor area that was accessible to the public. There was a birthday cake and party decorations including red and blue balloons, just as you would expect to find at a little girl's birthday party.

The day before, Timmy Earl Kinner, 30, had been asked to leave the property due to his behavior. What type of behavior it was that necessitated him being asked to leave isn't clear. He didn't live in the apartments but he did stay with a friend there when he had nowhere else to go.

At around 8:45pm, Kinner entered the area where the birthday party was being held, and began attacking the children with a knife. One of the victims was the 3-year-old girl, who the party was for. The other child victims were two 4-year-olds, a 6-year-old, 8-year-old and a 12-year-old. Three adults were also injured as they tried to intervene and stop the attack.

Of the victims, four received injuries that were classified as life threatening. The 3-year-old was taken to hospital but later died from her injuries.

Although the police didn't release her name, the International Rescue Committee, who works globally with refugees, identified the little girl as an Ethiopian refugee called Ruya Kadir. She had been living in the US with her mother since 2015, while her father lived in Turkey.

What made the death of Ruya even more upsetting to many people was not just her age or that it was her birthday party, but because her mother had fled with her to America to escape the conflict they had experienced in Ethiopia. Ruya was described as a child who 'sparkled' when she entered a room. She loved Disney princesses and the color pink, and was always the center of her mother's attention.

A History of Violence

The offender, Kinner, has an extensive criminal history, which spans across multiple states, and he had spent time in prison in Kentucky previously. Since 2012, he had been convicted of numerous offences, including aggravated assault, weapons offenses, assault, and unlawful possession of a controlled substance.

Kinner hadn't been living in Idaho for very long before he went on the murderous rampage. As mentioned, he stayed at a friend's apartment when he needed somewhere to go. When he was asked to leave the property the day before the attack, he left peacefully. Police believe that the whole reason he returned was to seek vengeance.

Tragically for those at the birthday party, the people who should have been the target of Kinner's revenge weren't there, and so he attacked the first people he saw. Unfortunately, the birthday party was only a few doors down from where Kinner's intended targets lived.

The true motive of Kinner's rampage is not known, as he has refused to cooperate with the police.

A Multi-Cultural Attack

The apartments where the attack occurred are home to a rather diverse community. Many who lived there were families with children, who had sought refuge in the US. The victims of the stabbing attack came from Ethiopia, Syria and Iraq, countries that have been the center of extreme violence for decades. The refugees at the party had left such awful living conditions to have a better life in the US, away from war and poverty. Instead, the war was brought right to their doorstep, in the form of Kinner.

Despite the cultural differences, there was no evidence found that would suggest Kinner had committed the attack as a hate crime. Despite this, the refugee community was struck with horror and fear over what had taken place.

Charges Laid Against Kinner

Kinner was charged with one count of murder and eight counts of aggravated battery, and was ordered to be held without bail. The Prosecutor's Office later announced that they would be seeking the death penalty in the case for the murder of Ruya.

The trial is set to take place on January 3, 2019. In recent hearings, Kinner's attorneys have voiced concerns over Kinner's mental health, and have requested he be committed to a state facility for treatment. A psychologist was appointed to evaluate Kinner, but he has refused to meet with him repeatedly.

During a plea hearing in August, Kinner chose to 'stand silent' rather than speak. The judge entered not guilty pleas on his behalf to all of his 13 charges. The total charges include the first degree murder and eight counts of aggravated battery, as well as one count of burglary for entering the apartment, and two counts of aggravated assault and a deadly weapon enhancement.

The Healthcare Murderer

In Britain, a nurse has been arrested, suspected of murdering eight babies in her care and the attempted murder of six more babies. These types of murders aren't as rare as they seem, and often they go unnoticed for long periods of time. These murders date back to 2015, and there are still further cases to be investigated.

The Suspected Murders

In total police have been investigating the deaths of 17 babies, and 15 cases of unexplained non-fatal collapses between a one year period, from June 2015 to June 2016. In July 2016, the Countess of Chester Hospital commissioned an independent review of the baby unit because there had been a rise in unexplained deaths in infants.

The same time as the review was commissioned, they stopped treating the really premature babies, or those that needed intensive care. By the end of the review, there was no explanation found for the increase of neonatal deaths, even though the medical consultants had noticed some similarities between the cases.

The report did highlight a failure by the hospital to investigate the cases, and although the babies underwent autopsies, they were basic and did not include systemic tests that would have found any changes in blood or sugar levels or detect any types of poison that may have been administered. With an autopsy, toxicology tests are not done routinely, but they are often performed when there is no apparent cause of death.

The report also noted that by mentioning to the staff that CCTV was going to be installed on the neonatal unit without a proper explanation most likely unsettled the nurses even further. In December 2016, the hospital began issuing electronic tracking wristbands to all patients and staff, supposedly to monitor free beds.

The Police Investigation

The police began an investigation in May 2017, as the trust who ran the hospital were still concerned about the increasing number of unexplained deaths in the baby unit. It started out studying the deaths of 15 babies, but then expanded to the 17 deaths and 15 near-deaths. Because the number of baby deaths that were being investigated was so high, it could become the largest scandal of this type in the history of the National Health Service.

In charge of the investigation, Detective Inspector Paul Hughes of Cheshire Police, stated: "This is a highly complex and very sensitive investigation and, as you can appreciate, we need to ensure we do everything we possibly can to try to establish in detail what has led to these deaths and collapses.

"As a result of our ongoing inquiries we have today arrested a healthcare professional in connection with the investigation. While this is a significant step forward, it is important to remember that the investigation is very much active and ongoing."

The Suspect - Lucy Letby

Nurse Lucy Letby, 28, had been employed at the neonatal unit since she graduated with a degree in child nursing from the University of Chester in 2011. She had also spent some time at the unit while she was undertaking her nursing training. Late in 2016, Letby was moved to administrative duties and removed from any patient care.

One source commented that if they were suspicious of Letby's involvement in the deaths, instead of moving her to administration, they should have suspended her immediately. This is another question the hospital may face when the case goes to court.

The Fallout

Tony Chambers, who was the chief executive officer at the hospital, resigned from his position two months after Letby was arrested on July 3.

The hospital chairman, Sir Duncan Nichol, claimed that the decision was not related to the investigation. However, there had been three reports criticizing the maternity care at the hospital.

As the investigation is still ongoing, there may be more charges laid against Letby in the months to come, In the meantime, she is awaiting her trial, which will take place next year.

Tragic Bus Crash a Criminal Act

On April 6, a horrific accident occurred between a semi-trailer and a coach bus nearly Armley, Saskatchewan, Canada. As a result of the accident, sixteen people were killed and thirteen injured, and tragically, most of those killed or injured were young members of the Humboldt Broncos, a junior ice hockey team. Normally this would seem just an awful accident, with a tremendous loss of life, but, in July it was decided that there was more to this than just an unforeseen accident. In fact, it could have been completely prevented, which is why criminal charges have been laid.

The Horrific Crash

The collision between the coach and the semi-trailer occurred at the intersection of Highways 35 and 335 at around 5:00pm. The semi-trailer had been traveling westbound on Highway 335, and the coach was heading northbound on Highway 35. It was a sunny afternoon and the roads were clear. Video footage of the scene showed the front of the coach had been obliterated, but the front of the semi-trailer remained undamaged.

A survivor told authorities that the coach had been broadsided by the semi-trailer. Normally, the seating plan of the coach would mean that the rookies were seated at the front, and the veterans took the seats at the back. This was verified by survivor Kaleb Dahlgren who recalled that the 18-year-olds were up the front, the 19-year-olds were seated in the middle of the coach, and the 20-year-olds were in the back.

The sheer force of the impact between these two large vehicles resulted in both coming to rest off the highway, and both vehicles were lying on their sides. There had been 29 people on board the coach. At the scene there were 14 dead, but two more died later on in the hospital.

The driver of the semi-trailer was uninjured and was initially detained by police for questioning, but was later released. The company he worked for stated later that the driver was receiving psychological support since the accident.

Sean Brandow, the team chaplain, arrived shortly after the accident to provide aid and offer prayers. Families of the team members were directed to a church in Nipawin by officers to await news. Because most of the veteran team members were relatively unscathed from sitting in the back, the majority of parents left waiting at the church towards the end were all those whose children were rookies.

Those who died as a result of the crash were:

- Dayna Brons, 24 (athletic therapist)
- Parker Tobin, 18
- Darcy Haugan, 42 (head coach and general manager)
- Brody Hinz, 18 (volunteer statistician)
- Logan Schatz, 20
- Jaxon Joseph, 20
- Adam Herold, 16
- Mark Cross, 27 (assistant coach)
- Tyler Bieber, 29 (play by play radio announcer)
- Stephen Wack, 21
- Logan Hunter, 18
- Conner Lukan, 21
- Glen Doerksen (driver of the bus)
- Evan Thomas, 18
- Jacob Leicht, 19
- Logan Boulet, 21

The First Responders

The first responders who arrived at the scene included three rescue helicopters and four air ambulances. Cities nearby and companies had loaned the aircraft so that the most critically injured patients could be transported to Royal University Hospital in Saskatoon, which was nearly 170 miles away. The hospital declared a Code Orange, an indicator that there were mass casualties on the way.

The Saskatchewan Health Authority which oversees ambulance and hospital services in the area encouraged the employees affected by the event to utilize the counselling available. This was largely because many of those who had been first responders had some sort of tie to the accident. It is an area where people tend to be obsessed with hockey, have a child that plays hockey, or acts as a billet for visiting hockey players.

Members of the Tisdale and Nipawin fire departments were sent peer counsellors to help those who had attended the crash, especially as they were the ones who were first on the scene and had to remove the victims from the mangled wreckage. As a crane operator who hoisted the coach roof off so the first responders could get in to the coach, said, "those poor first responders, them guys – they were the ones getting the people out of there, they were the ones making the decisions".

The number of first responders that were at the scene was estimated at 80 personnel. They had come from Tisdale, Nipawin, Carrot River, Zenon Park, Melfort, and other areas to provide assistance.

Investigating the Crash

On April 18, Assistant Commissioner Curtis Zablocki, the Commanding Officer of the Saskatchewan Royal Canadian Mounted Police (RCMP), announced that the semi-trailer driver had been in continuous contact with the RCMP. The investigation would be looking at the engine computers from both vehicles, as well as the driver's logs, and the experience of the drivers.

The RCMP went back to the scene of the crash on April 19, to reconstruct the crash and do further analysis of the scene. So that reconstructionists could recreate the crash more accurately, similar vehicles to those involved in the crash would be brought in. This would also allow for more precise measurements to be taken and sight lines to be analyzed.

A witness to the crash, Kelsey Fiddler, had stated in an interview with police that she had been forced to swing her vehicle out of the way just seconds before the crash so she wouldn't be 'sandwiched' between the two vehicles. She stated she had been waiting at the stop sign eastbound on Highway 335 and was going to turn on to Highway 35 when she saw the coach approaching. She believed the coach was traveling at normal highway speed.

Criminal Charges Laid

A news conference was held by the RCMP on July 6 to announce that they had made and arrest and charges had been laid in relation to the crash. The driver of the semi-trailer, Jaskirat Singh Sidhu, 29, of Calgary, was charged with 16 counts of dangerous driving causing death and 13 counts of dangerous driving causing bodily harm.

The investigation revealed that Sidhu had just one year of experience driving trucks when the crash occurred. He had only received two weeks of training on the semi-trailer he was driving that day. Following his arrest, he was released on $1,000 bail, and some conditions were placed on his release. These include that he must remain living at his home in Calgary, he was given a curfew, he was banned from driving, and his passport had to be surrendered.

In October, the owner of the trucking company Adesh Deol Trucking Ltd., Sukhinder Singh, was also charged with violating both federal and provincial safety regulations. The charges included two counts of failure to require a daily log, two counts of keeping multiple daily logs for a single day, three counts of failure to monitor their driver's compliance with the relevant regulation and one count of failure to have or follow a written safety plan.

The maximum sentence the driver of the semi-trailer may receive if found guilty would be 14 years for dangerous driving causing death and 10 years for dangerous driving causing injury. He has yet to enter a plea.

Civil Lawsuit

The parents of victim Adam Herold, Russell and Raelene Herold, filed a lawsuit on behalf of their son against the semi-trailer driver, the trucking company and the coach manufacturer. The lawsuit asks for court orders and unspecified damages. One of the court orders requested is that every coach that carries sports teams would have to have seat belts and other safety devices fitted. The case has not gone to trial yet.

The Aftermath

Prime Minister Justin Trudeau, along with many other politicians and dignitaries in Canada, expressed their condolences to the families of the victims. Queen Elizabeth II and Prince Philip were also among those who offered their condolences in the days after the tragic crash.

President Trump made a telephone call to Prime Minister Trudeau then tweeted his condolences to the victims and their families. Many celebrities such as Drake, Whoopi Goldberg and Ellen DeGeneres voiced their sympathy to all who were affected. Pope Francis also sent a message of condolence, which the Bishop of Saskatoon read out during a Sunday service two days after the crash.

The Swift Current Broncos of the Western Hockey League offered their condolences to the Humboldt Broncos organization, the players and the families. They had experienced their own tragic bus crash in 1986, and a group of survivors from that crash traveled to Humboldt to offer their support to the hockey team and to the community.

The SJHL immediately suspended its playoffs after the crash indefinitely. The board of governors of the league decided on April 11 to allow the two reaming teams in the play offs to play for the league championship. The Manitoba Junior Hockey League delayed their championship series for four days out of respect.

The trucking company involved in the crash had only been operating for one year, and following the crash, their safety certificate was automatically suspended while the Transportation ministry investigated.

On April 8, it was discovered that a mistake had been made in identifying one of the deceased players. The coroner had originally declared the victim to be Xavier Labelle, but it was in fact Parker Tobin. He issued an apology for the error.

Ryan Straschnitzki, a survivor of the crash, was paralyzed from the waist down as a result of the crash. It hasn't stopped him from sports though, as he told his parents he wants to continue with sledge hockey and hopes to compete in the Paralympic Games.

Danforth Avenue Mass Shooting

The night of July 22, a mass shooting took place on Danforth Avenue in the Greektown area of Toronto, Canada. The rampage left two young people dead and several others from ages 17 to 59, injured.

The Frightening Incident

AT around 10:00pm, a man armed with a gun walked along Danforth Avenue, randomly shooting at pedestrians in the street before opening fire on patrons in crowded restaurants, including Christina's and Demetre's. According to some witnesses, they heard up to 15 blasts that sounded like firecrackers, but other witnesses not only heard the gunshots but also saw the man with the gun.

The shooter walked westbound along Danforth towards Hampton Avenue, then crossed the street and fired into 7Numbers, a restaurant near Bowden Street. One victim was shot in this restaurant. When the Toronto Police Service arrived on the scene, they exchanged gunfire with the suspect on Bowden Street. The gunman then fled back to Danforth Avenue, and when police reached him, he was dead.

At the corner of Danforth and Logan, police detonated a package found there but did not disclose what the package was or why they thought it was suspicious.

The Innocent Victims

One of the victims killed in the shooting was Reese Fallon, an 18-year-old who was planning on attending McMaster University. The other deceased victim was a 10-year-old girl, Julianna Kozis. Both had been out on an innocent evening outing when their young lives were brought to a tragic and abrupt end by one man with a gun.

There were thirteen other victims with gunshot wounds. Eight of the injured, were transported to trauma centers. Four were taken to St. Michael's Hospital, three went to Sunnybrook Health Sciences Center, and the other patient was transported to The Hospital for Sick Children. Of those that went to St. Michael's, three required immediate lifesaving surgery. The others were in a serious condition but were stable.

Two further gunshot victims received treatment at Michael Garron Hospital, and they were classified as being stable. There were five other patients related to the shooting who were treated for other injuries, but not gunshots.

The Shooter - Faisal Hussain

Hussain, 29, had Canadian parents but they were of Pakistani origin. His parents made a public statement after the shooting declaring their son was psychotic and suffered depression throughout his life. He had apparently been seeing a psychiatrist back in 2010 for his mental health issues.

A former school teacher of Hussain's, described him as very disturbed, and on one occasion had to take him to a psychiatric facility because he was cutting into his face with a pencil sharpener blade. Another teacher had notified police after Hussain had allegedly stated, unprompted, "it would be really cool to kill someone."

The family of Hussain had suffered terrible tragedies, more than the average family. Hussain's sister had been killed in a car accident, and his brother was in a longstanding coma after having either a stroke or a drug overdose. Hussain did not follow religion, and refused to take part in Friday prayers.

The Investigation into the Shooting

Straight after the shooting, police had no information on the possible motive. They did state they were investigating every motive possible, and that included terrorism, even though Hussain had not been considered dangerous previously and was not on any federal watch lists.

A search warrant at Hussain's residence was executed on July 23. The following day, CBS News reported that a law enforcement source had told them Hussain visited ISIL websites, could have expressed his support for the terrorists, and may have lived in Pakistan or Afghanistan. Then on July 25, Amaq News Agency, also citing a source, reported that Hussain was 'from the soldiers of the Islamic State'. However, Toronto Police denied there was any evidence of a connection between Hussain and ISIL.

Because Hussain was discovered dead on the night of the shootout, an investigation had to be carried out to ascertain whether he had shot himself or he had been shot by police. A police cruiser was taken from the scene and the two officers who had been in it were investigated regarding their roles in the shooting. The handgun Hussain had used was also seized for analysis.

According to CBS, a police source had told them on July 25 that Hussain had committed suicide. Another news group reported the same day that the gun Hussain had used was from the US and had been obtained from a 'gang-related' source. It was believed it had been stolen during a burglary in Saskatoon in 2015.

Community Aftermath and Reactions

Following the shooting, business owners and residents in the area began a crowdsourcing campaign to raise money for the funerals of the two girls who had died.

Both the Prime Minister and the Minister of Public Safety and Emergency Preparedness tweeted their condemnation of the shooting and issued praise for the actions of the police. Other Canadian politicians and dignitaries also voiced their disdain for the actions of Hussain.

The Ministry of Foreign Affairs of Greece expressed condolence and solidarity with the people of Greektown, where the shooting had occurred. A prayer vigil was held at Calvary Church nearby, and they were joined by a congregation from the Madinah mosque.

Terrorist Attacks in Short for July

July 1

Jalalabad, Afghanistan: A suicide bomber detonated his explosives in the center of the eastern Afghan city of Jalalabad, killing at least 20 people, including several members of the small Sikh minority, and injuring 20 others.

July 6

Al-Busayrah, Syria: A car bomb went off in front of the Syrian Democratic Forces' base in the town of Al-Busayrah in the Syrian governorate of Deir Ez-Zor, killing a commander, ten other personnel and seven civilians, including three children.

July 7

Mogadishu, Somalia: At least 20 people were killed and two dozen others wounded when fighters of the Somali group Al-Shabaab attacked the compound of Somalia's interior and security ministries in the center of Mogadishu. The attack started when the terrorists detonated two car bombs outside the main gate of the interior ministry building before three militants stormed it. All three gunmen were killed by the security forces.

July 9

Latakia District, Syria: At least 27 regime forces, including eight officers, were killed in clashes and shelling in a village in the Latakia district of the Syrian governorate of Latakia. Another 40 government loyalists were wounded and six terrorists killed.

July 10

Jalalabad, Afghanistan: A suicide bomber detonated his explosives near a petrol pump, killing two officials working for Afghanistan's intelligence agency and ten civilians, including children, and sparking a big fire that burned eight cars in the eastern Afghan city of Jalalabad. Five other people were taken to hospital.

Zayzun, Syria: At least 14 regime and opposition fighters were killed in a suicide car bomb attack targeting a military position in Zayzun, a town in the western countryside of the Syrian governorate of Daraa.

Peshawar, Pakistan: A suicide bombing at an election rally in the northwestern Pakistani city of Peshawar killed at least 22 people, including prominent local politician Haroon Bilour. The attack at a campaign event organised by the Awami National Party also injured at least 75 people.

July 11

Jalalabad, Afghanistan: At least 12 people were killed and another nine injured in a militant attack on the building of the provincial education department in the eastern Afghan city of Jalalabad. One suicide bomber detonated his explosives, while two more were shot dead by the security forces in a gunfight lasting several hours.

Archi District and Khwaja Ghar District, Afghanistan: A series of simultaneous attacks by the Taliban killed at least 40 Afghan soldiers and injured ten others in the Archi district in the province of Kunduz and in the Khwaja Ghar district in the province of Takhar in Afghanistan.

July 13

Bama, Nigeria: Boko Haram terrorists ambushed a detachment of troops in the local government area of Bama in the Nigerian state of Borno. Ten corpses of soldiers were found and at least one officer and one soldier were injured.

Mastung, Pakistan: At least 149 people, including the Baluchistan Awami Party candidate Nawabzada Siraj Raisani, were killed and 186 others injured when a suicide bomber detonated his explosives in Mastung in the Pakistani province of Baluchistan.

July 14

Geidam, Nigeria: Islamist militants loyal to Abu Musab al-Barnawi, the leader of a Boko Haram faction, overran the base in the village of Jilli in the local government of Geidam in the Nigerian Yobe state. 62 soldiers were killed and at least 50 others injured in the attack.

July 15

Ménaka Region, Mali: Suspected jihadists shot dead 14 civilians in an attack on the village of Injagalane in the northeastern Malian region of Ménaka. The attackers also burned one truck and three other vehicles.

July 17

Sayyad District, Afghanistan: 27, including several Taliban militants, were killed and 23 others wounded in a suicide bombing that targeted a funeral for a deceased person in the Sayyad district of the northern Afghan province of Sar-e Pol.

Ngala, Nigeria: 30 persons were killed and dozens were missing when Boko Haram insurgents ambushed a convoy of vehicles along the Dikwa-Ngala road in the local government area of Ngala in the Nigerian state of Borno. The militants also torched 27 vehicles of various sizes and capacity that transported commuters and goods.

July 19

Daboua, Chad: Boko Haram jihadists attacked a village in the south of the sub-prefecture of Daboua in the Lac region of Chad. The attackers slit the throats of two people and shot dead 16 more. Two others were wounded and ten women were abducted by the terrorists, but one was able to flee and return home.

Imam Sahib District, Afghanistan: Twelve police officers were killed in a Taliban attack in the Imam Sahib district of the northern Afghan province of Kunduz.

July 20

Qarabagh District, Afghanistan: Taliban militants launched a wave of attacks on compounds and police security posts in the Qarabagh district in the eastern Afghan province of Ghazni, killing at least 12 local policemen and injuring 20 others.

July 21

Marivan County, Iran: At least 11 Iranian Revolutionary Guards were killed and eight others injured in an attack on a post near the city of Marivan in the province of Kurdistan in western Iran.

July 22

Kabul, Afghanistan: At least 23 people, including an AFP driver, were killed and 107 others injured in a suicide bombing near Kabul International Airport as scores of people were leaving the airport after welcoming home Afghan Vice President Abdul Rashid Dostum from exile.

July 23

Konduga, Nigeria: At least 11 people were killed and eight others injured in a suicide attack on a mosque in the local government area of Konduga in the northern Nigerian state of Borno.

Kismayo District, Somalia: An Al-Shabaab suicide bomber rammed a truck filled with explosives at a military base in a village, about 50 km north of the Somali city of Kismayo. After that, the base was stormed by gunmen. At least five soldiers and ten terrorists were killed and 30 others injured in the attack.

July 25

Quetta, Pakistan: At least 31 people, including five policemen and two children, were killed and 40 others wounded after a suicide bomber blew himself up outside a polling station in the Pakistani city of Quetta.

As-Suwayda Governorate, Syria: Islamic state militants carried out suicide bombings and gun attacks in the city of As-Suwayda and a number of villages in the southern Syrian governorate of As-Suwayda, killing 255 people, including 142 civilians, and injuring 180 others. At least 63 terrorists were also killed, including the suicide bombers. The jihadists also seized hostages from the villages they had attacked.

July 27

Borno State, Nigeria: Islamist militants attacked the checkpoint in the village of Bunari near the garrison town of Monguno in the Nigerian state of Borno, killing three civilians, including a woman and a child, and 11 soldiers. Four military vehicles, including an armored personnel carrier and a gun car, were carted away by the terrorists.

July 31

Bala Buluk District, Afghanistan: At least 11 civilians were killed when a roadside bomb hit a bus that was traveling through the Bala Buluk district in the Afghan province of Farah. 37 others were also injured in the explosion.

Jalalabad, Afghanistan: A suicide bomber blew up a car near the entrance to the Department of Refugees and Returnees in the Afghan city of Jalalabad and then two armed men stormed the building. The attackers took several hostages during the attack. Security killed both gunmen after about six hours. At least 14 people were killed and 26 others injured in the terrorist attack.

Lamitan, Philippines: A bomb exploded in a van and killed a suspected bomber, a soldier, four paramilitaries and four civilians, including a mother and her child, at a military checkpoint in the city of Lamitan in the province of Basilan in the southern Philippines. Twelve others were wounded in the attack.

Niono Cercle, Mali: At least six soldiers and eight militants were killed in an ambush near Nampala in the Niono Cercle of the Malian region of Segou. Several others were wounded and two vehicles of the Malian army and their occupants were missing. The attackers reportedly also set some vehicles on fire.

Chapter 8:
AUGUST

<u>Mass Shooting in Moss Side</u>

Yet another mass shooting occurred in 2018, and this time it was in Moss Side, a neighborhood of Manchester, in the UK. It was the first time a mass shooting had occurred in the UK since the Cumbria shootings that took place in 2010.

Background

The weekend of August 11-12, Moss Side was hosting the Manchester Caribbean Carnival, which included more than 16,000 attendees on the Saturday alone. The event happened every year, but this time it drew larger crowds because it was the 70th anniversary of the Windrush generation. One resident described Moss Side as being a volatile neighborhood, and it had long been associated with drugs, gun violence and gang territories.

The last shooting spree in the UK was Cumbria in 2010, and prior to that was the tragic school shooting in Dunblane in 1996. A DJ who was interviewed after this incident said he had come to the scene because he wanted to "see this thing, because 10 people is a major thing in Manchester." Prior to this, the last major violent incident in Manchester was the Arena bombing during the Ariana Grande concert in 2017, in which 22 people were killed.

The Mass Shooting

At 2:25am, Sunday August 12, shots were fired on Claremont Road that runs for two miles through Moss Side. Although Claremont is near Alexandra Park where the festival was taking place, the shooting was believed to be unrelated. Within a minute of gunfire being reported, police arrived on the scene. However, some witnesses thought it was much longer than that before police arrive.

Police reported that there were several hundred people in the area, despite being the early hours of the morning. A witness thought the initial gunshot noise was a balloon popping, but after hearing more shots, he hid behind a wall. Police believed a shotgun that had been loaded with pellets was used, but were treating it as an attempted mass murder.

Victims Injuries

There were twelve people injured in the gunfire, and ten of these were hospitalized with one being classified as serious. Most of the injuries were due to the gunshot pellets, but one man had suffered a broken leg. Two of the twelve victims were children, in their teens. None of the injuries were considered life threatening.

The motive for the shooting was not clear, and police considered the possibility that it had been targeted. Chief Supt. Chaudhry said, "There were no arrests at the event itself. At 2.25am my officers got the report of a sound of two large bangs in the Claremont Road area. What they were faced with was a large crowd of several people continuing to celebrate the carnival. There was a state of panic. Officers carried out first aid. Ten people have received injuries which were related to gun shot. Probably a shotgun discharge. How many times it was discharged is unclear.

"The injuries are serious for some but not life-threatening. This could've been far worse. Discharging a firearm like this completely reckless. These people need to be caught. I'd urge the community to pull together and work with the police. It's imperative that we catch these people and that we recover the firearm involved".

Arrests Made

On September 11, police arrested two individuals on the suspicion of attempted murder, for the Moss Side shooting. The two men, aged 24 and 30, were remanded in custody until further questioning and investigation was undertaken.

Horizon Air Plane Theft - Richard Russell

In one of the strangest cases this year that made global headlines, an airplane was stolen from the Seattle-Tacoma International Airport in Washington. What made it so strange, was that the man who stole the plane, Richard Russell, had no pilot training, and had never flown a plane before.

The Aircraft Stolen

The stolen plane was a Bombardier Dash 8 Q400 which belonged to Horizon Air and had been operating for Alaska Airlines. Horizon had owned the plane since 2012. The same day the plane was stolen, it had flown in from Victoria, British Columbia, at 13:35pm, and it was not scheduled for any further flights that day.

Russell Takes the Plane

Russell, 29, was a ground service agent for Horizon Air, and on August 10, he entered the aircraft at Plane Cargo 1 at the north end of the airport. He managed to maneuver the plane to runway 16C via taxiways. The Tower made several attempts to make contact and get the aircraft to identify itself but it received no response. An Alaska Airlines jet that was on the ground nearby reported seeing the aircraft begin a takeoff roll, and the wheels were smoking. The unauthorized takeoff happened at 19:32pm.

Because no contact had been made with the aircraft, two McDonnell Douglas F-15 Eagles from the Oregon Air National Guard's 142nd Fighter Wing were scrambled at 20:15pm. They took off from Portland Air National Guard Base to intercept the stolen aircraft. Onboard the F-15 Eagles were Sidewinder and air-to-air missiles, and as the planes went supersonic, sonic booms were generated on the way to Puget Sound. All flights coming in or leaving the airport were immediately suspended, temporarily.

Air Traffic Control (ATC) eventually made contact with the plane and Russell. Because the transmissions were broadcast on an open frequency, they were quickly posted on social media sites. Described as speaking in a 'frenzied stream of consciousness', Russell stated he was a man in crisis. He further said he was a "broken guy, got a few screws loose I guess. Never really knew it until now."

ATC made the suggestion to Russell that he land the plane at Joint Base Lewis-McChord, but he refused, saying "Those guys will rough me up if I try and land there. I think I might mess something up there, too. I wouldn't want to do that."

He went on to ask if he could get a job with Alaska Airlines as a pilot if he managed to land the aircraft successfully. ATC said, "they would give you a job doing anything if you could pull this off", to which he replied "Yeah right! Nah, I'm a white guy."

Russell told ATC that he wanted to attempt a couple of maneuvers so he could see what the aircraft could do, and he asked for the coordinates for an orca that had been national news, because he said he wanted to go see it. Russell said he didn't want to hurt anybody and in the last minutes of the communication with ATC he apologized to his family and friends.

Towards the end of the flight, the aircraft was filmed as it did aerobatic maneuvers over Puget Sound. The footage quickly appeared on social media. A veteran pilot who saw the footage said that the maneuvers "seemed pretty well executed, without either stalling or pulling the wings off."

ATC asked Russell again to land the plane, but he said, "I don't know. I don't want to. I was kind of hoping that was gonna be it, you know?" He added that he "wasn't really planning on landing it."

The two F-15 Eagles attempted to use their aircraft to direct Russell towards the Pacific Ocean, but they did not open fire on the plane. At 20:43pm, Russell crashed the plane on Ketron Island in Puget Sound. Russell was killed in the crash and the plane was completely destroyed. The first on the scene was a tow boat crew, followed by firefighters from West Pierce Fire and Rescue. Other emergency responders arrived about 1.5 hours after the crash because they had to wait for the ferry.

The plane crash caused a fire that covered two acres on the Island. Luckily there was a lack of dry brush and wind, so the fire was easily extinguished by the following morning.

Investigation into the Incident

On August 11 it was announced that federal agencies would be leading the investigation, with the Seattle office of the FBI in the lead role. The Pierce County Sheriff's Office thanked the public for providing accurate information regarding the theft of the plane and the suspect, Russell.

The FBI descried Russell as being suicidal and said his actions in no way constituted a terrorist incident. The flight data recorder was recovered along with some components of the cockpit voice recorder on August 12. The recording equipment was then sent to the National Transportation Safety Board as per protocol, for processing and assessment.

On November 9, the investigation had been completed, according to the FBI. It had been confirmed that Russell had acted alone and there was no suggestion of terrorism being a factor. The investigation determined that the plane's final descent and subsequent crash had been an intentional act, and the manner of death for Russell was deemed suicide.

Richard Russell

Russell had worked in a tow team at the airport, which is responsible for repositioning the aircraft on the airport apron. He had worked at the airport for four years, and a supervisor described him as quiet and well-liked by his co-workers. Airline employees do not receive the $15 minimum hourly wage like those in the city, and this came up in the communications between Russell and the ATC. He made a complaint about wages, saying "Minimum wage, we'll chalk it up to that. Maybe that will grease some gears a little bit with the higher-ups."

Born in Key West Florida, Russell and his family moved to Wasilla, Alaska, when he was seven years old. He was an athlete in high school, competing in track and field and wrestling. His nickname from his friends and family was 'Beebo'.

Russell met his future wife in 2011, at a religious meeting at Southwestern Oregon community College. They married in 2012, and opened a bakery in North Bend, Oregon. In 2015 they sold the bakery because his wife wanted to be closer to her family in Washington. They moved to Sumner, in Washington, and Russell got the job with Horizon Air.

Russell had been a keen traveler, and he majored in social science at Washington State University Global Campus. His goal was to attain a management position at Horizon Air, or possibly become a military officer once he completed his degree. He was a leader in Christian youth ministry 'Young Life' and was very active in his church.

Gary Beck, CEO of Horizon Air stated that the company was not aware of Russell having any flight experience or a pilot's license. He said that the aerial maneuvers Russell had performed were "incredible" and that he "did not know how he achieved the experience that he did."

While conversing with ATC, Russell said he knew "what I was doing a little bit" because he had experience playing video games. Following the incident, a pilot for SkyWest Airlines, Joel Monteith, told an emergency dispatcher that he had seen Russell and another man in 2017, pointing and flipping switches in the cockpit of a SkyWest aircraft. He further stated that the men had told him they were training how to use the auxiliary power unit so they could tow it, but Monteith thought it was suspicious that they left as soon as he confronted them. Monteith also stated that he had been in the cockpit of an Embraer 175 with Russell one time and Russell had questioned him about his flows, which was the preflight preparation done before takeoff.

On August 11, the family of Russell released a statement which stated that they were stunned and heartbroken, and devastated by the events.

The Watts family Massacre

The Watts family massacre was so heinous, it stunned and shocked people around the world. Over the weekend of August 12 and 13, Chris Watts systematically murdered his pregnant wife and their two young daughters. Committing the murders was atrocious, but what he did with the bodies of his children, is abominable.

Family Background

Chris Watts and Shanann had been married for six years, and they lived in a large home in Frederick, Colorado with their daughters Bella, who was born in 2013, and Celeste, born in 2015. They had previously experienced financial hardships, and declared bankruptcy in 2015. By 2018, Chris was working for an oil and gas company, Anadarko Petroleum. Shanann was working as an independent representative for a marketing company. At the time of the murders, Shanann was 15 weeks pregnant with a boy that the couple had decided they would name Nico when he was born.

Disappearance of Shanann and the Children

On August 13, Shanann returned home from a business trip in Arizona, and her friend and colleague, Nichole Utoft Atkinson had driven her home, arriving at about 1:40am. Later that day, Shanann missed her OB/GYN appointment, and was not returning any calls or text messages. Nichole was concerned, and after Shanann had also missed a business meeting, she went to the Watts' home.

Once at the house, Nichole rang the doorbell and knocked several times, but nobody answered. She contacted Watts, and then phoned the Frederick Police Department. The police went to the house to perform a welfare check at 1:40pm, and Watts gave them permission to search the house. They found Shanann's purse, keys and phone in the house. Her car and the children's car seats were also still at the house.

The following day, August 14, the FBI and Colorado Bureau of Investigation became involved in the case. Watts gave a television interview to a local TV station pleading for his family to be returned. During the interview, cadaver dogs could be seen in the background on the property.

On August 16, the bodies of Shanann and the two children were discovered on the property of Watts' former employer, Anadarko Petroleum. He had been fired the day before. Shanann's body was found buried in a shallow grave and the children's bodies were located inside the large oil tanks on the property.

Arrest and Charges

Late on August 15, Watts was arrested, upon which point he confessed that he had strangled his wife and disposed of the bodies. Watts had been having an affair, and claimed that he had asked Shanann for a separation. He claimed that by asking for the separation, Shanann strangled the children, and when he discovered what she had done, he strangled her in a fit of rage.

Watts was charged with multiple counts of first degree murder, three counts of tampering with a deceased human body, and unlawful termination of a pregnancy. To avoid the death penalty, Watts pleaded guilty to all charges on November 6. He was sentenced to life in prison without the possibility of parole on November 19. At the sentencing, Shanann's father Frank Rzucek stated, "I trusted you to take care of them, not kill them. They also trusted you, the heartless monster, and then you take them out like trash. You disgust me."

The Mistress

Shanann had confronted Watts on numerous occasions about her suspicions that he was having an affair. It turned out that her instincts were correct, and at the time of the murders, Watts had been having an affair with a woman he met at work, Nichol Kessinger. Prosecutors believed that this is why Watts had murdered his family, so he could have a fresh start with Kessinger.

According to Kessinger, Watts had lied to her, as he had told her he was in the process of getting a divorce from Shanann. When Kessinger learned that his wife and children were missing, she presented herself to the police.

Kessinger and Watts had met at work in June, and by July they were involved in a physical relationship. She described Watts as a good listener who was soft-spoken. But when she found out that Shanann was pregnant when she disappeared, her opinion of Watts as a nice guy collapsed.

Retrieving the Bodies - A Horrific Task

Early on the morning of August 16, the task of removing the bodies of the children from the oil tanks began. The tanks had the capacity to hold 400 barrels of oil, and before the bodies could be retrieved, the oil had to be manually emptied. As this was done, liquid then had to be poured over metal screens so any possible evidence could be retained. Pools of oil had to be kept aside to preserve the bodies in after they came out of the tanks.

Because of the toxic fumes given off by the oil, the troopers who were entering the tanks had to wear self-contained breathing apparatus, and were only able to be inside for a few minutes at a time.

Once they had emptied the two tanks, the bolts on the doors at the base of tanks were removed. Sergeant Armstrong went and looked through the 'thief hatch' at the top and said he could see what looked like a body face down on the south side of the tank. They took photos of the scene, and then began the awful task of removing the bodies.

As the troopers entered the tank, they confirmed there was a body face down on the south side. They could see that it was a small female child. One of the troopers grabbed hold of the upper portion of her right arm to turn her body over. He then lifted her up by both upper arms as another trooper held on to her right leg. The first trooper held her left leg and arm as they carefully moved the body towards the entrance.

As they moved the small girl's body out of the tank, the skin on her hand degloved, a term meaning it had slipped off, just like taking off a glove. The troopers retrieved the skin and it was handed to another member of law enforcement to take care of.

In the second oil tank, they found the second body. A trooper grabbed her right wrist area and moved her towards the entrance. The other trooper grasped her left leg and arm, and the two men were then able to pass the body out through the entrance.

The Weld County Coroner and Pathologist attempted to remove as much of the crude oil on the bodies as they could, using oil absorbent pads. The bodies were then placed into body bags and transported to the Coroner's office.

The troopers who had gone in to the tanks to retrieve the bodies had to be extensively decontaminated, even though they were only inside for a few minutes. They were hosed down with spray and firefighting foam by the Wiggins Fire Department.

The whole process of removing the little girls' bodies from the oil tanks took nearly 14 hours.

Where is Watts Now?

Watts was moved to a prison in Wisconsin after his sentencing, supposedly for his own safety, as he is classified as a high profile offender. The only people that know exactly where he is are law enforcement, the family of Shanann and the district.

Fredericton Mass Shooting

A mass shooting occurred in Fredericton, New Brunswick, Canada, on the morning of August 10. Four people were killed, including two police officers. The suspect, Matthew Vincent Raymond was arrested and is in custody.

How the Shooting Unfolded

Multiple witnesses reported hearing multiple gunshots on Brookside Drive at around 7:00am, August 10. Brookside Drive is a residential area between Main Street and Ring Road on the north side of Fredericton. Police locked the area down straight away and residents were warned to stay inside their houses. By 8:17am, police had announced they were investigating a shooting that involved multiple fatalities, and people were asked to avoid the scene.

Two civilian victims were already shot and on the ground when the first officers responded to the calls. The police officers who were killed where the first on the scene. An apartment building at 237 Brookside Drive was evacuated at 9:00am. Half an hour later, police entered an apartment and arrested the offender.

By 11:00am police confirmed there was no further threat to the public and they lifted the lockdown.

The Victims

Officer Lawrence Robert Costello, 45, and Sara Burns, 43, were the two officers gunned down that morning. Donnie Robichaud and his girlfriend Bobbie-Lee Wright were the two civilians killed.

The Suspect - Matthew Vincent Raymond

Raymond, 48, was shot during his arrest and he sustained serious injuries. He was transported to the hospital for treatment, along with his four deceased victims. Apparently, he was known to enjoy first-person shooter video games, and some thought he was ignorant and Islamophobic.

Investigating the Crime

The investigation was carried out by the RCMP Major Crimes Division and the Fredericton Police. Reporters who had been at the scene were asked by police to pass on any information that may be pertinent to the police.

During the investigation the authorities were able to work out that Raymond most likely was shooting at his victims from an elevated position, and he had used a long gun. Initially there was a publication ban on details from the shooting, but this was lifted on August 17.

On November 21, a psychiatric assessment of Raymond was ordered by Judge Julian Dickson. There is a publication ban on details regarding who should be conducting the assessment. Because Raymond is claiming he is innocent and had suffered from temporary insanity, it is essential to determine his state of mind and fitness to stand trial.

Changing Lawyers

The request for the psychiatric assessment sat for nearly a month as Dickson had to deal with Raymond's bid to get rid of his initial lawyer, Nathan Gorham. Eventually, the judge ordered that a new lawyer be appointed, and Alion Menard was given the job.

The trial will take place following the psychiatric assessment and recommendations the psychiatrist may or may not make.

Gamer on Shooting Spree at Jacksonville Landing

Often referred to as the Jacksonville shooting, a mass shooting took place at a video game tournament on August 26, at Jacksonville Landing, Florida. One gunman opened fire, killing two and injuring ten, before turning the gun on himself.

The Shooting Spree

At the Good Luck Have Fun Game Bar, which is a video game venue, the Madden NFL 19 video gaming tournament was taking place. There were up to 150 players and onlookers at the venue at the time of the shooting. David Katz, one of the players, lost a game and left the tournament after refusing to shake the hand of his opponent. He wasn't gone for long though, and when he returned he was carrying a handgun, one of two he had brought with him.

Katz entered the venue and opened fire, killing two people and ten others were injured. Two others were injured as they were fleeing the shooting. According to a tournament announcer at the venue, he was interviewing the first victim before he was shot, and he believed that victim had been targeted by Katz.

Social media first reported that there was gunfire at 1:34pm, and footage of the whole incident was streamed through the event's Twitch account. This recording was later uploaded on to YouTube.

Once alerted to the shooting, the Jacksonville Sheriff's Office ordered people to keep clear of the venue at 2:13pm. The building was then searched and evacuated by SWAT officers. Within two minutes of the first 911 call being received, first responders arrived on site, at 1:36pm. Members of the firefighters union were training nearby at the time, and some of the victims ran to them for help.

The location of the event was right next to the St. John River. Because of this the Coast Guard was called in to search the river, looking for victims or suspects.

Investigation into the Shooting

Using their Twitter account, the Jacksonville Sheriff's Office announced at 2:45pm that there were fatalities at the scene and that they had located the suspect, who was also dead, at 2:53pm. At first they were unsure if there were other gunmen involved, but they were later able to confirm that Katz was the only suspect.

According to the Sheriff's Office, Katz was armed with two guns, a 9mm handgun and a .45-caliber handgun. One of these was equipped with an aftermarket laser sight which was attached to the trigger guard. The guns had been legally purchased by Katz in Baltimore, and he had them stored in his vehicle prior to the shooting.

An update was released that evening informing that the FBI was getting involved in the investigation. They were also coordinating with police in Baltimore, where Katz had lived with his father. Publishers of the Madden NFL 19, Electronic Arts, fully cooperated with the authorities during the investigation.

Victims of the Shooting

One of the two people killed was Elijah Clayton, 22, from Woodland Hills, California. He originally wasn't going to attend but changed his mind more or less at the last minute. He was a professional gamer who went by the names 'True' and 'Trueboy'. When the video footage of the shooting emerged, at one point there appeared to be a red dot on Clayton's chest, most likely from the laser sight on the handgun.

The other person killed was Taylor Robertson. The 27-year-old was also a professional gamer, known as 'SpotMePlzzz'. He had traveled from his home in Ballard, West Virginia, to attend the tournament.

As a result of the shooting, eleven people were treated at hospitals for injuries. Many had been capable of leaving the site and sought help from first responders on their own. Another two had transported themselves to the hospital's emergency department for treatment. In total there were ten people non-fatally injured by gunshot wounds, and one was injured while trying to run from the shooter.

The injuries were not life threatening, and by the next day, most had been released from hospital.

Who Was David Katz?

Katz was a professional Madden player who had traveled from Baltimore to participate in the tournament in Jacksonville. He had lost some rounds in the competition which ended his chances of getting to the finals. Other competitors later reported he had been 'acting weird' and he refused to shake hands with his opponents after he lost each round.

Some of the pseudonyms used by Katz included, 'mrsslicedbread', 'Bread', 'ravens2012champ', 'RavensChamp', and 'TREXHAVAHARTATAK'. In the Madden Tournament the year before, he had won $10,000. He had been previously diagnosed with a mental illness from as young as 12, and had been treated with anti-psychotic medication.

Katz had seen many psychiatrists, and in a court filing from 2006, a therapist had stated Katz had experienced a 'psychiatric crisis'. Between 1993 and 2009, there had been 26 calls to the police from the Katz family home for mental illness issues and domestic disputes. There were reports involving arguments between Katz and his mother, but no record of any physical violence in any of the domestic-related reports.

After the shooting, Katz's parents, Richard and Elizabeth, fully cooperated with the authorities for the investigation. Both worked for the federal government, with Richard employed as an engineer with NASA and Elizabeth an employed by the Food And Drug Administration.

The divorce between Katz's parents was so acrimonious that both filed to have a guardian ad litem assigned to represent Katz. His parents disagreed strongly about the mental health treatment Katz required. As a child, Katz was first given psychiatric medicines including the antidepressant Lexapro, and the antipsychotic, Risperidone. He was taken to see several psychiatrists, an art therapist and a social worker by his mother.

Richard, his father, did not agree with the need for the psychiatric evaluations and medications prescribed to Katz at a young age. Instead he believed Katz needed a support group with peers. He certainly did not agree that Katz might be schizophrenic. Once when Katz refused to attend an appointment, he locked himself in the car.

Police were called to Elizabeth's home the day after Katz's 13th birthday to help her with Katz. Her complaint included the 'the volume of the television and his overall lack of respect toward her and his grandmother'. A similar occurrence took place the day after his 14th birthday, but this time Katz had called the police because his mother 'keeps punishing him by taking away his video games.'

Katz began taking classes at the University of Maryland three years after he graduated from high school. He majored in technology and environmental science, and lived off campus. The President of the University issued a statement which included a reference to a previous mass shooting that had occurred in Annapolis nearby. "Our community grieves for the families of those who lost their lives in yesterday's horrific shooting in Jacksonville. When our community was directly impacted by the shooting in Annapolis this summer, I said that more than silent reflection is needed to end the epidemic of gun violence in our country, and I will say that again today."

Those who knew Katz often described him as a 'loner' who was antisocial. Apparently he didn't' talk much, but most thought he was a 'good guy'.

How Was He Able to Purchase Weapons?

Many wondered how Katz was able to purchase the handguns when he had such a long history of mental illness. However, federal gun laws only prohibit anyone who has been involuntarily committed to a mental health institution, or adjudicated as 'mentally incompetent' from legally purchasing a firearm.

Even though someone has a history of psychological issues, it does not legally prevent them from being able to purchase a gun. Also, psychiatric or psychological medical records are protected patient information, and are considered to be private, so there is no way of knowing the background of someone who hasn't been committed.

In Maryland, a law came into action in 2013 that means residents have to obtain a handgun qualification license from state police before they can buy a revolver or pistol. Therefore, Katz would have been required to submit his fingerprints, undergone background checks and passed a firearms safety training course.

The Event Sponsor is Sued

Following the shooting, one of the tournament participants field a lawsuit on August 30 against the sponsor of the event, Elextronic Arts. The lawsuit also includes the mall, the restaurant where the tournament was being held and the manufacturer of the game. In the lawsuit it claims, "to hold those responsible accountable, and to ensure that gamers ... are able to get together to pursue their passion without having to fear for their lives".

Response and Aftermath

After the shooting, sponsors of participants and those who had been at the event competing took to social media to talk about what had happened. They talked about the injuries, safety, and recollections of how the events unfolded. The main sponsor, Elextronic Arts, released a statement 'their "most heartfelt sympathies" went out to the families of the victims and those who were injured and that their focus was on those affected and aiding law enforcement'.

The three remaining Madden Classic qualifier tournaments were subsequently cancelled so safety protocols for these events could be assessed and reevaluated. Elextronic Arts also donated $1million to a charity for the victims of the shooting. They also set up a fund so others could donate if they wanted to.

Other organizers of video-game based exhibitions that included Game Developers Conference, PAX and Electronic Entertainment Expo, and some esports tournaments, League of Legends Championship Series and Evolution Championship Series, announced that they would be adding further security measures at any future events. Their priority was to protect the exhibitors as well as the attendees.

Terrorist Attacks in Short for August

August 1

Chimtal District, Afghanistan: The Taliban attacked a police outpost in the Chimtal district of the northern Afghan province of Balkh, killing three local policemen and wounding four others. At least ten Taliban fighters were also killed in the gunfight.

August 3

Shaykh Najjar, Syria: A landmine placed by Islamic State militants exploded in the area of Shaykh Najjar in the northern Syrian Aleppo governorate, killing 14 civilians.

Gardez, Afghanistan: Two militants dressed in burqas entered a Shiite mosque in the town of Gardez in the province of Paktia and opened fire. Both attackers later blew themselves up. 48 people were killed and at least 70 others injured in the attack.

August 5

Mogadishu, Somalia: At least nine people were killed and seven others wounded when a car bomb explosion hit a busy restaurant in the Somali capital Mogadishu.

August 6

Mosul, Iraq: A family of 9 who were returning from a refugee camp was killed when their booby trapped house exploded by bombs left by ISIS.

August 7

North Kivu, Democratic Republic of Congo: 14 people were kidnapped and killed by the Allied Democratic Forces in Congo.

August 8

Borno, Nigeria: At least 17 Nigerian soldiers were killed in a fresh Boko Haram attack on a military base in the country's northeast.

August 10

Amman, Jordan: A bomb attack against a gendarmerie vehicle killed at least a police officer and injured six in Amman. After the attack, three members of the Jordan security forces were killed and dozens injured after several bomb attacks when they stormed an apartment with explosives. Four terrorists were also killed during the raid.

August 11

Madagali, Nigeria: 10 people were killed in twin suicide bombings and wounding 20 more in a crowded place in Madagali Nigeria.

August 12

Ghazni, Afghanistan: 14 people were killed when the Taliban assaulted on Ghazni killing at least 14 Afghan Police officers and wounding at least 20 others.

August 14

Jilib, Somalia: 9 people were killed and several others were injured when Al-Shabaab attacked farmers and caused clashes.

August 15

Baghlan, Afghanistan: The Taliban attacked an Afghan Army base killing 39 and wounding 2.

Kabul, Afghanistan: A suicide bombing in an educative academy of Kabul left at least 48 killed and 67 injured.

August 19

Maiduguri, Nigeria: At least 19 people were killed in an attack by militants on Northeast Nigeria several others are injured.

August 29

Al-Qa'im, Iraq: The Iraqi army and a government-backed militia manned checkpoint were targeted by the car bomber who killed at least 16 in western Iraq's Al-Qaim.

August 30

Borno State, Nigeria: Boko Haram militants launched an attack on a military base killing 31 and injuring 19 in Borno State.

Chapter 9: SEPTEMBER

Cincinnati Mass Shooting

In Cincinnati, Ohio, a mass shooting occurred on September 6. The suspect, Omar Santa Perez, 29, entered the lobby of the Fifth Third Center and opened fire, leaving three people dead.

The Attack

Just before the attack, Perez had gone into a sandwich shop and other businesses in the Fifth Third Center before he went back to the lobby of the bank. At 9:10am, he opened fire on employees and contractors. Two of those killed were employees of the bank, and the other fatality was a contractor. Two other persons in the area at the time of the shooting were injured. At one point Perez's gun jammed, which potentially prevented others from being shot.

As police approached the lobby after receiving reports, they discovered Perez still firing his gun. In response, four of the police officers returned fire at Perez, shooting him multiple times. Footage of the shooting recorded by police body camera showed Perez shooting at anyone he saw, rather than targeting specific individuals. The footage also showed Perez being shot through a glass pane, before collapsing.

The coroner later stated that although Perez only had one gun, he had a lot of rounds of ammunition on him. He further stated that Perez "never hesitated to pull the trigger, empty the clip, release and do it again and again."

Those who died were:

- Prudhvi Raj Kandepi, 25
- Richard Newcomer, 64
- Luis Felipe Calderon, 48

The Police Investigation

The investigation found that the amount of ammunition Perez was carrying was enough to kill more than 100 people. There was no indication that the victims that were shot had been involved in some sort of dispute with Perez.

Perez's family had previously wanted him to be committed to a mental health facility, claiming he was mentally unwell. Twice his mother and sister went to court in Palm Beach County and declared Perez was mentally ill and violent.

Omar Santa Perez

In the weeks leading up to the attack, neighbors claimed Perez had been acting more bitterly because he struggled to hold on to employment. At one former job in South Carolina, Perez had been arrested and charged with trespassing after he had been fired. A work colleague at the time said he remembered Perez as never showing any anger and that he was a quiet worker.

Perez had a history of committing minor offences, including marijuana possession in Palm Beach, entering or refusing to leave premises in South Carolina, traffic offenses in Lake Worth and Deerfield Beach, and disorderly conduct in Coconut Creek, Florida. He had also received a traffic violation for driving with an expired license plate. None of his offences had any sort of violent undertones.

Neighbors at the apartment building where Perez had lived prior to the shooting were shocked by what had happened. One of the neighbors,

Karen Rose, stated "It's disturbing to think someone like that lived here. He obviously wasn't who I thought he was. Something went wrong in his head."

Many of the other residents had similar opinions about Perez that he was becoming increasingly bitter leading up to the shooting. Some felt he was reclusive, and often didn't return pleasantries when greeted.

Another neighbor, Christina Fischer, said, "He kind of would hide when you'd come up the stairs. He didn't want anybody near him."

Fischer had thought there had been a woman living in the apartment with Perez up until a few weeks prior, and the woman stopped coming to the building. Despite the neighbors all thinking Perez was a bit strange, none of them ever expected him to go on a shooting spree.

Long History of Difficulty Keeping Jobs

When Perez was charged with trespassing in October 2014, he was discovered smoking a cigar and lying down on the ground outside the business. The police statement recorded, "The suspect appeared to be upset and disoriented. When I would ask the suspect questions but he would respond with strange answers," the report said. "The suspect mumbled something about the war and the economy, but for the most part talked about the fact that he was upset that he was terminated."

Perez was asked to leave the premises but he refused, and instead began crying. He completely stopped complying with orders and requests by police, and he had to be forcibly removed and arrested.

A former work colleague who worked with Perez for two years at an oil well shaft manufacturing company remembered Perez as very hardworking, but quiet. The colleague, Daniel Noel said, "He walked out of work every day filthy. He was the manual labor for this department."

According to Noel, Perez never showed any type of aggression while he was at work. He was a little awkward socially. Because of the masculine environment, conversations often revolved around guns. It's through these conversations that Noel knew Perez did not own a firearm back in 2015.

Lawsuit 'Borders on Delusional'

In 2017 Perez filed a lawsuit against TD Ameritrade Holding Corp, and CNBC Universal Media LLC. In the lawsuit he alleged the two companies had undertaken extensive searches and investigations of his personal devices and then published personal and private details about his life.

Federal Magistrate Karen Litkovitz recommended on June 25, 2018, that the case be dismissed. She wrote that the allegations made by Perez were "rambling, difficult to decipher and borders on delusional."

Perez subsequently filed a motion to have a hearing to clarify his complaint and to also defend himself from the label imposed by Litkovitz, that he was delusional. Because of the shooting, and Perez's death, the case never went back to court.

Border Patrol Serial Killer Juan Ortiz

Juan David Ortiz had been working as an American border patrol agent when it was discovered that he was in fact a suspected serial killer. He was eventually accused of murdering four women, but it is likely there were more yet to be discovered.

Personal Life of Ortiz

Ortiz had worked for the Border Patrol for a decade, and his role was of intelligence operator. He had also spent time in the US Navy, and was a veteran. He served between July 2001 - May 2009. He achieved the class of Hospital Corpsman 2nd Class by the time he left the Navy. He received the Joint Meritorious Award, the National Service Award, and the Rifle Marksmanship Medal.

Throughout his military service there is no record of him having any disciplinary issues. While in the Navy, Ortiz gained a bachelor's degree from the American Military University, followed by a master's degree from St. Mary's University, Texas.

Ortiz was married and was the father of one child.

The Arrest

A friend and fellow sex worker of Melissa Ramirez, who had disappeared while with Ortiz, got into his vehicle on September 15, 2018. They had a conversation about Ramirez, and then Ortiz allegedly pulled out a gun and tore her shirt off. Terrified, she jumped out of Ortiz's truck, and as luck would have it, there happened to be a state trooper nearby. She reported what happened in the truck with Ortiz.

In the early hours of the following morning, Ortiz was tracked down at a hotel parking lot where he was supposedly hiding, and was arrested by Texas police. The Chief Deputy claimed Ortiz had planned to commit 'suicide by cop'. He had stocked up on weapons and had been attempting to goad the police by pointing his telephone at them just before his arrest. In the previous hours, Ortiz had posted goodbye messages on Facebook.

Confessed and Suspected Victims

After his arrest, Ortiz confessed to the following homicides:

- Melissa Ramirez, 29, killed on 3 September 2018
- Claudine Anne Luera, 42, killed on 13 September 2018
- Griselda Alicia Hernandez Cantu, 35, killed on 15 September 2018
- Nikki Enriquez Ortiz, 28, killed on 15 September 2018

Three of the victims were female sex workers, and one was transgender. Ortiz told investigators that his first murder was on September 3, and that he had known the first two victims personally. The last two victims were killed just five hours between assaulting the woman who escaped and raised the alarm, and his arrest.

Ortiz admitted picking up Melissa Ramirez, 29, and mother of two, on September 3. He drove two miles out of the city to a rural country road in

Webb County. When Ramirez got out of the vehicle to urinate, Ortiz got out also and shot her multiple times. The next day her body was discovered.

Then, ten days later, Ortiz picked up Claudine Anne Luera, 42, and a mother of five children. She confronted Ortiz about the disappearance and murder of Melissa Ramirez, knowing that Melissa had previously been seen with Ortiz. She got out of the vehicle, and like with Ramirez, Ortiz shot her in the head. Miraculously she was still alive when she was found, but she succumbed to her injuries and died hours later.

With the last two victims, Ortiz had picked them up in Laredo, and in two separate trips, taken them to a section of Highway 35 and killed them. They were both shot. After he was arrested, Ortiz took them to the scene of the crime. These murders were different than the others because Ortiz did not know them, nor had he had any previous contact with them.

Legal Aftermath

Ortiz was charged with four counts of murder and one count of aggravated assault with a deadly weapon, and unlawful restraint, by the Webb County court. During his interrogation, Ortiz did confess to the murders and the assault. He told investigators he had a hatred of prostitutes. They have not ruled out the possibility that there may be more victims of Ortiz that they are yet to find out about.

The Webb County District Attorney Isidro Alaniz stated that the investigators considered Ortiz to be a serial killer. Each of the victims had been involved in sex work or drugs, or both. The motive is not clear, even though Ortiz voiced his dislike of prostitutes.

Webb County Chief Deputy Federico Garza stated, "He took advantage of the vulnerability of this community. They didn't have a defense against him. He found a crime of opportunity to take advantage of these victims."

Throughout his killing spree that lasted ten days, Ortiz continued to go to work as usual. DA Alaniz said, "As law enforcement was looking for the killer … he would be reporting to work every day like normal.

It is clear that none of the murders or attacks occurred while Ortiz was on duty. However, authorities are still analyzing his service weapon to see if it was the weapon used in the murders.

The US Customs and Border Protection issued a public statement in which it offered its sincerest condolences to the families of the victims. It also stated that criminal activity by their employees was not tolerated. The Chief, Carla Provost, claimed Ortiz was a 'rogue' individual and that she is "sickened and saddened" over the killings. Their Agency was cooperating fully with the local police.

Tragically, Ortiz is not the only Border Patrol agent working in Laredo that has been arrested this year on murder charges. Fellow agent Ronald Anthony Burgos-Aviles has been charged with killing a romantic partner and her 1-year-old child, and prosecutors will be seeking the death penalty for that case.

Bedford Mass Murder

A young father was arrested after killing his wife, three daughters, and the children's grandmother in Bedford, Perth, Australia.

A Horrific Massacre

On September 3, Anthony Robert Harvey allegedly killed his wife Mara Lee Harvey, 41, in their house. He also is alleged to have killed his daughters, Charlotte Kate, 3 ½, Alice Ester, 2, and her twin sister Beatrix. The following day, he is accused of killing his mother-in-law, Beverley Ann Quinn, 73, at the same house. It was believed that Harvey had used knives and a blunt instrument to carry out the murders.

Harvey allegedly stayed in the house with the bodies of his murder victims for five or six days. He then drove 1,400km to Pannawonica in the Pilbara region and handed himself into the police station there.

When police arrived at the house, the television was still on. Then they discovered the bodies. The bodies of the two adults were located in the kitchen, and the children's bodies were found in other rooms of the house.

Charges Laid

Harvey was charged with the murders and appeared at his first hearing wearing jeans and a dark grey t-shirt, no shoes, and sporting a beard. He displayed very little emotion as the charges and names of his victims, including his own children, were read out. When asked if he understood the charges, he replied briefly with 'yes' or 'I understand'.

He reappeared in court on September 19 via video link. The hearing was brief, and he is still to enter a plea. His next court appearance is scheduled for January 2.

No Hint of Conflict in 'Perfect Family'

Neighbors of the Harvey family claimed there were no signs that anything was terribly wrong. They recalled they had never heard any loud arguments or conflict coming from the Harvey house, and the children were always happily playing. Ms. Quinn, the mother-in-law, was at the house all the time helping with the children.

Harvey ran Jim's Mowing franchise alone with his wife. He had recently confided in a neighbor that he was financially struggling and was pressured to work even when he was physically unwell, just to keep everything afloat. According to neighbor Richard Fairbrother, 'There was a couple of times he had been quite ill with the flu and he was having to get up and go to work anyway, he told me. He said there was no money coming in unless he was out there."

The home the family lived in on Coode Street was owned by Harvey's wife. Friends and family described her as being 'unlucky in love' in the past, and when she met Harvey, who was 18 years her junior, they finally thought she had found the right man.

They lived together in the small brick house, and Harvey proposed in 2014. Then Charlotte was born, followed by the twins a year later.

No Known Motive

To date no motive has been given or identified. There is no obvious reason as to why Harvey would suddenly butcher his wife, small children, and mother-in-law in such a gruesome manner. The fact that he stayed with the bodies for a number of days makes the deed even more disturbing.

It has also not been explained why Harvey had traveled so far away to a remote area to report the homicides. If he really wanted to give himself up, why didn't he go to his local police station? Maybe his original intention wasn't to give up, perhaps what he really intended to do was disappear but changed his mind during the journey.

Whatever his reason was for killing his family, there is no crime more powerfully tragic than that of a family massacre. It is one thing for a man or woman to kill their spouse, and maybe even the mother-in-law, but to kill tiny toddlers goes above and beyond what is 'normal'.

Naturally the family of the victims has been absolutely devastated by their terrible loss. Even they didn't suspect anything was wrong with the Harvey's. The loss of a mother, a beautiful sister, and three young nieces is incomprehensible.

Mass Shooting in Aberdeen, Maryland

Those who went to work at the Rite Aid Distribution center in Aberdeen, Maryland on September 20, had no idea what was about to happen. The last thing they expected was for one of their fellow employees to come to work with a weapon and open fire. The shooting resulted in three deaths, and others were wounded.

Bad Day at Work

On the morning of September 20, Snochia Moseley, 26, reported to work as usual at the Rite Aid Distribution Center, where she had been employed for just two weeks. Almost immediately, she pulled out a gun and began to fire randomly at people that were inside the building and outside on the street. Reports of 'shots fired' came into the Harford County Sheriff's Office at around 9:06am.

Within 3 minutes of receiving the call, police officers responded to the scene. Agents from the FBI and the Bureau of Alcohol, Tobacco, Firearms and Explosive (ATF) also responded. It was quickly ascertained that the shooter had shot herself in the head. As officers began evacuating the injured, one officer tried to perform CPR on the suspect before she was taken to hospital, where she later died.

The Victims

Two of the victims died at the scene, while a third died at the hospital along with the shooter. Surviving victims were taken to Johns Hopkins Bayview Hospital in Baltimore and the Christiana Hospital in Delaware.

The victims who were killed were:

- Sunday Aguda, 45
- Brindra Giri, 41
- Hayleen Reyes, 21
- Those who were injured and survived were:
- Hassan Mitchell, 19
- Wilfredo Villegas, 45
- Acharya Purna, 45

As the shooting was unfolding, some family members received terrifying text messages from their loved ones. Alexie Scharmann received a text from her mother saying there was a shooter in her workplace. The text read, "I love you both more than u will ever know. There's a shooter in the building. I am hiding. I love you."

It wasn't until around 10:30am that Alexie Scharmann heard that her mother had safely been removed from the building.

Reggie Rodriguez's mother also worked at the distribution center, and when word broke about the shooter, his wife kept trying to call her without any answer. The employees normally keep their cell phones in lockers while they are working, so it was difficult to reach his mother. It wasn't until the afternoon that she finally answered the phone and informed him she was alive and uninjured.

Mike Carre, who worked at a furniture company next door to the Rite Aid Distribution Center, said he had barely started work when a stranger staggered into the office. The man had a bullet hole above his knee and blurted out that there was a shooter next door. Carre and his coworkers helped the injured man into a chair. They removed his pants and used them to put pressure on the bleeding from the wound. Then emergency services stated arriving.

Snochia Moseley

Identified as the shooter, Moseley had no past criminal record, and the Glock 9mm she used in the shooting legally belonged to her. At the end of August and beginning of September, Moseley had been pulled over while driving three times. She was given tickets for having a suspended registration, not having current registration plates, not having insurance, and failing to update her address with the MVA. Instead of paying the tickets, Mosely put a request into the courts on September 14, asking that the cases be taken to trial.

Moseley was 26 years old at the time of the shooting, and was an African American woman from Baltimore County. It was understood that she had suffered from some form of mental illness for years. She also had issues with her sexual identity, which caused her a great deal of emotional turmoil.

According to her family members and friends, Moseley had become more agitated in the two weeks leading up to the shooting, and that they had been concerned for her mental wellbeing.

Response and Aftermath

Larry Hogan, Maryland Governor, expressed his condolences as well as his thoughts on the incident through Twitter. He tweeted, "We are closely monitoring the horrific shooting in Aberdeen. Our prayers are with all those impacted, including our first responders."

Rite Aid, where the shooting took place, issued a statement of their intention to continue to work with authorities closely as they continued their investigation. The company also announced they would provide grief counselors to their staff for as long as they were required. They also offered their prayers and thoughts to all of those affected by the shooting.

Motive?

No motive has been uncovered during the investigation. Moseley hadn't confided in anyone or left a note to say why she felt compelled to take her gun to work that day and start shooting at everyone. There was no indication that she had specific issues with anyone at work or the company she worked for. Considering she had only worked there for two weeks it was highly unlikely she could have developed such a hatred for the people or the place that would drive her do what she did.

Sometimes a motive is never identified, especially with these types of mass shootings where the perpetrator kills themselves. In some cases, religious beliefs are a contention, but there was no evidence of this with Moseley. It seems that she was just a mentally unwell person who obviously wasn't getting the help she needed.

Female mass shooters are rare, and in the US, only 4% are women.

Australian Strawberry Contamination

Strawberries have always been the kind of fruit you can give your children, because they are small, sweet, and most kids love them. In September 2018, a major health safety crisis evolved in Australia, and later in New Zealand, as people began finding needles in their strawberries. By November, at least 186 reports had been filed in Australia alone.

Fruit Contamination Fears

Before there was any sort of official announcement that strawberries had been found with needles in them, a member of the public uploaded a warning on Facebook specifically aimed at strawberries that had been purchased from the Woolworths Strathline Center in Moreton Bay, near Brisbane.

According to the Facebook poster, his friend had inadvertently swallowed part of a needle and was in the hospital receiving treatment. Then, a second complaint was made to Woolworths on September 11. The store did not withdraw the fruit from the shelves, and the first public report occurred on September 12.

Over the ensuing days, dozens of punnets of strawberries were found to be contaminated. They weren't at one isolated store however, and had spread to other states in New South Wales, South Australia, Tasmania and Victoria. The strawberries affected had been grown in Western Australia and Queensland.

Even though many of the complaints received were legitimate, there were some that were a hoax. One man in South Australia was arrested and charged on September 21, after he had faked a contamination.

The Affected Brands

By September 16, the following brands of strawberries had been confirmed by the authorities as being involved in the contamination:

- Donnybrook Berries
- Love Berry
- Delightful Strawberries
- Oasis brands
- Berry Obsession
- Berry Licious
- Mal's Black Label
- Australian Choice

The health authorities and the police had recommended that the public dispose of any brands from that list or return them to where they had purchased them. It was also recommended that consumers cut the strawberries up before eating them.

Two major chain stores, Coles and Aldi, removed all of the punnets of strawberries from their shelves. They planned to restock them after September 18. Woolworths removed just the brands that were known to be affected, and also stopped selling sewing needles temporarily.

The strawberry contamination wasn't just restricted to Australia, unfortunately. On September 23, strawberries sold in Auckland, New Zealand, under the 'Australian Choice' brand were found to contain needles.

Investigating the Contamination

Initially, the Queensland Strawberry Growers Association stated that it may have been a 'disgruntled' former packing employee who was responsible. However, the Acting Chief Superintendent of Queensland Police, Terry Lawrence, commented on that theory saying, "This was an earlier comment by the Strawberry Growers Association, it's something we don't subscribe to".

The vice-president of the Queensland Strawberry Growers Association Adrian Schultz described the act of putting needles in the strawberries as 'commercial terrorism'. A grower from Western Australia said he believed it was carried out by someone with some sort of vendetta against the strawberry industry, and if it wasn't, then it could be a terrorist act.

On November 11, farm supervisor My Ut Trinh, 50, was arrested in Brisbane and charged with seven counts of contamination of goods. The charges related to one of the very first incidences of contamination that had involved the brand Berry Licious. Trinh was born in Vietnam, but twenty years ago she traveled to Australia by boat as a refugee. She had worked at the Berrylicious/Berry Obsession fruit farm as a picking supervisor north of Brisbane. The police were lead to Trinh through her DNA which was present on a needle in one of the contaminated strawberry punnets.

Australian Government Response

The Premier of Queensland Annastaciz Palaszczuk announced on September 15 that a reward of $100,000 was being offered for information that would lead an arrest and conviction for the contamination. Then on September 18, she announced that a $1million assistance package was being made available for the strawberry industry in the state of Queensland. The same day, Premier of Western Australia Mark McGowan announced a $100,000 reward for information that would lead to a prosecution.

In New Zealand, the two major food retailers, Foodstuffs and Woolworths NZ announced that they would be taking all Australian-grown strawberries off the shelves.

Criticism of the Formal Response

By September 17, a consumer-level recall of the affected brands had yet to be issued, and instead, only a trade recall had been issued. A trade recall is described by the Food Standards Australia New Zealand as a recall 'conducted when the food has not been sold directly to consumers. It involves recovery of the product from distribution centers and wholesalers.' A food safety expert commented that she was surprised there had not been a consumer-level recall as the products had been sold to individuals. Also, the recall wasn't stated on the government or supermarket food safety websites. Criticism was also given regarding the delay between the first report of contaminated strawberries on September 9 and the public warning issue on September 12.

The Queensland Strawberry Industry Development Officer Jennifer Rowling, made accusations that some 'authoritative spokespeople' had mishandled the response to the contamination of the strawberries. She also criticized the media and said they had cost the agricultural business millions. She insisted that the contamination had only affected three brands, not all of them.

Grower Measures Taken and Responses

Suncoast Harvest farm on the Sunshine Coast announced via Facebook on September 15 that they would cease from growing strawberries for the rest of the year. This move resulted in 100 workers losing their jobs. Other growers began installing metal detectors to check all further strawberries for contamination.

Some of the farms had to dispose of strawberries. Donnybrook Berries in Queensland had to dump truckloads of strawberries, which they filmed and the footage went viral, receiving more than one million views in one day. Another Queensland strawberry farm found it more financially viable to destroy 500,000 plants rather than harvesting.

Related Incidents

On September 17, a woman who suffered from a mental illness was cautioned after allegedly contaminating a banana at a supermarket in Maryborough, Queensland, with a metal object.

New South Wales Police announced on September 18 that needles had been found in apples and bananas in Sydney. The public were reminded to report any contamination issues they experienced. They were also prompted to be cautious when purchasing any fruit in New South Wales.

On September 20, police in New South Wales arrested a young boy after he had admitted hiding sewing needles in strawberries as a prank. The same day, a needle was found inside a mango in West Gosford, New South Wales.

In New Zealand, a 50-year-old woman was arrested on November 11 after she had contaminated strawberries with needles.

Ahvaz Military Parade Attack

A military parade was taking place in the city of Ahvaz, southwestern Iran, on September 22, when armed gunman attacked. The 25 people who were killed were both civilian bystanders and soldiers of the Islamic Revolutionary Guard Corps. At that time, it was the deadliest terror attack in Iran since 2010.

Responsibility for the attack was claimed by the Ahvaz National Resistance, in the name of the Arab Struggle Movement for the Liberation of Ahwaz. The Amaq News Agency attributed it to followers of the Islamic State of Iraq and the Levant (ISIL).However, none of these claims were rejected. Later, responsibility was claimed by an ISIL spokesman who also warned of further attacks. Iran felt that the US and the Gulf states enabled the attack, and they vowed to seek revenge. Involvement was denied by the American defence secretary, and Saudi Arabia also condemned the accusation.

The Parade Attack

The military parade occurs each year as part of an annual commemoration, the Sacred Defence Week which commemorates the start of the Iran-Iraq War that began in 1980. The Islamic Revolutionary Guard Corps marched along Quds Boulevard. As the parade made its way through the street, five gunmen who were in a nearby park, opened fire. The gunmen were dressed in military uniforms and were disguised as volunteers and members of the Islamic Revolutionary guards Corps.

As well as the marching parade, the gunmen targeted a viewing stand where civilian bystanders were watching the parade from. The gunfire attack went on for around ten minutes, and in that time, 25 people were killed and 70 were left wounded. The dead included 12 soldiers from the Islamic Revolutionary Guard Corps, and a four-year-old boy was also killed. Many of those injured were in a critical condition when they arrived at the hospital.

Initially, reports were confused. At first the Iranian state media announced that four assailants that had committed the attack had been killed. The deputy governor claimed that two had been placed under arrest. Senior spokesman for the armed forces, Brigadier General Abolfazl Shekarchi, said, "All four terrorists were quickly neutralized by security forces". In a further conflicting report, Fars News Agency stated a fifth suspect had been killed but he had initially been confused with other victims.

Who Was Responsible?

Multiple groups claimed responsibility, which made it difficult to work out exactly who was behind the deadly attack. The Iranian state media reported that the assault had been carried out by 'takfiri gunmen', at first.

The first to claim responsibility was a splinter group of the Arab Struggle Movement for the Liberation of Ahwaz (ASMLA). Yaqoob Al-Ahvaz claimed responsibility through comments they made to the UK based Iran International TV. He stated that his group "Ahvaz National Resistance has no choice but to resist". On September 23, a statement appeared on the website of ASMLA that denied any responsibility for the parade attack, and said that the claim had been made by a group that had been removed from the organization back in 2015.

When the Amaq News Agency claimed ISIL was responsible, they uploaded videos of three men, two who spoke Arabic and one who spoke Persian, who were supposedly discussing the upcoming attack.

ISIL's Al Furqan Media Foundation published an audio statement on September 26 with the title of "The Muwahhidin's Assault on the Tower of the Mushrikin". The statement was from spokesman Abul-Hasan Al-Muhajir, and it stated "A group of men of the Khilafah and guardians of the creed in the land of Persia have pounced in defense of the religion, acting to deter and suppress their enemy and to fulfill the Islamic State's promise to all who have the blood of Ahlus Sunnah on their hands."

Photographs of the alleged five attackers, who were masked, were released by ISIL's newspaper al-Naba on September 27.

International Reactions

Ali Khamenei, the Supreme Leader of Iran, said on his website: "This crime is a continuation of the plots of the regional states that are puppets of the United States, and their goal is to create insecurity in our dear country." He called on security forces to bring the men responsible to justice.

The Ministry of Foreign Affairs asked the governments of the United Kingdom, the Netherlands and Denmark to "condemn the attack and extradite people linked to it to Iran to be put on trial." The British ambassador to Iran Rob Macaire sent condolences to the victims' families on behalf of the British nation and condemned the attack.

The United Arab Emirates' chargé d'affaires was summoned by the Iranian ministry on September 23, regarding a tweet that had been made by Emirati professor Abdulkhaleq Abdulla about the attack. The tweet said: "A military attack against a military target is not a terrorist act and moving the battle to the Iranian side is a declared option". The comments were deemed thoughtless and irresponsible by Iran's Foreign Ministry spokesman.

Khamenei alleged that the attackers had been paid by Saudi Arabia and the UAE. The UAE denied the allegations that it had anything to do with the attack.

Russian President Vladimir Putin claimed he was horrified by the attack and presented his condolences to the victims. The Syrian Ministry of Foreign Affairs also condemned the attack and warned against those who finance terrorism in the region.

Minister of Intelligence Mahmoud Alavi announced on September 24 that most of those behind the attack had been located and arrested. The United Nations Security Council called for those perpetrators to be brought to justice.

The Funerals

A mass funeral took place on September 24 near Ahvaz's Sarallah Hussainiya, and it was attended by thousands of Iranians. The coffins were wrapped in the Iran flag, and some of the mourners clutched photographs of the victims or waived Iranian flags. ABC News described it as 'a collective outpouring of grief'.

Retaliation

On October 1, the Aerospace Force of the Islamic Revolutionary Guard Corps launched six missiles against the Hajin headquarters of takfri militants who were allegedly behind the military parade attack. The Fars New Agency reported that at least one of the missiles had slogans 'death to America', 'death to Israel' and 'death to Al Saud' on it.

The missile attack was described as a revenge attack for the Ahvaz people. As a result of the missile attack, Brigadier Amir Ali Hajizadeh, head of the Aerospace Force of the Islamic Revolutionary Guard Corps claimed that 40 of the top leaders of ISIL had been killed. However, Colonel Sean Ryan, spokesmen for the US-led Combined Joint Task Force - Operation Inherent Resolve, there was no damage at all caused by the missiles.

Terrorist Attacks in Short for September

September 1

Borno State, Nigeria: 30 Nigerian soldiers died in combat with Boko Haram jihadists who overran a military base in the northeast near the border with Niger.

September 4

Bria, Central African Republic: Suspected Seleka rebels massacred at least 42 Christians by shootings and stabbings in Bria, Central African Republic.

September 5

Kabul, Afghanistan: 26 people were killed and 91 were injured in a blast in a Kabul Wrestling club killing 4 then another attacker exploded when emergency forces arrived, in total 26 were killed and 91 were injured, among the dead were two journalists and the Islamic State claimed responsibility for the bombing.

September 6

Badghis Province, Afghanistan: Taliban militants carried out an attack on a security post killing 11 and injuring 6 officers the Taliban militants suffered at least 10 deaths as well.

September 7

Muhradah, Syria: Jihadists linked to Al-Qaeda fired several rockets towards the large Christian town of Mhardeh killing at least 12 and injuring 20.

September 8

Herat Province, Afghanistan: Taliban insurgents attacked a checkpoint in the western province of Afghanistan of Herat killing 9 and injuring 6 the militants suffered 10 losses as well.

September 10

Khamyab District, Afghanistan: The Taliban attacked multiple checkpoints in Northern Afghanistan province killing at least 52 and injuring at least 27, 42 Taliban insurgents were also killed and many were wounded.

September 11

Momand Dara District, Afghanistan: 68 people were killed and at least 165 were injured when a suicide bomber targeted a gathering of protesters in the eastern Afghan area of Momand Dara District, the Islamic State is suspected, while the Taliban denied that this was anything to do with them.

As-Suwayda, Syria: At least 21 Syrian soldiers were killed and other 30 others were kidnapped during an ambush and coordinated attack in the city of As-Suwayda, last bastion of Islamic State jihadis in the region.

September 14

Deir ez-Zor Governorate, Syria: Islamic State fighters ambushed US backed SDF fighters and opened fire on them killing at least 20 and wounding several more.

Dara-I-Suf-Paen, Afghanistan : At least 7 police died and another 17 were injured when the Taliban attacked a Police Checkpoint in the Dara I Suf Paen District.

Kompienga Province, Burkina Faso: Islamist militants killed at least nine people and injured two in two twin attacks at villages of the Kompienga Province of Burkina Faso, in one attack they attacked a mosque killing five including an imam and in another attack they killed three people of the same family and wounded two.

Borno State, Nigeria: At least ten villagers were killed by a Boko Haram ambush in Nganzai local government area of Borno State.

September 16

Afghanistan: The Taliban launched attacks all over Afghanistan killing 27 security forces and injuring several, 22 Taliban Militants were killed and another 16 suffered injuries.

September 18

Balkh Province, Afghanistan: Nine Afghan Local Police (ALP) personnel, including a commander, were killed in a Taliban attack in the northern Balkh province of Afghanistan.

September 19

Borno State, Nigeria: Boko Haram insurgents killed at least 9 people and injured 9, when they raided villages in Borno State and set them on fire after shooting.

September 20

Palma District, Mozambique: 12 people were killed and 14 were injured in a brutal attack on a village in the Palma District of Cabo Delgado, Mozambique when jihadists raided the village, 10 were shot to death and another 2 were burnt to death and a person was beheaded after being killed.

September 22

Beni, Democratic Republic of The Congo: At least 27 people were killed and 9 were injured when ADF Rebels attacked the town of Beni in the Democratic Republic of the Congo most of the dead were church members as well, at least 4 rebels were killed as well.

September 25

Gao Region, Mali: Gunmen attacked civilians at a camp in the Northeastern region of Mali killing at least 17 civilians. The Islamic State Greater Sahara (ISGS) is suspected.

September 26

Baraboulé Department, Burkina Faso: At least nine Burkina Faso soldiers were killed and several others were injured when their vehicle crossed over a landmine in the Baraboulé Department of the Soum Province in Burkina Faso.

September 28

Amalaoulaou, Mali: Suspected Jihadists killed at least 25 Tuaregs in coordinated attacks on Dates 28-29 in Amalaoulaou, Mali, the attack was blamed on "jihadists'.

Yambio, South Sudan: 9 people were killed and 35 were injured when a man lobbed a grenade at a memorial service, at Yambio South Sudan.

September 29

Lake Chad, Chad: Boko Haram militants ambushed people near Lake Chad killing 6 including soldiers and injuring Several, Chadian Soldiers later announced that they had killed at least 17 militants.

Chapter 10:
OCTOBER

The Disappearance of Jayme Closs

An emergency call was placed on October 15 from the home of the Closs family, and when police arrived at the scene, the parents had been shot and killed and teenager Jayme, 13, was missing. It is believed by police that Jayme played no part in the deaths of her parents and it was most likely she had been abducted.

Death and Disappearance

On the night of the killings and disappearance, someone from the house made a 9-1-1 call at around 1:00am. The operator didn't hear anyone speak on the call but they could hear a lot of yelling and sounds of a disturbance. A call was placed back to the house number, but it went to the voicemail of Denise Closs, Jayme's mother.

Four minutes after receiving the call, police arrived at the house. Straight away they observed that the front door had been kicked in. They entered the house and found the bodies of Jayme's father James, 56, and her mother Denise, 46. Both had been killed by gunshot wounds.

Police believe that Jayme was still in the house when her parents were shot, as suggested by evidence in the home and from the 9-1-1 call. After a thorough search of the home, no gun could be found.

Surveillance footage showed two vehicles near the home on the night Jayme disappeared and they were quickly considered to be of interest. One was a red or orange colored 2008-2014 Dodge Challenger, and the other vehicle was black, possibly a 2004 -2010 Acura MDX or a 2006-2010 Ford Edge.

When neighbors were questioned, some claimed they had heard two gunshots at around 00.30am but because hunting was common in the area, they didn't feel concerned.

Police Investigation

A search was undertaken on October 18 focusing on the roadsides of US Route 8, which was near the Closs house. A second search occurred on October 23, and volunteers spent the day looking for the missing teenager. A reward of $25,000 was offered on October 24 for any information that could lead to the location of Jayme. Two days later, that offer was doubled to $50,000.

Although thousands of volunteers had help police in searching for Jayme, her whereabouts were still unknown. Police had put in hundreds of hours of work trying to work out who could have taken her or why. On November 1 it was announced that because the number of tips coming into police were decreasing, the authorities were scaling back their efforts to find Jayme to 'a more deliberate and methodical effort to progress the investigation'.

As of January 2019, Jayme Closs has been discovered alive, after she escaped from her alleged captor. A man has been arrested for the murders of Jayme's parents and her abduction.

Pittsburgh Synagogue Mass Shooting

A synagogue is meant to be a place for peaceful worship, not the scene of multiple shootings such as what occurred at Tree of Life in the Squirrel Hill neighborhood in Pittsburgh. A single suspect entered and opened fire on October 27, leaving nearly a dozen people dead and several injured, including police officers.

How the Shooting Unfolded

There were three services underway at the Tree of Life synagogue, which housed three congregations, by 9:45am. Both New Light and Tree of Life had just started separate Shabbat morning service, with New Light in the basement and Tree of Life in the Pervin Chapel.

Five minutes later, a heavy-set white man with a beard entered the building and immediately opened fire. He was apparently shooting for nearly twenty minutes, using a Cold AR-15 semi-automatic rifle and three Glock .357 SIG semi-automatic pistols. According to witnesses and authorities, the gunman used all of the weapons in the attack.

There were 75 people in the building at the time of the shooting. The first victims shot were the Rosenthal brothers who were at the main entrance. The shooter then went downstairs. Some of the people who heard gunshots didn't realize what they were.

Calls started coming into the police at 9:54am from people inside the building who had barricaded themselves for safety. Melvin Wax, the leader of services for New Light, came out of hiding in a closet and was shot. However, the shooter did not realise there were three other people still hiding in the closet.

By 9:57am, the shooter was headed back upstairs to Tree of Life, where 12 worshippers had gathered for the Shabbat service. Four of them managed to escape through a side door, but eight didn't have time to flee. Seven of those left behind were killed, and one was wounded. Witnesses said that at one point the shooter had shouted "All Jews must die!"

Police arrived at the synagogue at 9:59am, and the gunman opened fire on them from the entrance. He was apparently leaving the building at the time, and police returned fire, which made him retreat back inside. Tactical teams entered the synagogue at 10:30am, and were met with gunfire.

The officers fired back at the gunman and wounded him, and he retreated to the third floor. During the gunfight, two of the SWAT members were also shot, with one being critically wounded. At 11:08am, the gunman crawled out from the room he had been hiding in and surrendered to police. He was given medical care once he was in police custody, at which time he told a SWAT officer that he wanted all Jews to do, and that Jews were committing genocide against his people.

Those Who Died

The gunman had killed eleven people during his shooting rampage at the synagogue. A further six people were injured, including four police officers, and it is remarkable the numbers weren't much higher considering the amount of weaponry the gunman was armed with.

Five of the wounded were taken to UPMC Presbyterian Hospital, with four needing surgical treatment. One of the wounded had minor injuries and was released by the afternoon. Another victim went to UPMC Mercy for treatment. The shooter was transported to Allegheny General Hospital where ironically, three of the staff who treated him there were Jews.

Those who tragically lost their lives were:

- Joyce Fienberg, 75
- Richard Gottfried, 65
- Rose Mallinger, 97
- Jerry Rabinowitz, 66
- Cecil Rosenthal, 59
- David Rosenthal, 54
- Bernice Simon, 84
- Sylvan Simon, 86
- Daniel Stein, 71
- Melvin Wax, 88
- Irving Younger, 69

The Suspect - Robert Gregory Bowers

Bowers, 46, lived in Baldwin, Pennsylvania. His parents got divorced when he was only a year old, and when Bowers was 6, his father committed suicide at the age of 27. His mother remarried, and they moved to Florida, but the marriage didn't last and it was over within a year. Bowers and his mother returned to Pennsylvania, and moved in with his maternal grandparents in Whitehall.

Bowers' mother had health issues, so his grandparents took most of the responsibility for taking care of him and raising him. From about 1989, Bowers had dropped out of high school and was working as a truck driver. His neighbors described him as someone who rarely interacted with other people.

For more than twenty years, Bowers had actively engaged in conversations and media posts that started as 'staunch conservatism' but transitioned to white nationalism. He became a follower of websites like Gab, which promoted anti-Semitic conspiracy theories through social media.

Gab is often descried as being 'extremist friendly' for the alt-right, the neo-Nazis and white supremacists. Bowers profile had been registered with Gab as of January 2018, and his handle was 'onedingo'. The description of his account read: "Jews are the children of Satan (John 8:44). The Lord Jesus Christ [has] come in the flesh."

Despite the apparent Christian identity beliefs, the cover photo contained the number 1488 which neo-Nazis and white supremacists use to evoke David Lane's 'Fourteen Words' and the Heil Hitler. Bowers had published posts on his account supporting the white genocide theory. Content by other anti-Semitic, neo-Nazi, white supremacist/nationalist, Holocaust-denying users was reposted by Bowers. He also reposted comments that supported the Southern California-based alt-right fight club, Rise Above Movement.

Bowers criticized President Donald Trump for being a 'globalist not a nationalist'. He also claimed Trump was being surrounded and controlled by Jews. In a post he wrote, "There is no #MAGA as long as there is a kike infestation." A month prior to the shooting, he had posted photos online of his target practice results. He also had a photo of his three handguns, which he called his 'glock family'.

Bowers made anti-Semitic posts online that were directed at the Hebrew Immigrant Aid Society (HIAS), who sponsored National Refugee Shabbat.

Tree of Life participated. He made claims that members of the Central American caravans heading toward the US border were being assisted by Jews. He also referred to those caravans as 'invaders'.

A post that Bowers had put on Gab read: "HIAS likes to bring invaders in that kill our people. I can't sit by and watch my people get slaughtered. Screw your optics, I'm going in."

The Southern Poverty Law Center explained that "the mention of 'optics' is in reference to a disagreement that has raged within the white nationalist movement since the Unite the Right rally in 2017 about how best to get their message across to the general public".

Following Bowers' attack at the synagogue, Gab suspended his profile and said they would cooperate with police in the investigation. Not long after the attack, the main supporters of Gab including Stripe, PayPal, Medium and Joyent, along with Go Daddy, where the domains for Gab were registered, pulled their support. Gab had to relocate to a different hosting service, which resulted in Gab being shut down in the short term.

Criminal Charges and Proceedings

The US Department of Justice charged Bowers with 29 federal crimes. These include eleven counts of obstruction of exercise of religious beliefs resulting in death, eleven counts of use of a firearm to commit murder during a crime of violence, four counts of obstruction of exercise of religious beliefs resulting in bodily injury to a public safety officer, and three counts of use and discharge of a firearm during a crime of violence.

Bowers also received 36 state criminal charges, including eleven counts of criminal homicide, 6 counts of aggravated assault, 6 counts of attempted criminal homicide and 13 counts of ethnic intimidation.

On October 29, he appeared in federal court to hear the charges against him. He was appointed an attorney by the court and remanded in custody without bail. On October 31, he was indicted by the federal grand jury. The charges laid against Bowers carry a maximum penalty of death or 535 years in a federal prison.

Bowers entered a plea of 'not guilty' on November 1, which is quite normal at this stage in the legal proceedings, and a jury trial was requested.

Reactions - United States

President Trump stated through Twitter that the shooting was a 'wicked, anti-Semitic act of pure evil'. He further offered an opinion that the shooting was preventable, saying: "If there was an armed guard inside the temple, they would have been able to stop him". Trump suggested that the death penalty was suitable for crimes such as this.

Other politicians and dignitaries that commented on Twitter their opinions were Pennsylvania Goerner Tom Wolf, Braddock Mayor John Fetterman, and Pittsburgh City Councilman Corey O'Conor. All denounced what the shooter had done and expressed their sympathies.

Cecilia Wang from the American Civil Liberties Union claimed that this attack and other recent unrest was inspired by 'elements of Trump's rhetoric'. Vice President Mike Pence denied any connection in an interview with NBC News.

Between October 27 and 31, all American flags that were on military or public grounds were flown at half-staff in memory of the victims.

Reactions - International

The Prime Minister of Israel, Benjamin Netanyahu, condemned the 'horrifying anti-Semitic brutality" adding that "the whole of Israel grieves with the families of the dead." Naftali Bennett, the education and diaspora affairs minister of Israel, travelled to Pittsburgh immediately to visit the synagogue, meet with members of the community and to participate in the victims' funerals. The Ministry of Diaspora Affairs was also directed to "assess and prepare to assist the Pittsburgh Jewish community, including the need for emergency and resilience teams that immediately left Israel for psychological assistance and community rehabilitation."

On October 28, Israel's cabinet stood for a minute of silence in honor of the victims. Chief Rabbi of Israel David Law said: "Any murder of any Jew in any part of the world for being Jewish is unforgivable". He described the synagogue as "a place with a profound Jewish flavor". Several news reports said that Lau refused to refer to the Conservative congregation as a 'synagogue' because it is non-Orthodox. But when he was interviewed, he questioned, "Why does it matter in what synagogue or what liturgy they were praying?!"

In Tel Aviv Municipality, their city hall building was lit up with the colors of the American flag. It showed their solidarity with the Pittsburgh victims. On Jerusalem's Western Wall and image of the American flag beside the Israeli flag was projected.

During his Sunday prayers in St. Peter's Square on October 28, Pope Francis denounced the 'inhuman act of violence'. He led prayers for the dead, the wounded and their families. He asked God," to help us to extinguish the flames of hatred that develop in our societies".

The Iranian Minister of Foreign Affairs offered his prayers and thoughts to the victims. He stated: "Extremism and terrorism know no race or religion, and must be condemned in all cases".

Reactions - Local

Following the dreadful attack, the American flag at Carnegie Mellon University was lowered to half-staff as a symbol of mourning. Immediately after the attack had taken place, the campus of the University was placed on lockdown. Residents were at the same time being advised to stay off the streets.

A very large number of people from the Pittsburgh Jewish community including all denominations came together to participate in local Jewish rituals related to death and mourning. Tradition requires someone to guard a corpse until it has been buried. Volunteer 'guards' took shifts of one hour at a time at the morgue until all of the bodies had been transported to funeral homes.

At the joint funeral service for the Rosenthal brothers on October 30, members of the Pittsburgh Steelers attended. The sister of the brothers was a former employee of the team.

Media and Organizations

On October 28, the lights on the Empire State Building were darkened in a way of honoring the victims. The top of the building was left glowing as a symbol of 'an orange halo shining a light on gun violence awareness'. In Paris, the Eiffel Tower also darkened its lights, and on October 27, the Victory Lights on the top of the Cathedral of Learning at University of Pittsburgh were darkened. Also at the university, the Victory Lights were altered on November 2 so that the blue beam only shined for 11 seconds, one second for each victim.

Many sports teams across America and Canada honored those who died in the attack. During a game between the Pittsburgh Steelers and the Cleveland Browns, a minute of silence was observed. The same with games between the New Orleans Saints and the Minnesota Vikings, the Winnipeg Jets and the Toronto Maple Leafs, the Pittsburgh Penguins and the Vancouver Canucks, the Pittsburgh Panthers and Duke, and the Philadelphia Eagles and Jacksonville Jaguars, who were playing in London.

At the World Series Game 4 at Dodger Stadium, a moment of silence was observed. When the Pittsburgh Penguins played the New York Islanders on October 30, their jerseys had a patch which said 'Stronger than Hate'. They later auctioned the jerseys to raise money for the synagogue. The Pittsburgh Panthers similarly had a decal on their helmets with the same saying during their game against University of Virginia on November 2.

Rallies and Vigils

On the same night as the shooting, a vigil was held at the intersection of Forbes and Murray Avenues in Squirrel Hill. More than 3,000 people attended the vigil which had been organized by the students at Taylor Allderdice High School. Two further vigils also took place in the neighborhood.

An interfaith vigil organized by the regional Jewish Federation was held the day after the shooting. It was held at the Soldiers and Sailors Memorial Hall, and the crowd numbered an estimated 2,500, including numerous local and national dignitaries. The Israeli ambassador to the US and during the event a video stream of Israeli president Reuven Rivlin offering comments and leading the crowd in reciting the Kaddish.

Within a week of the attack, solidarity rallies and vigils were being held in countries all over the world. In the US, some of these involved thousands of people, in cities all across the country. These included the following:

- Ann Arbor
- Atlanta
- Austin
- Boston
- Buffalo
- Charleston
- Chicago
- Cincinnati
- Cleveland
- Columbus
- Denver
- Houston
- Jacksonville
- Knoxville
- Los Angeles
- Madison
- Memphis
- Middletown
- New Haven
- New Orleans
- New York City
- Philadelphia
- Portland
- Rochester
- Salt Lake City
- Seattle
- St. Louis
- Washington
- Wilkes-Barre
- Woodbridge

Vigils and rallies were held in Montreal, Ottawa, Vancouver and Halifax, as well as other parts of Canada. On the evening of October 28, a gathering at Zion Square in Jerusalem involved around 500 people, both Israelis and Americans, and they all lit candles. Jewish communal vigils were also held in Liverpool, London, Brighton and Paris.

The Presidential Visit

President Donald Trump flew to Pittsburgh on October 30 along with several of his family members and the Treasury Secretary Steven Mnuchin, to visit the area. Their first stop was at the synagogue where they met with Jeffrey Myers, the spiritual leader of Tree of Life, and Ron Dermer, Israeli ambassador to the US.

Inside the synagogue, Trump lit candles for the victims, and then outside he placed a small stone of each of the 11 Star-of-David memorial markers for those who had been killed. Trump had brought the stones form the White House grounds. From there they traveled to the UPMC Presbyterian Hospital and met with the victims who had been wounded and their families, and medical staff and law enforcement officials.

Unites States Mail Bombing Attempts

Sixteen pipe bombs were sent through the postal service to critics of President Donald Trump. At first it was thought that they were live bombs, but when they were analyzed, it was found that they were not capable of exploding. Investigators weren't sure if they were meant to be duds or if they just hadn't been made correctly.

The Intended Recipients

The first bomb was found on October 22, at the home of George Soros in New York. Soros was often the targeted subject of many conspiracy theorists. On the day the bomb was delivered, Soros wasn't at home, and the employee who discovered it carefully carried it away from the house to a wooded area. The bomb squad arrived and detonated it without incident.

On Tuesday October 23, another bomb was intercepted by the United States Secret Service before it could reach the targeted addressee, Hillary Clinton. It had been sent to her address in Chappaqua, New York.

The Secret Service also intercepted a bomb that had been sent to former President Barack Obama. The mail had been screened in Washington, which lead to the discovery, on October 24. The same day, a package arrived at the mail room at CNN addressed to former CIA Director John O. Brennan. It had been delivered by courier, and on inspection contained an explosive and a suspicious powder.

Brennan had served as an intelligence and national security analyst for MSNBC and NBC News since February, and had made appearances on CNN previously. The bomb alarm sounded while Poppy Harlow and Jim Sciutto were in the Newsroom, and after they left the building, they kept reporting via Skype using a cellphone.

Also on the same day, a package was intercepted by the United States Capitol Police, addressed to US Representative Maxine Walters. Another package addressed to her resulted in the US Postal Service facility in Los Angles to be evacuated. US Attorney General Eric Holder was meant to receive a package but it hadn't been addressed correctly and was sent back to the sender. The sender's address was the office of US Representative Debbie Wasserman Schultz.

Early on October 25, a package addressed to actor Robert De Niro was found in Tribeca, New York City. It was addressed to De Niro's company, TriBeCa Productions. A package was also found addressed to Vice President Joe Biden in New Castle Delaware. It had insufficient postage on the package and was returned to the post office. A second one was sent to Biden, but it had the wrong address on it and was sent to a facility in Wilmington, Delaware. Federal authorities and the Miami-Dade Police Department thought many of the packages had been sent through a mail center in Opa-locka in Florida, and subsequently searched it along with a bomb squad and a K-9 unit.

On Friday October 26, four more packages were discovered by the authorities. One was addressed to former National Intelligence Director James Clapper and was found in a New York City postal facility. Another addressed to US Senator Cory Booker was discovered in a postal facility in Florida. The other two were addressed to US Senator Kamala Harris in Sacramento, and billionaire Tom Steyer in Burlingame, California. A second package addressed to Steyer was found on November 1.

President of CNN Jeff Zucker alerted employees on October 29 that a suspicious package addressed to the CNN center had been found at a post office in Atlanta. This one wasn't addressed to anyone in particular, and looked very similar to the other bomb packages that had been sent.

Explosive Devices and Envelopes

The explosive device sent in the package to Soros's house was made from a six inch piece of PVC pipe that was filled with explosive powder. The bombs that were found on October 24 were packed with glass shards. The packages sent to both Clinton and Obama were constructed similarly to the one sent to Soros.

With the bomb and mysterious white powder sent to CNN, the bomb was a pipe bomb but the powder was completely harmless. The bombs contained pyrotechnic powder but there was no trigger mechanism, so they wouldn't have exploded. It's just as well, because the FBI said that if they had triggered, they were 'potentially destructive devices'. They contained timers and batteries but would not explode.

Each bomb was sent in a yellow manila envelope that was lined with bubble wrap, and they each had a printed address label. The return address on the packages was that of US Representative Debbie Wasserman Schultz. It was noted that the spelling of Schultz was incorrect on each parcel, and Florida had also been spelt incorrectly.

On each package was a 'meme parody' of the ISIL flag, and contained the message 'Git 'Er (sic) Done'. The phrase was a catchphrase of Larry the Cable Guy, a standup comedian.

The Investigation

Because of the nature of the bombs and their intended targets, the FBI lead the investigation along with assistance from the US Secret Service, the US Postal Inspection Service, the Bureau of Alcohol, Tobacco, Firearms and Explosives, and police departments from New York City, Los Angeles, Atlanta, and Miami-Dade.

Many of the bombs and their packaging were sent to be analyzed at the FBI Laboratory in Quantico. On one of the packages a fingerprint was found, and DNA was found on two others. This lead to the identification of the suspect, Cesar Altieri Sayoc Jr. His image was found on video surveillance near a post office in South Florida, and he was found through cell phone tracking.

Sayoc was arrested on October 26 in Plantation, Florida, in a parking lot of an AutoZone store.

Cesar Sayoc Jr.

Sayoc was born in Brooklyn in 1962, and his family moved to Florida when he was a child. His mother had Italian heritage and was born in the Bronx, whereas his father was a Filipino immigrant. When he was young, his father left the family. Sayoc graduated from high school and spent three semesters at Brevard College and University of North Carolina, but he did not declare a major or attain a degree.

He had quite a long criminal history, and in 2002, he was convicted of calling a bomb threat in to Florida Power & Light. There were multiple other arrests for battery, drugs and theft, and received convictions in 1991, 2013 and 2014. He has previously been connected to two businesses which are no longer active. These were the Proud Native American One Low Price Dry-cleaning in 2001 and the Native American Catering & Vending LLC in 2016. In 2009, Sayoc's home was foreclosed and he filed for bankruptcy in 2012. At that time his debt was more than $21,000.

Sayoc, a body builder, was known to abuse steroids. Over the years he has made a number of false claims about himself. In 2014, during a deposition, he stated he had played soccer for A.C. Milan, which was untrue. He also stated he had played arena football for the Arizona Rattlers, and this was also untrue. Sayoc claimed to have been a stripper and said he had owned a strip club. He also said he was a partner in famous strip group Chippendales, but he has never worked for them nor been associated with them in any way.

When he declared bankruptcy, his employment was listed as store manager at a company called Hassanco Investments, in Florida. Between January 2017 and January 2018, he had been making pizza deliveries part time. At the time of his arrest for the bomb packages, he was working as a doorman and DJ at a strip club in West Palm Beach.

Sayoc registered with the Republican Party in 2016. He even filmed himself at one of the president's rallies wearing a MAGA hat (Make America Great Again). He was known in social media for having extreme views and for his support of Trump.

As part of the arrest process, Sayoc's van was also seized, and inside it was covered with images of Donald Trump and Mike Pence. There was also a sticker that said 'CNN Sucks'. Some of the posters in the van supported a Native American tribe, the unconquered Seminoles.

Sayoc had claimed that he was of Native American heritage, but the Seminole Tribe stated there was no record of him being a member. Other stickers found in the van had images of Hillary Clinton, Barack Obama, Van Jones, Michael Moore and Jill Stein, each with a gun crosshair design on their face.

Also inside the van were a number of items suggesting the bombs were constructed inside the vehicle. These include stamps, envelopes, soldering equipment, a printer, powder and paper. There was also a 'hit list' with more than 100 people's names on it, and although the names haven't been publicly released, each person was contacted by the authorities and informed.

The Legal Proceedings

Sayoc was arraigned on October 29 for five federal crimes, including:

- Interstate transportation of an explosive
- Threats against former presidents and certain other persons
- Illegal mailing of explosives
- Threatening interstate communications
- Assaulting federal officers

He entered a plea of not guilty. He was transferred to New York on November 2 to await his trial. A New York judge ordered on November 6 that he be held without bail.

Reports of Previous Threats

According to Ilya Somin, a scholar at the Cato Institutes and law professor at George Mason University, Sayoc made death threats towards him through Facebook in April 2018. He had threatened to murder Somin and his family, and stated he would 'feed the bodies to Florida alligators'. The comments were reported to Facebook which did nothing. The incident was also reported to George Mason University police and Arlington law enforcement by Somin.

Sayoc sent a threatening tweet to Democratic strategist Rochelle Ritchie on October 11. The threat said, "Hug your loved ones real close every time you leave you home". Twitter didn't act upon the threat until after Sayoc was arrested, at which time they apologized to Ritchie and suspended Sayoc's accounts permanently.

Kerch Polytechnic College Massacre

In what was the largest loss of life during school violence since 2004, the Kerch Polytechnic College massacre was a shooting and bomb attack that took place in Crimea. By the end of the attack, 20 were dead and 70 were wounded. The final death was that of the perpetrator.

School under Attack

On September 8, Vladislav Roslyakov bought a shotgun and on October 13, he purchased 150 rounds of ammunition. He had been planning this attack for a while. On October 17, at around 11:46am, he entered the Kerch Polytechnic College grounds, and began to shoot.

Many witnesses saw the gunman walking up and down the halls and shooting randomly at teachers and classmates. He even shot at the computer monitors, a fire extinguisher and any locked doors he came across. He detonated a large nail-bomb, and later, the police found other explosives he had planted around the campus.

As the explosion occurred, the windows of the building erupted, and as people ran from the blast, Roslyakov shot at them at point blank range. The bomb went off on the first floor, but the shooting rampage took place on the second floor. According to Russia-24, the state television channel, 200 military personnel were sent to the scene.

There is some discrepancy among witnesses as to how long it took for help to arrive. Some reported it only took 5 minutes for police to arrive, while others claimed it was closer to 20 minutes. Remarkably, there is a police station only 330 yards away.

At the end of his rampage, Roslyakov ended his life by shooting himself in the college library.

So Many Victims

The majority of the victims were teenagers, as expected at a college. Of those who died, 15 were students and 5 were teachers. All were killed by gunshot. Six of the students killed had not even turned 18 at the time of their death. In total, there were 20 deceased victims, and the dead perpetrator.

There were 70 people wounded in the massacre, with some in critical condition and comas.

Those who were killed were:

- Ksenia Boldina, 17
- Vladislav Verdeborgo, 15
- Victoria Demchuk, 16
- Ruden Djuraev, 16
- Anna Zhuravleva, 19
- Alina Kerova, 16
- Alexey Lavrynovich, 19
- Egor Perepelkin, 17
- Vladislav Lazarev , 19
- Ruslan Lysenko, 17
- Roman Karymov, 21
- Danil Pipenko, 16
- Sergey Stepanenko, 15
- Nikita Florensky , 16
- Daria Tjeherest ,16
- Anastasia Baklanova, 26
- Svetlana Baklanova, 57
- Larisa Kudryavtseva, 62
- Alexander Moiseenko, 46
- Lyudmila Ustenko, 65

The Boy Behind the Gun

Roslyakov, 18, was a fourth-year student at the college. He had a troubled family background that started when he was about ten years old. His father had sustained a serious head injury, leading to him being aggressive and disabled, so his parents separated. At school Roslyakov had poor grades and few friends. His hobbies were centered on violence, including video games and weapons.

He enrolled in college in 2015 so he could study to be an electrician. While there he developed a keen interest in more weapons and explosives. He even started carrying a bayonet. One day in class he released pepper spray but couldn't explain why he had done it.

His mother, a Jehovah's Witness, was strict on Roslyakov by limiting his social life, searching his pockets all the time, and wouldn't let him go to the cinema or use a computer until he was 16 years old. Just days before he went on attack at the college, he had made the comment that he did not believe in the afterlife. The night before the attack, he burned a Bible that he had highlighted verses in.

He Hated the Polytechnic College

Roslyakov had reportedly told a friend that he hated the polytechnic college and he had vowed to seek revenge on the teachers. Some reported he may have been bullied, and an ex-girlfriend claimed he lost his faith in people after he was ridiculed by his classmates because he was different.

Days leading up to the attack, he had commented that he lacked any sense in his life, and discussed ignorance by others. He also mentioned suicide and shooting on social media. He was also involved in many online groups dedicated to serial killers.

The surveillance footage of the massacre showed Roslyakov carrying an eight-shot 12 gauge Hatsan Escort Aimguard pump-action shotgun that had a pistol grip. He was wearing a white t-shirt with a Russian word for hatred on it and black trousers. He was dressed similarly to Eric Harris, one of the shooters at the Columbine High School massacre in the US in 1999. This led some to believe that this was a copycat crime.

Investigating the Crime and the Perpetrator

The main focus of the investigation in the days following the massacre was trying to identify what the motive was for Roslyakov to walk into his school and start killing people. They also were looking into how he could have been able to afford to purchase the weapon, which would have cost the equivalent of $450-$600 USD. They also wanted to know where he learned how to use such a weapon.

Later it was determined that he had purchased the weapon legally and that he had obtained a weapon permit in 2018. He had completed training on weapon security which is a legal requirement before getting the permit and being able to purchase a firearm. He occasionally attended a shooting club, which is where he most likely learned how to use the gun.

A psychiatric evaluation of Roslyakov was ordered postmortem by the Investigative Committee. On October 18, Prime Minister Segey Aksyonov stated there was a possibility he hadn't acted alone, and the police were looking for someone who could have been 'coaching' Roslyakov on how to commit the crime. But, on November 9, the Investigative Committee stated that he had acted alone and there was nobody else involved.

Reactions to the Crime

The Prime Minister of Crimea announced after the massacre that there would be three days of mourning, and it was also announced by the Crimean State Council speaker that the families of the victims would receive financial compensation. The initial figures suggested were 1 million rubles ($17,140.9 USD) from the federal budget and that same from the local budget.

According to Russian President Vladimir Putin, the attack seemed to be the result of social media, the internet and globalization. He further mentioned, "everything started with the tragic events in schools in the US...we're not creating healthy (Internet) content for young people...which leads to tragedies of this kind."

Similarly, Sergey Mikheyev, a Russian political analyst, blamed it on 'Western subculture'. He claimed that it "builds its matrix on the cult of violence...the one who has a weapon in his hands is right. This is a purely American approach to the matter."

Aftermath at the School

When students returned to the school on October 23, they were met with checkpoints at every entrance. Their identities were checked and confirmed before they were allowed to enter.

<u>The Assassination of Jamal Khashoggi</u>

Jamal Khashoggi - journalist for the Washington Post, Saudi dissident and general manager and editor-in-chief of Al-Arab News Channel met a grisly death on October 2 that sent shockwaves of horror, anger and disgust around the world. It wasn't just that he was killed, but how he was killed, who was present at the death, and who ordered it.

A Record of Horror

On October 2, Khashoggi had gone to the Saudi consulate in Istanbul, Turkey, to obtain some documents he required before he could marry his fiancée. He never returned. On investigation, there was no security camera footage at the consulate of him ever leaving the building, and so he was declared missing. Meanwhile, reports were coming in through various news agencies that he had in fact been assassinated inside the consulate. Even worse, the rumors were that he had been dismembered.

When questioned, the Saudi Arabia government claimed that he had left the consulate and that they knew nothing about what had happened to him since. Media in Turkey published proof that he never left the building.

The Turkish police believe that Khashoggi was tortured, killed and dismembered in the consulate, and that a 15-member team had arrived from Saudi Arabia to carry out the gruesome task. One anonymous source claimed that the body had been cut into pieces before quietly being removed from the building. The source also claimed it had been "videotaped to prove the mission had been accomplished and the tape was taken out of the country". Allegedly, the squad took Khashoggi's severed fingers to Mohammad bin Salman in Riyadh as proof that the assassination had been carried out.

Turkish officials said they would release evidence of the murder, but within a few days, Yasin Aktay, an adviser to the president of Turkey, stated that 'the Saudi state is not blamed here'. Speculation was rife that the statement was made so that the trade ties Turkey had with Saudi Arabia would not be affected, as they were very lucrative.

It was claimed by Turkey that they had both video and audio evidence of the murder as it occurred inside the consulate. President Donald Trump said the US had asked for the recordings, and it was believed the audio recording was shared with Central Intelligence Agency agents (CIA).

On October 15, CNN reported that Saudi was going to admit to the killing but would claim it wasn't planned and carried out by a death squad. Criticism of this statement was widespread, given he was dismembered, the murder was premeditated, the circumstances of the death and the arrival and departure of 15 men which included forensic specialists.

An anonymous source reported that it took around seven minutes for Khashoggi to be killed. They stated that Salah Muhammed al-Tubaigy, a forensic specialist, had cut the body into pieces while Khashoggi was still alive, using a bone saw he had brought along with him. Throughout this there was music playing. Allegedly, Khashoggi was dragged from the office of consul general Mohammad al-Otaibi into the study where he was cut up. There had been no interrogation; they had purely come to slaughter him.

The Daily Sabah newspaper, which is pro-government, reported on October 18 that neighbors of the consul's residence had noticed an unusual barbecue party. The newspaper made the suggestion that this may have been to cover up the smell of the corpse as they incinerated it. The neighbor said, "We have been living here for twelve years but I have never seen them having a barbecue party. That day, they had a barbecue party in the garden."

Reports from an anonymous source were published in the Wall Street Journal that Khashoggi was tortured in front of Mohammad al-Otaibi. The report included the information that al-Otaibi had left Istanbul on October 16, and had gone to Riyadh. Interestingly, he left just hours before a search was to be undertaken at his home in relation to the disappearance of Khashoggi.

The Saudi Foreign Ministry reported on October 20 that the preliminary investigation showed that Khashoggi had died during a fight that he was engaged in at the consulate. This was the first time Saudi had acknowledged Khashoggi was dead. The same day, both Ahmad Asiri and Saud al-Qahtani were fired by Saudi Arabia due to their involvement in the murder.

Another explanation came out on October 21, when an anonymous Saudi official said that Khashoggi had been threatened with kidnapping and drugging by Maher Mutreb, and that when he resisted he was restrained by chokehold, which lead to his death.

On October 22, a Turkish intelligence source said that Saud al-Qahtani had called the consulate via Skype and insulted Khashoggi, to which Khashoggi returned an insult. Then Qahtani asked the team to kill him, and told them to "Bring me the head of the dog".

Nazif Karaman from the Daily Sabah reported that the last words of Khashoggi on the audio recording were:

"I'm suffocating... take this bag off my head, I'm claustrophobic".

A Hürriyet columnist reported on November 16 that Turkey was in possession of a second audio recording, which contains discussions on how to execute Khashoggi. The reported also stated: "Turkish officials also did not confirm [Saudi prosecutor's claim] that Khashoggi was killed after they gave him a fatal dose of drug. They say that he was strangulated with a rope or something like a plastic bag."

A Major Investigation

Khashoggi's fiancé, Hatice Cengiz, begged the US government to take action in helping to locate Khashoggi. On October 9, she wrote in the Washington Post, "At this time, I implore President Trump and first lady Melania Trump to help shed light on Jamal's disappearance. I also urge Saudi Arabia, especially King Salman and Crown Prince Mohammed bin Salman, to show the same level of sensitivity and release CCTV footage from the consulate."

On October 11, Turkish officers were investigating whether the Apple Watch Khashoggi had worn would reveal any clues as what had happened inside the consulate. They were looking to see if the data from the watch had transmitted to his phone, which Cengiz was in possession of, or to the cloud.

King Salman and President Erdoğan announced on October 14 that a joint working group would be examining the case. The Turkish Foreign Ministry announced on October 15 that the consulate would be inspected by both Saudi and Turkish officials that day. Sources claimed the Turkish officials discovered evidence of tampering during the inspection, and that evidence supports Khashoggi's death. A statement by President Erdoğan was made that the "investigation is looking into many things such as toxic materials and those materials being removed by painting them over".

The search by Turkish police has been expanded to include Belgrade Forest and farmland in Yalova Province. These areas were targeted based on the movements of vehicles from the Saudi consulate. Samples taken from the consulate and the consul's residence were also being DNA tested. Allegedly, fingerprints belonging to Salah Muhammad al-Tubaigy were found inside the consulate.

Confirmation of Death

Following the statement from the Saudi Foreign Ministry on October 20 that Khashoggi had died during a fight in the consulate, six US and Western officials stated on October 22 that they believed the crown prince

Mohammad bin Salman was ultimately responsible for the disappearance of Khashoggi. The Director of the CIA was sent to Turkey to investigate due to "a growing international uproar over Saudi's explanation of the killing". Khashoggi's fiancée was given 24 hour police protection.

Footage from the Turkish authorities was broadcast by CNN on October 22, which showed Mustafa al-Madani, a member of the 15 man team, leaving the consulate through the back exit. He was wearing Khashoggi's clothes, minus the shoes. He was also wearing a fake beard, Khashoggi's glasses and his Apple Watch. He then went to Istanbul's Blue Mosque, where he changed into his own clothes in the bathroom and discarded Khashoggi's clothes.

He was smiling and laughing later on during a dinner with another Saudi agent. One Turkish official thinks that Madani was brought in specifically to be a body double for Khashoggi as he was about the same height and weight. It was most likely an effort to prove their first statement that Khashoggi had walked out the back door of the consulate. The fact that they even had a body double further bolstered the claims that the murder was premeditated, or that they had planned to take Khashoggi back to Saudi Arabia.

Although Saudi Arabia vowed to conduct a thorough criminal investigation and deliver justice, the Turkish investigators have dealt with numerous delays by Saudi. Turkish police found a car on October 22 with diplomatic number places that had been abandoned in a car park in Istanbul. The car belonged to the Saudi consulate, and the Saudi diplomats asked for permission to search it. A video emerged from October 3 showing consulate staff burning documents.

At first the Saudi officials refused to let the Turkish police search a well that was located in the consul's garden on October 24, but later that day, they agreed. Samples of the water were taken from the well but no DNA traces were found of Khashoggi.

UN Special Rapporteur on Extrajudicial, Summary or Arbitrary Executions, Agnes Callamard, called from an international investigation on October 25. She explained that the Saudi officials that had been implicated in the death were "high enough to represent the state. Even Saudi Arabia has admitted that the crime was premeditated ... From where I sit, this bears all the hallmarks of extrajudicial executions. Until I am proven otherwise I must assume that this was the case. It is up to the Kingdom of Saudi Arabia to prove that it was not."

Saud al-Mojeb, Saudi public prosecutor, arrived October 28 in Istanbul, just days after he had contradicted previous official Saudi statements. His arrival in Istanbul was amid suggestions by Turkey of a lack of cooperation by the Saudis, and alleged attempts to ruin evidence. He held talks with Istanbul's chief prosecutor Irfan Fidan on October 29, and during the meeting, the Saudi officials asked for the investigation folder including statements, footage and evidence. They were given the findings in a dossier but the Turkish investigators refused to share information on the evidence they had gathered.

Turkey also requested that the identified 18 suspects be extradited to Turkey, but the Saudi foreign minister had said a couple of days beforehand that the men would face trial on Saudi soil. The Saudi officials were asked where the body of Khashoggi could be found and the identity of the local person that the Saudis claimed was the one who got rid of the body.

As there was a level of distrust between the two countries, the meeting lasted just 75 minutes. A second round of talks took place on October 30, and then he inspected the Saudi consulate. Fidan also asked Mojeb to do another search at the consul's residence because in the previous search, the Turkish investigators weren't allowed to enter three locked rooms.

Cover Up Attempt

A senior Turkish official told The Washington Post on October 31 that the Turkish authorities were looking into the theory that the body had been destroyed in acid at either the consul's residence or in the grounds of the consulate. Apparently, some biological evidence was found in the consulate garden.

Erdoğan made comments in the Washington Post that the murder was inexplicable, and a "clear violation and a blatant abuse of the Vienna Convention on Consular Relations". By not punishing the perpetrators, a very dangerous precedent could be set. He passed criticism against the Saudis for not taking action against consul general Mohammad al-Otaibi, as he had not only misled the media, but had fled the country soon after the murder. He further wrote, "As responsible members of the international community, we must reveal the identities of the puppet masters behind Khashoggi's killing and discover those in whom Saudi officials — still trying to cover up the murder — have placed their trust... We know that the order to kill Khashoggi came from the highest levels of the Saudi government."

The Daily Sabah reported on November 5 that an investigative team of 11 people had been sent to Istanbul by Saudi Arabia on October 11. Two members of the team were Khaled Yahya al-Zahrani, a toxicology expert, and Ahmad Abdulaziz Aljanobi, a chemist, and it's suggested they were sent to get rid of any evidence. The team visited the consulate every day until October 17.

The Audio Tapes

Erdoğan acknowledged during a speech on television on November 10 that the audio tapes of the killing do exist. He said, "We gave the tapes. We gave them to Saudi Arabia, to the United States, Germans, French and British, all of them."

He discussed what to the next steps should be with President Trump and Secretary-General Antonio Guterres of the UN during World War I Centennial commemorations in France. Both President Trump and the French President Emmanuel Macron agreed that more details of the murder were needed. They also all agreed that it was important the situation didn't cause further destabilization in the Middle East.

Charges Laid

The Saudi Prosecutor's Office announced on November 15 that 11 Saudi Nationals had been charged with Khashoggi's murder, and five of the charged would face the death penalty for being directly involved in ordering and carrying out the crime. The prosecutors stated that it is alleged that shortly after Khashoggi entered the consulate, he was bound and injected with a sedative overdose which lead to his death. They also allege that his body was dismembered and removed by five of the men charged in the killing. The body parts were then given to a local collaborator who disposed of them. They continued to deny that any member of the Saudi Royal Family was involved in ordering or sanctioning the murder.

Many news organizations reported on November 16 that the CIA was 'unequivocal in assessing with high confidence' that the crown prince Mohammad bin Salman had ordered the assassination. Intelligence gathered included a phone call between Khashoggi and the brother of the crown prince, Khalid bin Salman.

President Trump made a statement on November 20 denying the CIA's conclusion, saying "Our intelligence agencies continue to assess all information, but it could very well be that the Crown Prince had knowledge of this tragic event — maybe he did and maybe he didn't!" He further stated that the CIA did not have the 'smoking gun' and was acting on 'feelings' rather than evidence.

The following day, communist of the Hürriyet, Abdulkadir Selvi wrote, the "CIA holds 'smoking gun phone call' of Saudi Crown Prince on Khashoggi murder and that the Director of the Central Intelligence Agency Gina Haspel has possession of a intercepted phone call in which crown prince Mohammad is giving order to his brother Khalid 'to Silence Jamal Khashoggi as Soon as Possible'. The subsequent murder is the ultimate confirmation of this instruction."

Alleged Perpetrators

A report indicated that seven of the fifteen men suspected of carrying out the murder were personal bodyguards of Mohammed bin Salman. The fifteen men have been named as:

- Maher Abdulaziz Mutreb, born 1971: former diplomat in London has been photographed with Mohammad bin Salman on numerous international trips.
- Salah Mohammed al-Tubaigy, born 1971: Head of Saudi Scientific Council of Forensics.
- Abdulaziz Mohammed al-Hasawi, born 1987: Personal bodyguard to Mohammed bin Salman.
- Thaer Ghaleb al-Harbi, born 1979: Member of the Saudi Royal Guard.
- Mohammed Saad al-Zahrani, born 1988: Member of the Saudi Royal Guard.
- Meshal Saad al-Bostani, born 1987: Lieutenant in the Saudi Air Force. Died in a car accident on return to Saudi Arabia.
- Naif Hassan al-Arefe, born 1986
- Mustafa Mohammed al-Madani, born 1961: Khashoggi's body double.
- Mansur Uthman Abahussein, born 1972
- Waleed Abdullah al-Shehri, born 1980
- Turki Musharraf al-Shehri, born 1982
- Fahad Shabib al-Balawi, born 1985
- Saif Saad al-Qahtani, born 1973
- Khalid Aedh al-Taibi, born 1988
- Badir Lafi al-Otaibi, born 1973

The investigation is still a worldwide concern, despite Saudi Arabia saying they would never accept an international investigation into the murder. It is only a matter of time before it is known what will happen to those who have been arrested, and whether or not the crown prince will ever face scrutiny.

The Sagay Massacre

A brutal massacre occurred when several sugarcane famers, including women and children were shot and killed in Sagay, Negros Occidental, Philippines, on October 20. It was suspected the massacre may have been motivated by land reform conflicts in the Philippines.

Slaughtered While Having Dinner

While the sugarcane famers were sitting in a makeshift tent on a farm having dinner, a group of gunmen entered and opened fire on all inside, including the women and children who were present. Nine farmers were killed, and three of them were also burned after they had been slaughtered. It took the gunmen ten minutes to carry out the massacre, which occurred at 9:45pm. Some survivors managed to flee and escape.

The nine victims were identified as being:

- Eglicerio Villegas
- Paterno Baron
- Rene Laurencio
- Rannel Bantigue
- Angelife Arsenal
- Morena Mendoza
- Marcelina Dumaguit
- Jomarie Ughayon Jr.
- Marchtel Sumicad.

Investigating the Massacre

The majority of the victims were members of the Negros Federation of Sugar Workers (NFSW). The NFSW stated the massacre occurred on the first night of 'bungkalan' activity, which is where "farmers occupy idle lands and collectively cultivate to make them productive". The police are looking into whether land conflict could be the possible motive for the shootings.

The Sagay City Acting Chief of Police Chief Inspector Robert Mansueto, said during an interview on CNN Philippines that the victims had farmed the land in question before, and that they were land reform beneficiaries. Initial reports on the shooting claimed that 40 armed men had been involved, but police later determined there were 5 or 6 that night.

A survivor of the massacre stated that because it was such a remote area, they had not heard the men arrive on foot. Western Visayas police director, Chief Supt. John Bulalacao, said that some of the farmers were 'linked to the New People's Army (NPA)' and he claimed that the NFSW was a 'legal front' of the NPA.

Mansueto commented that the incident appeared to have been a shootout between some of the farmers and gunmen, but none of the gunmen were injured or killed. But three of the survivors denied this occurred, saying that none of the farmers had guns. When the police gathered evidence at the scene, they found seven bullet casings from a .45 caliber handgun and 12 empty bullet casings from a 5.56 mm rifle.

Philippine National Police Chief Oscar Albayalde stated in an interview that the NFSW is "used by the Communist Party of the Philippines to take over private lands for profit". He further said that the victims were not legitimate tenants or tillers of the plantation. According to the Department of Agrarian Reform, the farmers weren't beneficiaries of the land distribution program.

On October 23, police announced they had identified one of the NPA members who was allegedly behind the massacre. The Armed Forces of the Philippines (AFP) claimed the plantation was a 'vigorous' site for the NPA.

Suspects Identified

The PNP identified two suspects on October 28. Rogelio Arquillo and Rene Manlangi, who were recruiters of the farmers to the NFSW. Murder charges were filed against the two men, but they had yet to be captured. The statement by Western Visayas Police Chief Supt. John Bulalacao was "Sagay City Police Station already filed a case of multiple murders against the recruiters, Rene Manlangi and Rogelio Arquillo, both members of the National Federation of Sugar Workers and other John Does."

The recruiters were being accused of getting the victims to join their association by deception and 'promising them a parcel of land once their cause would succeed'. The victims had been recruited on the morning of October 20, and killed the same day.

The police also stated that some of the members of the sugar workers' association had ties to the NPA, who they thought were behind the massacre. The police and the military believed the NPA set it up to raise public doubt against the government. The Communist Party of the Philippines had denied this.

There are eight complainant-witnesses working with police including a minor. Bulalacao said, "All of them were willing and voluntarily signed their affidavits, including the minor whom we turned over to the Local Social Welfare Development Officer who also witnessed the taking of the minor's statement by our investigators."

Accusations of Illegal Arrest

The NFSW posted an allegation that the minor survivor of the massacre had been illegally arrested, and on their Facebook page, posted 'Urgent Alert'. However, this has been completely disputed by the Negros Occidental Police Provincial Office. The office said, "The statement of NFSW was meant to deceive the public and disrupt the investigation."

The Negros Occidental Police Provincial Office stated that the boy had been sent to the custody of the Social Welfare Development Office located in Sagay City, in the presence of his father who gave his consent.

The police produced a copy of a section of a report that stated the boy's father had arrived at the police station and endorsed his son to the City Social Welfare Department Office without being coerced, forced, intimidated or being offered a reward.

The NFSW had declared in its post that the NUPL lawyer was set to assist his (referring to the minor) grandparents to turn him over after being held in custody of the CSWD."

But the provincial police said, "The grandparents mentioned by the NFSW who were supposed to fetch the survivor are not his legitimate grandparents."

The Negros Occidental Police Provincial Office also said that the statement of the boy as a minor witness to the massacre was important to the investigation, but because he had experienced a traumatic incident, he went to social welfare custody to help him recover from his ordeal.

Terrorist Attacks in Short for October

October 2

Kama District, Afghanistan: A suicide bomber killed 14 people and injured around 40 at an election rally in the Kama district of the Nangarhar Province, the Islamic State claimed responsibility through Amaq.

Nimruz Province, Kandahar Province and Faryab Province, Afghanistan: A series of violent attacks by the Taliban targeting security forces checkpoints at the Nimruz Province, Kandahar Province and the Faryab Province, left 9 security forces dead and 10 injured while at least 4 Taliban militants were killed in the fighting.

October 4

Plateau State, Nigeria: 19 people were killed and 4 were seriously injured when gunmen belonging to Fulani Herdsmen attacked a community in the Plateau State, Nigeria.

October 6

Saydabad District, Afghanistan: 14 security officers including a district police chief were killed when the Taliban attacked them in the Saydabad District of the Wardak Province, Afghanistan.

Faryab Province and Nimruz Province, Afghanistan: 13 people were killed and 4 were wounded in clashes with the Taliban at the Faryab Province and Nimruz Province, 3 Taliban militants were also killed.

October 7

North Kivu, Democratic Republic of the Congo: Mai-Mai militants armed with machetes killed 14 people and injured 9 people in DRC's Rubaya Village located in the North Kivu region.

Saydabad District, Afghanistan: Militants killed the district police chief along with nine other policemen, burned the police headquarters, and blew up the bridge along the arterial highways in Sayeed Abad district, Maidan Wardak Province, Afghanistan.

October 8

Borno State, Nigeria: Boko Haram militants attacked a military base in a village in the Borno State leaving 18 soldiers dead and at least 157 soldiers and police officers were left missing, they were probably kidnapped or later killed by the militants.

October 9

Al-Safa, Syria: 15 Syrian Soldiers were killed when the Islamic State ambushed them and opened fire in the Al-Safa region of As-Suwayda, Syria.

October 10

Deir ez-Zor Governorate, Syria: Over a hundred people were kidnapped from a displacement camp by the Islamic State in the Deir ez-Zor Governorate, Syria, fighting between US backed Syrian Democratic Forces (SDF) and the Islamic State between October 10 and October 13 has resulted in 37 deaths of the SDF and at least 58 of the Islamic State.

Lake Chad, Chad: Eight Chad soldiers were killed and at least eleven were injured in clashes with Boko Haram jihadists in the Lake Chad region, 48 Jihadists were allegedly killed afterwards in a counter-terrorism operation by Chad Soldiers.

Al Anbar Governorate, Iraq: At least 10 Iraqi security forces were killed when Islamic State insurgents attacked a gas field on the western part of the Anbar Province.

October 11

Qalay-I-Zal District, Afghanistan: 15 Afghan Security Officers were killed and 13 were wounded when the Taliban attacked them at a checkpoint in the Qalay-I-Zal District of the Northern Province of Afghanistan Kunduz.

October 13

Rustaq District, Afghanistan: An explosive packed motorbike blew up near a rally for Nazifa Yousufi Bek, killing 22 and injuring 36 more. The candidate had not yet arrived. The attack occurred in the Rustaq District of the Takhar Province, Afghanistan, which has been frequented by Taliban attacks in the past.

Baidoa, Somalia: At least 22 people were killed and 30 were wounded when twin suicide bombings targeted a restaurant and a coffee shop in Baidoa, Somalia. A grenade was also thrown into a nearby hotel.

Ménaka, Mali: 12 Tuaregs were killed when armed militants on motorcycles opened fire on them near Menaka, Mali, the Islamic State Greater Sahara is suspected for the attack.

October 14

Sifontes Municipality, Venezuela: The ELN is believed to be behind an attack on miners at the Sifontes Municipality of Venezuela, at least 16 miners were shot dead in the ambush and at least 6 others were injured in the attack.

Farah Province, Afghanistan: 20 Afghan National Army (ANA) soldiers were killed when the Taliban attacked soldier checkpoints in the Farah Province, at least two other Afghan soldiers were captured alive by the Taliban.

October 15

Mopti Region, Mali: 11 civilians were killed when militants on motorcycles opened fire on them on the Mopti Region of Mali, on a separate incident a woman was blown up by a roadside bomb and other two were injured nearby.

Daykundi Province and Farah Province, Afghanistan : Taliban militants attacked Afghan security checkpoints in the Daykundi Province and the Farah Province killing 16 and injuring 17, the Taliban also seized many weapons.

October 20

Borno State, Nigeria: At least 12 farmers were killed in a Boko Haram attack on a remote village in the Borno State, the death toll could rise as they are still searching for missing people, and the militants had used machetes in the attack.

Kabul, Afghanistan: Multiple explosions hit Kabul due to sticky bombs causing at least 3 deaths and 37 blast related injuries, after that a suicide bomber detonated at a polling station in a school killing 15 (10 civilians and 5 police) and injuring at least 25 people.

Beni, Democratic Republic of the Congo: The Allied Democratic Forces (ADF) attacked Congolese army positions and several neighborhoods in Beni, they killed 15 people and abducted at least a dozen children.

October 21

Achin District, Afghanistan: At least eleven people including six children and a woman were killed and a little girl was seriously injured when a vehicle was hit by a bomb at the Achin district of the Nangarhar Province, Afghanistan, no group has claimed responsibility but the Islamic State has done similar attacks in that area in the past.

October 26

Al-Baghuz Fawqani, Syria: Islamic State fighters ambushed and killed at least 70 SDF fighters (Syrian Democratic Forces) and at least 100 were also injured and 6 were also captured alive at the Al-Baghuz Fawqani village, Syria.

October 30

Jonglei State, South Sudan: Murle gunmen killed at least 15 people and injured an additional 20 in attacks targeting cattle herders and rival ethnic people in South Sudan's Jonglei State.

Chapter 11:
NOVEMBER

Hot Yoga Killing in Tallahassee

On November 2, a gunman walked into a hot yoga studio in Tallahassee and started shooting people. Six people received gunshot wounds, with two receiving fatal injuries. Another person was pistol-whipped before the perpetrator shot and killed himself.

Tallahassee Hot Yoga - Unexpected Gunfire

At 5:37pm, a lone gunman entered the hot yoga studio, killing two women. Police responded within three and a half minutes of receiving gunfire reports. When they entered the studio, they found the gunman dead from a self-inflicted gunshot wound.

People who were in a bar across the street told how they had seen people running from the studio and one man in a white t-shirt with blood on it ran into the bar claiming to have been pistol-whipped after charging at the gunman. Survivors of the shooting confirmed this, saying the male customer had used a broomstick and a vacuum cleaner to attack the shooter which enabled other students in the studio to escape unharmed.

The Tallahassee Police Chief Michael DeLeo gave credit to the students who not only tried to save themselves but also tried to help others.

Tallahassee Hot Yoga studio was part of a plaza that also contained other businesses and restaurants. People dining at the restaurant underneath the yoga studio heard the gunshots, and stated the owner of the studio came into the restaurant looking for a doctor.

The Victims

Six people in total were shot, not including the gunman. The two women who were killed were Maura Binkley, 21, and Nancy Van Vessem, 61.

Binkley was a student at Florida State University and was a member of the Delta Delta Delta sorority. She was expected to graduate from University in 2019.

Van Vessem was the chief medical director for Capital Health Plan and a doctor. She had gained her medical degree from St. Louis University and her research focus was on health care for people with multiple chronic diseases. She was also a faculty member at Florida State University.

The Gunman - Scott Paul Beierle

Beierle was a teacher of English and social studies at Meade High School in Maryland, and a military veteran. He had worked as a substitute teacher at many other schools but never lasted long at any one place due to his inappropriate behavior and performance issues. In one incident, he had asked a female student if she was ticklish then touched her below the bra line on her stomach, which led to him being fired. He had also been charged with battery twice, both times for grabbing a woman's buttocks, in 2012 and 2016.

Beierle had posted YouTube videos in 2014 that indicated he identified with the involuntary celibate community. He regularly complained about being sexually rejected by women. He was a sympathizer of Elliot Rodger, the shooter of the 2014 Isla Vista killings, as he felt unloved and lonely like Rodger had.

He had posted other videos in which he ranted about interracial relationships and African-Americans, and the title of one of the videos was 'Dangers of Diversity'.

The Aftermath

A vigil for the victims was held by Florida State University and further tributes were planned along with the Delta Delta Delta sorority to take place on November 5. The day after the shooting, a yoga instructor from Hot Yoga Tallahassee lead a healing yoga class in the middle of Adams Street.

Thousand Oaks Mass Shooting

In yet another mass shooting for 2018, a gunman opened fire at the Borderline Bar and Grill in Thousand Oaks, California on November 7. A popular location for college students, twelve people were killed including a police officer. Once again the shooter committed suicide before he could be arrested and charged for his heinous crimes.

A Bar Full of Terror

At around 11:20pm, a gunman approached the Borderline Bar and Grill and shot the security guard who was standing outside. Armed with a .45-caliber Glock 21 semi-automatic pistol that had a banned high-capacity magazine, he entered the bar. Other security guards and employees were shot before he began shooting the patrons inside the bar. He fired an estimated 30 rounds, and threw smoke bombs as he moved around inside the bar.

There were over 200 people inside the bar that night, not including staff and security. It was 'College Country Night', a regular event that students from local universities and colleges enjoyed attending.

Following the first 9-1-1 calls, Ventura County Sheriff Sgt. Ron Helus accompanied by a California Highway Patrol officer arrived at the bar after three minutes of the first call. They heard gunshots from inside, which prompted Helus to run inside. He was shot almost immediately as he entered. Helus was dragged outside by the Highway Patrol officer to safety outside. The Highway Patrol officer returned fire at the gunman.

Other police officers and the SWAT team arrived shortly after Helus was shot. When they entered the bar, they discovered the gunman deceased having shot himself in the kitchen area of the bar. Agents were deployed to the scene from the FBI, the Department of Homeland Security, and the Bureau of Alcohol, Tobacco, Firearms and Explosives. While the gunman had been shooting at the innocent people in the bar, he had been making posts on Instagram about his thoughts.

Chaos Inside - Witness Reports

The scene inside the bar turned to utter chaos once the gunman began shooting. According to a woman who had been inside the bar, "All of a sudden you hear the bang bang of the gun shot and it just started going crazy. We didn't take it seriously at first because it just sounded like firecrackers."

She continued, "Everyone just dropped down onto the floor. We couldn't get out because the shooting was on that side. So our friends got the bar stools and started slamming them against the window so we could get out."

A man who had been close to the front door when the shooting started said he had been talking to his stepfather and started hearing big 'pops'. When he looked up, he noticed the security guard had been shot. The gunman started throwing the smoke grenades all over the bar and just kept firing.

Tragic Loss of Life - The Victims

Those who were killed were three women and nine men, and seven were college students with another a graduate. Others killed included police officer Helus, a Marine Corps veteran and a Navy veteran who had already survived one horrific mass shooting the year before.

Telemachus Orfanus

Orfanos, 27, had survived the massacre at the Las Vegas Country Music festival in 2017, where 58 people were killed. It's incredibly tragic that he survived that horrific event only to be killed in a similar circumstance a year later. He had spent the night helping first responders and carrying the injured at the massacre in Las Vegas.

Orfanos had spent two and a half years in the US Navy, and on the night of the shooting, he was at the Borderline Bar and Grill meeting friends for dinner. His mother told a reporter, "I don't want prayers. I don't want thoughts. I want gun control."

Daniel Manrique

Manrique, 33, was a Marine Corps veteran who had started the Ventura chapter of Team Red, White and Blue in 2014, which helped veterans make the transition from military to civilian lifestyle. His friend, Sara Bergeron who had served with him at the Navy said, "I've never met anyone my whole life that was so selfless and committed to helping veterans succeed and just thrive. He never quit on people. He never gave up, even if someone tried to push him away. He always still reached out."

She suspected Manrique had suffered from PTSD but he never talked to her about it. Her first thought when she heard the shooter was a former Marine with PTSD was that she wished the man had met Manrique. She said, "The shooter killed someone who could have been his lifeline, who could have helped him with his PTSD, who could have understood more than anyone what he was going through," she said. In fact, that's what Manrique was doing that night at Borderline, Bergeron said, "He was there to support and work with other veterans."

"A lot of people when they separate from the military have a hard time moving past their past. He definitely honored his military service but he was focused on his current service to his current community," she said. "Instead of going into the darkness, he became a light for others to follow."

Justin Meek

Meek, 23, was also a friend of Sara Bergeron. He had been attending California Lutheran University studying criminal justice. He never stayed idle, and was involved in choir, water polo, and was the president of Club Italia. He also worked in his spare time as a Coronado lifeguard.

The night of the shooting, Meek was working at the bar as a security guard, and he apparently died while trying to save other people, by shielding them with his body. He was described as "a big, huge beast of a man, a big tall man. He was a security guard, but he was also a pussycat, one of the sweetest guys in the world," said Tony Duran, owner of Goode Time Productions, which supplies carolers like Meek to Disney venues.

He was a classically trained singer and had memorized all 100 songs in the repertoire and dreamed of singing at Disneyland's Club 33 with his girlfriend. They had discussed their future together as both spouses and singers.

Alaina Housley

Housley, 18, was a freshman at Pepperdine University, and had gone to the bar that night to line dance with her friends. As news of the shooting emerged, her aunt Tamera Mowry-Housley of 'The Real' and 'Sister, Sister' fame, desperately searched the media for news of her niece. Her husband asked his Twitter followers, 100,000 of them, for prayers as they waited for news.

When they found out the terrible news, they said, "Our hearts are broken. Alaina was an incredible young woman with so much life ahead of her, and we are devastated that her life was cut short in this manner."

At high school Housley played on the varsity soccer team, served in student government and was an honors student. She was an accomplished violinist and pianist, and was described by a former teacher as a natural leader.

Cody Gifford-Coffman

Cody, 22, was the older brother to two younger brothers, and was about to become a brother again, this time to a baby girl. He was good with children and been the head umpire for the Camarillo Pony Baseball League. He had planned to join the Army.

His father said losing his beloved son would change his life forever, and he wondered if Cody would have run towards the gunfire not away from it because he always stood up to bullies.

Noel Sparks

Sparks, 21, was a college student at Moorpark College where she majored in art. She loved going to the bar and had posted a photo of herself dancing that night. She worked part time at Calvary Community Church in Weslake Village, helping with the children's programs.

The Rev. Shawn Thornton said, "She loved kids. We had a lot of parents show up today to say, 'She made my child feel important and that they mattered."

Kristina Morisette

Morisette, 20, was employed at the bar as a cashier. She always had a ready smile, and many described her as sweet. Her world revolved around her friends. She had only just recently bought herself her first car with the money she earned at the bar. Recently she had told her parents that she wanted to apply for an animal training program.

Sean Adler

Adler, 48, was a bouncer at the bar and at another nearby bar, Azar's Sports Bar. He was also a strength and conditioning coach at Royal High School and a father of two. He finally realized his dream to open a coffee shop in August.

Adler apparently tried to disarm the gunman.

Jacob Dunham

Dunham, 21, was at the bar with his friend Blake Dingman that night, and both were killed. They were off-road enthusiasts, and a memorial meet was organised for them by No Sways Offroad.

Dunham had recently graduated from Conejo Valley High School, which had been difficult due to being blind in one eye following an accident as a young child.

Blake Dingman

Dingman, 21, had worked in the commercial electrical field since he had left high school. He had just been offered a new job with a local company. His family said he always seemed to have grease under his fingernails from working on motorcycles and cars, and had always liked taking things apart since he was a child, just to see how they worked.

A patriotic young man, Dingman along with Dunham and other friends went on a 'Flag Run' every Fourth of July during which they attached large American flags on their trucks and drove from Ventura County through Los Angeles.

According to his mother, he had always been the helper if they were planning a trip. She said, He was the one who made sure everything was in order, fixed and ready to go. I'm going to miss his hugs and his heart. He gave the best hugs and always told me he loved me. I am in utter disbelief that I will not be able to hold or hug my son again."

Mark 'Marky' Meza

Meza, 20, worked as a busboy and food runner at the bar and was just about to celebrate his 21st birthday. His family made a statement, "Marky was a loving and wonderful young man who was full of life and ambition. His family is devastated by his loss. Marky would have turned 21 on November 19. His family asks for peace and respect at this time to allow them to grieve privately."

Ron Helus

Helus, 54, was a 29 year veteran of the Ventura County Sheriff's department. He had been thinking about retiring in the next year or two. Ventura County Sheriff Geoff Dean said, "Ron was a hard-working, dedicated sheriff's sergeant. He was totally committed. He gave his all. Tonight, as I told his wife, he died a hero because he went in to save lives, to save other people."

Steve Mayorga had worked on and off with Helus for nearly 30 years, and when he heard Helus had died after rushing inside to save people, he wasn't surprised. "That's who Ron was," said Mayorga, who retired two years ago. "He was very dedicated to his job. When people call him a 'cop's cop,' what they're saying is that he was the type of cop who other cops looked up to, someone who goes beyond what a normal cop does."

Just before he went to the scene of the shooting that night, Helus spoke to his wife, saying, "Hey, I gotta go handle a call. I love you. I'll talk to you later."

A Disturbed Perpetrator

The gunman was identified as Ian David Long, 28, a Marine Corps veteran. Though he had previously been living with roommates, he was living with his mother at the time of the massacre.

While Long was at high school, claims were raised by a teacher that Long had physically assaulted her, but she was encouraged not to pursue the incident in case it endangered his future in the Marines. She claimed Long had issues before he did his military service.

Long's neighbor stated he had suffered from posttraumatic stress disorder (PTSD) after his time in the military. Hombre, clinical psychologist and behavioral scientist Lisa Jaycox said that it was too early to say that he suffered from PTSD or that it had any role in the massacre.

FBI investigators were trying to determine what Long's motive was, and they were looking at his state of mind leading up to the tragedy. They were investigating if he had any associates or if there was any potential radicalization. The gun Long used that night had been modified illegally with an extended magazine. Witnesses from the bar said he didn't speak while he was shooting.

The police had been involved in several incidents with Long. They had been called to his home in April following a report of a 'disturbance'. A mental health crisis team had assessed Long and the specialist determined that he did not qualify for involuntary commitment, under California law at that time. He had been acting irrationally and was irate.

It was after that incident that the mental health specialist was concerned Long was suffering from PTSD. Long had also been assaulted at a local bar in 2015, but it's unclear if this was a factor in his decision to open fire in a bar.

Long was trained as a machine gunner in the Marine Corps from 2008 to 2011. He was deployed in Afghanistan from November 2010 to June 2011. He received the Marine Corps Good Conduct Medal, the Afghanistan Campaign Medal and the Global War on Terrorism Service Medal.

His unit had been based in Hawaii, and he got married in Honolulu in 2009. They later separated in 2011 and divorced in 2013. There were no children from the marriage.

After leaving the Marines, Long went to college but didn't complete his degree. He had majored in athletic training from 2013 to 2016 but didn't graduate.

A former roommate of Long's, Winnet Blake, said that he was shocked when he found out about the massacre and that Long was responsible. They had shared a house twice, and that while they lived together Long kept to himself mostly.

The Melbourne Stabbing Attack

On November 9, a man went on a stabbing attack in Melbourne, Australia. Three people were stabbed, one of whom died. The suspect was shot and killed by police, who are now treating the incident as 'terror-related'.

Fire and Knives

At around 4:10pm on Bourke Street in Melbourne's Central Business District, a man set fire to a Holden Rodeo vehicle. Just before it burst into flame, the man came out from behind the vehicle then went on a stabbing spree, armed with a large knife.

Three pedestrians were stabbed, one fatally, then the attacker was confronted by two officers from Victoria Police. A member of the public attempted to ram the attacker with a shopping cart to stop him from attacking anyone else.

The attacker slashed at the police officers, at which time one of the officers fired one shot into his chest. They restrained the man and he was taken to hospital for medical treatment under guard. He died later that day in the hospital.

Police confirmed after the perpetrator was identified that the attack was ISIS inspired. The Islamic State took responsibility for the incident through its Amaq news website.

Hassan Khalif Shire Ali

Ali, 30, had moved to Australia in the 1990s from Somalia, along with his parents and siblings. He was married and had a young son. The Chief Commissioner of Victoria Police, Graham Ashton, told the media that Ali was known to federal intelligence agencies but he was not being monitored.

Ali had a criminal history which included the possession of cannabis, use of cannabis, theft, burglary and the possession of a dangerous article in a public place. A previous lawyer of Ali's described him as unremarkable, and he could not recall any prior problems with drug addiction or mental health.

However, he had been sentenced to a year of drug testing and treatment at one stage though the details about the addiction and his compliance are not available.

Ali's young brother, Ali Khalif Ali, was arrested in November 2017 for plotting to commit a mass shooting at a New Year's Eve celebration in Melbourne.

Australian Federal Police's acting national manager of counter-terrorism stated that Ali's passport had been cancelled in 2015. ASIO believed at the time that he was planning on going to Syria to fight for ISIL. However, he was never a target of counter-terrorism investigations because they did not believe he was a real threat.

In the space of three years leading up to the attack, Ali had:

- Had his passport cancelled
- Became somewhat isolated from his family who were increasingly concerned with his erraticism
- Was incidentally monitored during a covert investigation of which he was not the target
- Separated from his wife
- Was charged on three separate occasions with driving offences.

Family members and acquaintances of Ali claimed he had substance abuse problems and mental health issues, and he was allegedly delusional and agitated before the attack. He had been complaining of "being chased by unseen people with spears."

Ali's Victims

Sisto Malaspina, 74, had been walking over to the burning car to offer help when he was stabbed by Ali. The stab wound went in above his collar bone.

A former nurse performed CPR but he could not be revived. The knife had punctured a major artery leading to severe blood loss. He was the co-owner of Pellegrini's Espresso Bar, an Italian coffee bar nearby.

One of the wounded was a 58-year-old retired businessman from Tasmania. He suffered stabbing injuries to the head and had to have surgery at the Alfred Hospital. A 24-year-old security guard from Hampton Park received lacerations and he was taken to the Royal Melbourne Hospital.

The Aftermath

Victorian Premier Daniel Andrews announced on November 12 that Malaspina's family had accepted the offer of a state funeral. Andrews described Malaspina as a 'Victorian icon'. The possibility of Crossley Lane which corners where the Pellefrini's coffee bar was to be renamed in honour of Malaspina was being considered by the City of Melbourne.

Prime Minister Scott Morrison made a statement on television that received criticism. His statement suggested that Muslim communities in Australia were partly responsible for failing to report extremism.

Ten-Year-Old Charged with Murder

In perhaps one of the most disturbing cases of child murder, another child was being charged. What made it even more unbelievable, apart from the horror she inflicted, was that she was being charged with first degree intentional homicide.

What, How and Why

On the afternoon of October 30, police responded to an emergency call at a licensed day care center in Wheaton, a rural town west of Chippewa Falls. On arrival, they found a 6 month old baby boy unresponsive and bleeding from the head. The baby was rushed to a local hospital, and then transported by air to Gillette Children's Hospital in St. Paul. Tragically, the baby died on November 1.

One adult and three children were present at the day care at the time, and they were all interviewed. Police quickly identified the 10-year-old girl as the prime suspect. She told police she had been holding the baby and she dropped him, hitting his head on a footstool. When the baby started crying, she panicked and stomped on the baby's head.

A doctor who examined the baby determined that the injuries were not accidental.

A Day in Court

The young girl had a bond hearing, during which she cried the whole time. The hearing lasted 10 minutes, and she was ordered to be held on $50,000 cash bond. The girl buried her head in her mother's arms as the charges were described, crying and moaning throughout.

Although her parents were in court with her, she had actually been removed from their home in September. She was placed in foster care, and the day care center was their business.

It is possible the case will go to juvenile court, but because the charges are so severe, it must be initially be brought in adult court if the child is over 10 years.

Other Child Killers

As awful as it is to contemplate how a 10-year-old girl could purposefully stomp on the head of an innocent baby, child killers are not that uncommon. It's surprising to learn just how many there have been, and it's hard to understand what drives these young kids to kill. Following is a list of child killers, how old they were at the time, and the number of lives they took.

- Dedrick Damell Owens, aged 6, killed 1, year 2000
- Amarjeet Sada, aged 8, killed 4, year 2007

- Jason Osmanson, aged 10, killed 1, year 1994
- Robert Thompson, aged 10, killed 1, year 1993
- Jon Venables, aged 10, killed 1, year 1993
- Joseph Hall, aged 10, killed 1, year 2011
- Mary Bell, aged 10, killed 2, year 1968
- Jordan Brown, aged 11, killed 1, year 2009
- Nathaniel Abraham, aged 11, killed 1, year 1997
- Andrew Golden, aged 11, killed 5, year 1998
- Natsumi Tsuji, aged 11, killed 1, year 2004
- Nathan Ferris, aged 12, killed 1, year 1987
- Piedad Martinez del Aguila, aged 12, killed 4, year 1965
- Jose Reyes, aged 12, killed 1, year 2013
- Lionel Tate, aged 12, killed 1, year 1999
- Christopher Pittman, aged 12, killed 2, year 2001
- Evan Drake Savoie, aged 12, killed 1, year 2003
- Jake Lee Eakin, aged 12, killed 1, year 2003
- Jasmine Richardson, aged 12, killed 3, year 2006
- Eric Smith, aged 13, killed 1, year 1993
- Mitchell Johnson, aged 13, killed 5, year 1998
- Nathanial Brazill, aged 13, killed 1, year 2000
- Craig Price, aged 13, killed 4, year 1987
- Heather Smith, aged 14, killed 2, year 1985
- James Ortega, aged 14, killed 1, year 1989
- Brandon McInemey, aged 14, killed 1, year 2008
- Caril Ann Fugate, aged 14, killed 11, year 1958
- Michael Carmeal, aged 14, killed 3, year 1997
- Josh Philliips, aged 14, killed 1, year 1998
- Barry Dale Loukaitis, aged 14, killed 3, year 1996
- Seito Sakakibara, aged 14, killed 2, year 1997
- Andrew Jerome Wurst, aged 14, killed 1, year 1998
- Todd Cameron Smith, aged 14, killed 1, year 1999

- Kenneth Bartley Jr., aged 14, killed 1, year 2005
- Jesse Osborne, aged 14, killed 2, year 2016
- Charles Andrew Williams, aged 15, killed 2, year 2001
- Jaylen Ray Fryberg, aged 15, killed 4, year 2014
- Sergey Gordeyev, aged 15, killed 2, year 2014
- Eric Hainstock, aged 15, killed 1, year 2006
- Paula Cooper, aged 15, killed 1, year 1985
- Kip Kinkel, aged 15, killed 4, year 1998
- Akiyoshi Umekawa, aged 15, killed 5, year 1963
- William Cornick, aged 15, killed 1, year 2014
- Kazutaka Komori, aged 15, killed 2, year 1960
- Nick Clatterbuck, aged 15, killed 1, year 1984
- Jamar Siler, aged 15, killed 1, year 2014
- Edgar Yoevani, aged 15, killed 1, 2014
- Toni Lawrence, aged 15, killed 1, year 1992
- Hope Rippey, aged 15, killed 1, year 1992
- Nehemiah Griego, aged 15, killed 5, year 2013
- Luke Mitchell, aged 15, killed 1, year 2003
- Rafael Solich, aged 15, killed 3, year 2004
- Jared Padgett, aged 15, killed 1, year 2014
- Don Steenkamp, aged 15, killed 3, year 2012
- Jason McLaughlin, aged 15, killed 2, year 2003
- James Fairweather, aged 15, killed 2, year 2014
- Lisa Borch, aged 15, killed 1, year 2014

The Colts Neck Mansion Murders

The Caneiro family was killed in their mansion home on November 20. A massive fire was lit after the murders, most likely to hide the evidence, but it wasn't long before the true nature of what happened in the house became apparent.

A Cold Hearted Killing

In the early hours of November 20, while it was still dark, Paul Caneiro drove to his brother's house. Keith Caneiro, 50, lived in a mansion in the Colts Neck Township in New Jersey. The two brothers, and business partners, met on the front lawn, at which time Paul pulled out a gun and shot his brother to death.

Paul then went into the mansion and stabbed his sister in law Jennifer, 45, repeatedly, until she was dead. He then stabbed his niece, Sophia, 8, and nephew Jesse, 11, until they were all dead.

After he had killed them all, he removed 'items of evidence' from the home before setting it on fire, at some point before 5:00am. Paul then went back to his own home and set it on fire to make it look as though he was a victim as well.

The fire wasn't discovered until 12:30pm, when a grounds keeper at the neighbors reported it. By the time firefighters arrived on the scene, the fire had become an inferno which required 20 fire departments to put out. It was discovered that the fire had started in the basement.

Alleged Offenses and Charges

Paul was arrested on November 21 and charged with one count of aggravated arson in relation to the fire he set at his own house. Fortunately the family members who lived in the house had all managed to escape the fire. Then on November 29, police announced that they had filed seven more charges against Paul. These included four counts of first degree murder, one count of aggravated arson, one count of possession of a firearm for an unlawful purpose and one count of possession of a knife for an unlawful purpose.

All of the added charges related to the murders of his brother, sister in law, niece and nephew, and the setting fire of their home. At a brief court appearance for the first aggravated arson charge on November 30, Paul pleaded not guilty.

Police believe that the motive behind the murders was greed.

His next detention hearing is scheduled for December 4.

Two Fires, Two Burns

Although Paul allegedly set fire to both houses, the fires themselves were quite different. The one at the mansion was a raging fire, designed to destroy as much of the house as possible. The fire at Paul's own home was much different, in that instead of one big fire, two small fires were lit to create as little damage as possible.

The main reason behind lighting two different fires is because the one at the mansion was a necessity to cover up the murders of Keith, his wife and children. Whereas at Paul's house, the priority was to protect his family, not risk harming them. In fact, it was Paul that raised the alarm at home and enabled his family to escape completely unharmed.

In his wife's eyes, Paul was a hero for saving his wife and children. When he was standing outside his burning home, his neighbor stated he put on an 'Oscar-worthy display of grief'.

Brotherly Bond

Keith and Paul grew up in Brooklyn and later after they moved to Staten Island, they met the women who would become their wives. The two families then moved to suburban New Jersey, and then they shifted within roughly 10 miles of each other and settled.

The brothers were business partners in two IT companies - Square One and Jay-Martin Consulting, both based in Asbury Park. The companied provided data security, tech support and surveillance equipment installations. Their clients included law firms in New York, advertising agencies, and major companies including Nike, HSBC, Citibank and Sabrett.

Paul's house had a lot of surveillance equipment including cameras and infrared technology. The investigators have not revealed what evidence they have from both crime scenes, but some wonder whether it was Paul's own surveillance equipment that provided the evidence leading to his charges.

Mercy Hospital Shooting

A mass shooting occurred on November 19 at the Mercy Hospital and Medical Center in Chicago, Illinois. AS a result, three people were killed, including a police officer, an attending physician and a pharmacy resident, along with the gunman.

An Emotional Attack

Between 3:00pm and 3:30pm, a verbal argument occurred between an emergency room doctor and her ex-fiancé in the carpark of the hospital. The doctor, Tamara O'Neal, was shot and killed. She had run to a group of people for help and was trying to call 9-1-1, saying that the gunman was going to kill her. He came over to her and shot her six times when she was unable to give him a ring he had requested to have back from her.

He then entered the hospital and started shooting. Police arrived on the scene and gunfire was exchanged with the gunman as he retreated further into the hospital. During the shootout, police officer Samuel Jimenez, 28, was shot and later died. Pharmacy resident Dayna Less, 25, was also shot and killed, and the gunman was killed as well.

By 4:40pm, the hospital was secured by police and there was no further threat.

Juan Lopez - the Gunman

The shooter was identified as Lopez, 32, who had previously been engaged to O'Neal. He was located in the hospital with a gunshot wound to the head.

Lopez had threatened previously to shoot up the Chicago Fire Academy following his dismissal as a trainee. He was fired from the academy due to improper conduct towards women and aggressive conduct.

In 2014, Lopez's former wife filed for an order of protection against him. She alleged he was threatening and was harassing her. She also documented his threatening and unsafe conduct with a gun.

Police found that Lopez had a concealed carry gun permit and a valid FOID card, and in the five years leading up to the shootings, he had purchased four weapons.

At the time of the shooting, his ex-wife had taken him to court for unpaid child support to the value of $6,000. He moved houses constantly and always refused to tell her where he was living. Since their divorce, he had inconsistent employment, and worked a variety of jobs. He was entitled to six hours a month visitation with his son, but he didn't do it.

Clear Motive

It's fairly obvious that the shooting was the result of the domestic dispute he was engaged in with his ex-fiancé. Witnesses said he had asked for the ring back and she had said she didn't have it, right before he shot her. There didn't seem to be any premeditated planning involved, it was most likely driven by the rage he felt in that moment.

But why take other lives as well? Perhaps he realised that people had seen him kill O'Neal and there was no way he was going to get away with it. He may have run into the hospital thinking he could hide easily then eventually sneak out. Once he was confronted with the police, he most likely thought he had no chance of getting away with what he had done.

Those that died in the hospital could almost be considered collateral damage. They happened to be in the wrong place when Lopez decided he needed to shoot his way out of a bad situation.

Terrorist Attacks in Short for November

November 1

Boron State, Nigeria: Boko Haram insurgents set fire on many houses and burned them down while killing at least 15 people in a spate of attacks at villages of the Boron State, Nigeria.

November 2

Deri ez-Zor, Syria: 11 security officials including 7 Russian soldiers were killed in their headquarters at Deir ez-Zor when a land mine exploded as they were touring the building.

November 3

Djugu, Democratic Republic of the Congo: Armed Mai-Mai gunmen attacked a military camp in Djugu with rifles and arrows killing at least 11 people and injuring 9 according to witnesses, civilians were among the dead and at least 3 soldiers were also killed.

November 4

Hajin, Syria: At least 12 US backed SDF fighters were killed and 20 injured in a large scale Islamic State attack near Hajin that began with a suicide car bomber and subsequent clashes afterwards.

Ghazni, Afghanistan: Talban overran a security checkpoint in the city of Ghazni, killing around 13 Afghan soldiers and wounding 13. They also seized a large amount of weapons and ammunition.

November 6

Farah Province, Afghanistan: The Taliban attacked an Afghanistan army checkpoint in the Farah Province, killing 20 Afghan soldiers and leaving several wounded and missing, 15 Taliban were also killed.

November 7

Khujand, Tajikistan: In the city of Khujand, Tajikistan, a detained Islamic State member attacked a guard at the high-security prison where he is detained, seizing his assault rifle and a riot started, the rioters initially took over a building before security forces coming and subduing the attack. At least 25 inmates and two security guards were killed and six security guards were also injured. It is unknown if the attacker is among the casualties.

November 8

Mosul, Iraq: A car bomb exploded near a restaurant in the Iraqi city of Mosul killing at least 13 people and injuring 23.

Khwaja Ghar District, Afghanistan: The Taliban attacked a military base in the Khwaja Ghar district of the northern Takhar province, killing 14 soldiers and injuring 7 others at least 8 Taliban fighters were killed in the shootout and more fled afterwards.

Ghazni Province and Maidan Wardak Province, Afghanistan: The Taliban attacked simultaneously police outposts in the Ghazni Province and in the Maidan Wardak Province killing 13 policemen and injuring 3 more, the Taliban also set several civilian houses on fire.

November 9

Kunduz Province and Nimruz Province, Afghanistan: 11 Afghan security forces were killed and several were injured in Taliban attacks on checkpoints located in the Kunduz and Nimruz Provinces of Afghanistan.

Mogadishu, Somalia: Three car bombs, including two suicide car bombs, were detonated near two hotels in central Mogadishu, Somalia. After that, four gunmen tried to storm the hotel, but security forces killed them all. At least 58 people were killed and 106 were injured. The Al-Shabaab terrorist group claimed the responsibility for these attacks.

Ngala, Nigeria: Boko Haram jihadist's ambushed convoys on a highway near the town of Ngala killing at least 9 people including 8 civilians and a soldier, several people were also injured or are missing.

Baghdad Province, Afghanistan: Three security personnel were killed and 11 were wounded when the Taliban attempted to storm checkpoints in the

Baghdad Province, however the attacks were met with resistance resulting in 12 Taliban killed and 8 wounded.

November 10

Bagola Province, Afghanistan: A shooting and bomb attack by the Taliban on an army base in the Bagola province resulted in 16 people dead including 12 soldiers and four tribal elders and injured 3, the Taliban also abducted two soldiers and set the base on fire.

Al-Safe, Syria: The Islamic State attacked Syrian Army positions in the Al-Safe area resulting in 7 deaths of the Syrian Army and 11 of the Islamic State.

November 11

Johore District, Afghanistan: The Taliban attacked Ghazi's Jaghori district resulting in 25 people dead including 15 civilians and 10 security forces, 17 people including 11 civilians and 6 security forces were also injured in the attack

Al-Karmah, Iraq: Nine people including eight civilians and one tribal fighter were killed when the Islamic State attacked a house of a fighter of the Tribal Mobilization Forces near the Al-Karmah area in Iraq.

Farah Province, Afghanistan: At least 50 security personnel were killed in Taliban attacks in the Farah Province, nine security officers were injured and ten others were arrested by the Taliban, one Taliban insurgent was killed and three others were injured in the clashes.

November 13

Chahar Burjak District, Afghanistan: A Taliban attack killed at least 12 security officers that were guarding the Kamal Khan Dam in Chahar Burjak district of southwestern Nimroz province, a Taliban insurgent was also killed in the clash.

Borno State, Nigeria: Boko Haram attacks on Farmers in villages of the Borno State left at least 16 Farmers dead and at least 35 missing.

Urozgan Province, Afghanistan: The Taliban attacked security posts in the Urozgan Province killing at least 10 security officers and injuring around 5, 15 Taliban terrorists were also killed in the attack.

November 14

Maidan Wardak Province, Afghanistan: A Taliban attack on the Maidan Wardak Province killed at least 9 Afghan Soldiers, 5 Taliban were also killed in the clashes.

November 15

Farah Province, Afghanistan: The Taliban surprise attacked an army base in the Farah province killing at least 40 security personnel and wounding several as well as seizing many weapons and vehicles from the base.

Beni, Democratic Republic of the Congo: 20 people including 8 UN Peacekeepers and 12 Congo Soldiers were killed as well as 10 others injured in an attack by the Allied Democratic Forces during a military operation by the UN Soldiers near Beni.

Alindao, Central African Republic: Attacks by armed groups killed at least 60 civilians in the town of Alindao, the attacks begun when Anti-Balaka fighters attacked Muslims, afterwards a Seleka group killed dozens of Christians in an attack on a cathedral and many of the people killed were sheltering at a church while also setting many homes on fire, one person was left missing and dozens were injured, in total 60 people were killed in the attacks.

November 16

Hama Governorate, Syria: Jihadist rebels operating in Idlib led by the Al-Qaeda linked group Hurras-al-Deen killed at least 22 Syrian regime fighters in the northwest part of the Hama Governorate.

November 18

Latakia Governorate, Syria: Militants shelled several areas of the Latakia Governorate killing 18 Syrian Soldiers and wounding another one.

Borno State, Nigeria: Boko Haram fighters loyal to ISIS attacked a military base in the Nigerian town of Metele, killing at least 118 soldiers while at least 153 others were still missing as of today, the militants also seized tanks, armored vehicles, weapons, and ammunition.

November 19

Borno State, Nigeria: Nine farmers were killed and an additional three were injured, when Boko Haram terrorists opened fire on the farmers as they were working in the Borno State, Boko Haram also kidnapped and abducted 12 farmers.

November 20

Kabul, Afghanistan: A suicide bomber detonated his or her explosives inside a wedding hall in Kabul where hundreds of scholars and clerics had gathered to mark the birthday of Islam's Prophet Muhammad, the suicide bombing killed at least 55 people and injured 94, no group has claimed responsibility yet for the blast, but the Islamic State is suspected, while the Taliban denied any involvement in the attack.

November 22

Nangade District, Mozambique: Presumed Ansar-al-Sunna attacked a village in the Nangade district using machetes killing 12 villagers the insurgents afterwards set on fire and burnt at least 40 homes.

Tadmur District, Syria: An Islamic State attack on Syrian Soldier positions in the Tadmur area of Homs left at least 10 Syrian Soldiers killed.

November 23

Kalaya, Pakistan: A suicide bomber detonation in a market killed 34 people and wounded around 56 people at a market in the Shi'ite dominated region of Kalaya, Khyber Pakhtunkhwa, northern Pakistan, the Islamic State claimed responsibility.

Khost Province, Afghanistan: A suicide bombing left 27 Afghan National Army personnel dead and another 57 wounded in a mosque at an army base in the Khost Province, Afghanistan, the Islamic State claimed responsibility for the attack.

Tazirbu, Libya: Multiple armed gunmen believed to be ISIS attacked a police station in the town of Tazirbu killing 9 police officers as well as kidnapping 11 locals and police officers.

Deir ez-Zor Governorate, Syria: The Islamic State attacked positions of the Syrian Democratic Forces in the Deir ez-Zor Governorate, killing 92 SDF soldiers, and injuring an unknown amount of others. 61 Islamic State fighters were also killed in the attacks, while 51 civilians died but due to airstrikes.

November 24

Balad, Somalia : A bomb and shooting attack by Al-Shabaab on an armored vehicle carrying soldiers in the town of Balad as they were heading to Mogadishu killed 10 soldiers and injured several others.

November 25

Qaysar District, Afghanistan: The Taliban stormed a security checkpoint in the Qaysar district of the northern Faryab province, killing 10 personnel and injuring 3 others, the Taliban ran off after the attack.

Farah Province, Afghanistan: The Taliban ambushed a police convoy and opened fire in the Farah Province killing 22 police officers and wounding 2 others.

Galkayo, Somalia: A suicide car bomber detonated at the gate of a religious center in Galkayo ran by a controversial cleric killing 17 people (including the cleric), afterwards four gunmen stormed the building and began an exchange of fire killing 3 officers and resulting in 3 militants dead and one arrested, in total 20 people were killed and 20 were injured, the attack was claimed by Al-Shabaab, it is said that the cleric was killed for having music in religious ceremonies.

November 28

Kabul, Afghanistan: A suicide car bomber detonated targeting a British security contractor's compound in the Afghan capital Kabul, several gunmen then attacked the G4S compound right after the car bomb, in total 10 people died and 19 others were injured, the Taliban also claimed responsibility.

CHAPTER 12: DECEMBER

A Date with Death

New Zealand is supposed to be a safe place to visit, and thousands of young people are drawn there every year, as an ideal place to travel and explore. But for one young woman, on her big O.E., it was to be a trip that would end in tragedy.

Grace Millane

Born December 2, 1996, in England, Grace Millane was the daughter of David Millane, a wealthy property developer. After attaining a bachelor's degree in advertising and marketing, Grace decided to take the time to travel and see a bit of the world.

Grace spent six weeks in South America, before traveling to New Zealand. She arrived on November 20, 2018, and journeyed around the North Island, before reaching Auckland on November 30. She had planned to spend two weeks in New Zealand before moving on to her next destination.

Disappearance of Grace

Grace was staying at the CityLife Hotel on Queen Street in Auckland, and the alarm was raised when her birthday came and went on December 2, and family and friends received no response to their messages. She had always kept in touch regularly throughout her overseas trip, so it was completely out of character for her.

Her parents contacted the New Zealand Police on December 5 and reported her missing. On investigation, the CityLife Hotel stated that she had not gone back to her room on the night of December 1, and had not been seen by the staff since. At first the police felt there was no evidence of any foul play related to Grace's disappearance, but rather quickly, they determined that she had in fact been murdered.

Investigation Leads to Tragedy

Police checked all CCTV footage around the central business district in Auckland to search for clues to where Grace may have gone. One camera showed her on Victoria Street at 9:00pm on December 1. Shortly afterwards, her image appeared on CCTV at Sky City. The last time she was seen was at the CityLife Hotel at 9:41pm.

On December 8, it was formally announced by police that the case was now being treated as a homicide. They uncovered a suspect quickly, and a 26-year-old man was charged with her murder. It was reported that Grace and the man had met through a dating app, but this has not been confirmed by police.

Grace's body was discovered on the afternoon of December 9, in the Waitakere Ranges, a forest area west of central Auckland. Almost no details have been released about the circumstances of her death, or the manner in which her body had been disposed of. Police did state however, that her body was intact, so there were no signs of dismemberment or disfigurement.

Who Killed Grace?

The man accused of killing Grace had also been staying at the CityLife Hotel at the same time as Grace. The 26-year-old appeared in court on December 10, charged with the murder, and was subsequently remanded in custody until his next court appearance on January 23. Initially, his request for name suppression was denied, but it was immediately appealed. This resulted in an automatic interim name suppression order for 20 working days, until the appeal had been considered.

A member of the accused's family made statements regarding the case and the man charged with the murder, the first of which was a plea for people to stop trying to contact them. They had been overwhelmed by people sending them messages and questioning them.

The second statement said that they were sorry for the loss suffered by the Millane family, and that she didn't deserve what had happened to her. They also said that they, along with the rest of New Zealand, were heart-broken over it. They claimed that after their relative was arrested, they cried, and barely slept.

The statement further added that if the accused was guilty, then it was 'despicable, atrocious and disgusting'.

It is believed that the man accused of killing Grace was estranged from his family, and had returned to New Zealand after a period in Australia.

New Zealand Name Suppression Laws

Name suppression in the New Zealand legal system prohibits anyone from publishing the name of the person or any identifying details. If the suppression order is breached, it is called contempt of court, and it can result in a penalty of up to $100,000NZD for a corporation or up to 6 months imprisonment for an individual.

However, contempt of court is not an extraditable offence, so it cannot be enforced internationally. Therefore, several media organizations overseas chose to publish the accused murderer's name and details about who he is. Media in the United Kingdom in particular chose to publish his name, and Google included the name in an email it sent to its newsletter subscribers, listing it as a 'trending topic'. Over 100,000 searches were recorded where people had tried to find the man's name.

As a result of the international media choosing to publish the details, the Justice Minister of New Zealand, Andrew Little, and the New Zealand Bar Association criticized the foreign publishers. They stated that by publishing the accused's name and personal information, it could affect the man's right to a fair trial.

Many international media outlets have subsequently stopped publishing the man's name.

National Reactions

Murders do happen in New Zealand, but seldom are they random killings of visitors to the county. For this reason, the New Zealand public reacted in an unexpected way, with a shared outpouring of grief for what had happened to Grace. A public apology was made to the Millane family by Prime Minister Jacinda Ardern, on behalf of the country. She said, "on behalf of New Zealand, I want to apologize. Your daughter should have been safe here, and she wasn't". Media reported that the Prime Minister was close to tears as she read out her statement.

Two of the biggest monuments in Auckland, the Harbour Bridge and the Sky Tower were lit up with white lights in the shape of a ribbon between December 10-13, to mark Grace's death. Numerous candlelight vigils by the public also took place in several parts of New Zealand.

Just before David Millane was to return to England with Grace's body, he released a public statement thanking the New Zealand public for their compassion and support, and he also praised the police for their professionalism. He added that Grace had loved New Zealand and that "in some small way she will forever be a Kiwi".

Timeline of Grace's Last Days

November 20

Grace arrives in New Zealand following her stay in Peru. She is part way into a round the world trip.

December 1

Grace is seen in the city centre of Auckland, on Victoria Street. Fifteen minutes later, she is seen on Sky City's CCTV.

She is then seen later in the evening with a male companion at the CityLife Hotel.

December 2

Grace's birthday. Her family has had no response to messages. A red Toyota Corolla hatchback is hired in central Auckland by a male.

December 3

The Toyota is believed to have been in the West Auckland area.

December 5

Grace's family reports her missing. A public appeal, including Facebook posts and shares, is issued.

December 7

David Millane arrives in Auckland. He makes a plea for any information. Police announce they have identified the male seen with Grace and have spoken with him.

December 8

A 26-year-old man is taken into police custody. He is charged with Grace's murder.

December 9

Police locate the body of Grace in the Waitakere Ranges shortly after 4:00pm.

Murders of Maren Ueland and Louisa Vesterager Jespersen

Maren Ueland of Norway and Louisa Vesterager Jespersen of Denmark were discovered murdered in the foothills of Mount Toubkal near Imlil in

Morocco. The shocking details of the murders, and the link with terrorism, made these awful deaths the subject of international outcry.

'Chasing Experiences'

As many young people do, Louisa Vesterager Jespersen, who was born in 1994, and her friend Maren Ueland, born in 1990, embarked on a trip to find new experiences and enjoy the wildlife in other countries. The two women were students at university in Norway, and had been studying outdoor recreation and nature guidance, prior to their trip.

They arrived in Morocco on December 9, first in Marrakesh before they traveled further to the village of Imlil, located in the Atlas Mountains. This is a popular tourist area for those who are planning on climbing Toubkal, the highest peak in North Africa. For Jespersen and Ueland though, this small village would be the last place they saw.

A Horrific Discovery

Two French hikers were walking a trail between Imlil and Mount Toubkal on December 17, when they came across an awful sight. Near their tent, they found the bodies of Jespersen and Ueland, and both had been savagely murdered, with stab wounds and decapitation. They quickly raised the alarm, and police began an investigation into what had befallen the two young women from Norway.

It didn't take them long to find a suspect, after an ID was found in the tent belonging to Jespersen and Ueland. The owner of the ID was Abderrahim Khayali, and he was promptly apprehended. Police also checked CCTV footage in the area and found three more suspects: Rachid Afatti, Abdessamad Ejjoud and Younes Ouaziyad. Police located theses suspects on a bus in nearby Marrakesh, and they were arrested. These three suspects were all carrying weapons with blades.

It was believed that Abdessamad Ejjoud was the leader of the group of men, and the week before the murders, they had made a video recording in which they all pledged their allegiance to ISIS. The group had planned to carry out a terrorist attack on either foreign tourists or on security services in the county. They eventually decided to look for foreigners, as Imlil was a well-known tourist attraction.

Vile Video Circulation and Further Arrests

The Wednesday following the murders, an absolutely disturbing video recording appeared on social media sites, starting in Morocco then travelling more worldwide. The video shows a man cutting off the head of a woman with blonde hair. The victim can be heard screaming for her life. The man committing the atrocious act and his colleague, who was filming it, spoke in Darija, which is Moroccan Arabic. They also spoke in standard Arabic, and stated that they were 'acting to avenge Hajin, a city in eastern Syria recently retaken from ISIS'.

At first there was some speculation over the authenticity of the video, and whether the victim depicted was either Jespersen or Ueland. However, after a thorough investigation into the video footage, both Norway's National Criminal Investigation service and the Moroccan authorities confirmed that the footage was real.

Following the release of the murder video, and the arrest of the first four suspects, the authorities identified and located another nine suspects who were all believed to be involved in the murders of Jespersen and Ueland. The suspects were located in Marrakech, Tangier and Casablanca.

On December 28, a man of Swiss-Spanish descent was arrested as a suspect in the murders. He had a long history of criminal activity, including domestic violence, robbery, damaging property, aggression and drugs, in Switzerland. He had converted to Islam and left Switzerland after becoming radicalized, and moved to Morocco in 2015. According to the investigation into the murders, this suspect had allegedly taught the other men arrested as suspects in how to commit the murders.

To date, 22 suspects have been arrested in connection with these gruesome murders. On December 30, 15 of the suspects had their first appearance before the judge, and the others were expected to face the court within days.

In Court

When the first 15 appeared in court, the public prosecutor called on the judge to investigate the men for the 'terror acts they committed against the tourists, including the crimes of forming a gang to prepare acts of terror.' The judge was also asked by the prosecutor to place the suspects into custody.

The Safety of Tourists in Morocco

Although Morocco has typically been considered a relatively safe place for foreign tourists, there is a history of tourists being attacked by terrorists. The last terrorist attack occurred in 2011, when a bomb was detonated at a restaurant in Marrakesh, leaving 17 people dead. However, since that time, more than 1600 people have travelled from Morocco to join the Islamic State.

At first the Moroccan authorities weren't concerned about those who left the country to join ISIS, but they eventually realized that these people could return to Morocco and commit terrorist acts. Because of this, the Moroccan authorities created the Bureau Central d'Investigations Judiciaires (BCIJ) to investigate any potential terrorist threats.

Morocco Reacts

Following the horrific murders of Jespersen and Ueland, many Moroccan citizens launched a petition through the Change.org forum to impel the government to sentence the suspects to death if found guilty.

On the Saturday following the murders, many Moroccans had said they would gather in front of the Denmark and Norway embassies in Rabat to honor the victims.

Timeline of Events

Monday, December 17

The bodies of Jespersen and Ueland are discovered a short distance from Imlil by French hikers.

No details about the murders or the identities of the victims are released at first.

Police travel to the site and begin their investigation.

Tuesday, December 18

The first suspect is apprehended.

The identities of Jespersen and Ueland were released but details of their deaths are not.

Wednesday, December 19

Following the receipt of further information, police and the public prosecutor announce that the suspect in custody was part of a radicalized group.

Video of the murders starts to circulate.

Thursday, December 20

Three more suspects are arrested.

The video of the suspects pledging their allegiance to ISIS is released.

The murder is officially called a terrorist act by Government Spokesperson Mustapha El Khalfi.

Friday, December 21

Another nine suspects are apprehended.

Police in Norway comment, that it cannot be proven that the murder video is a fake.

Sunday, December 30

First 15 suspects appear in court and remanded in custody awaiting trial.

The Strasbourg Attack

On the evening of December 11, a busy Christmas market was underway in the city of Strasbourg, France, when those shopping at the market were set upon by a man with a gun and a knife. By the time the attack was over, five people would lose their lives and eleven more would be injured.

The Christmas Market Tradition

The Christmas market, called Christkindelsmärik in the Alsatian dialect, was held every year on the square in front of the Strasbourg Cathedral. The market was an incredibly old tradition, with records showing it had begun back in the year 1570.

Because of a previous terrorist bomb threat on the market back in 2000, security had been reinforced for the market since. The market always attracted a large crowd, which could be difficult to manage. Another terrorist attack had been foiled in 2016, and the market was almost canceled at the time, but instead was rescheduled.

Shoppers Under Attack

The attacker entered the market through Pont du Corbeau, walking through Rue des Orfèvres, before unleashing gunfire. The first victims were shot and stabbed at Carré-d'Or, then Rue des Grandes-Arcades. For ten long minutes, the man raced around the streets, attacking people and shouting "Allahu akbar".

When soldiers of Opération Sentinelle and officers from the National Police approached, gunfire was exchanged with the attacker. One soldier received a gunshot wound to the hand, while the attacker was shot in the arm. The attacker then jumped into a taxi cab and escaped, heading towards Neudorf and Place de l'Étoile. Luckily for the taxi driver, he wasn't harmed by the attacker, and as soon as he was free, he reported to the police about the injured man he had transported.

During the taxi ride, the attacker had bragged to the driver that he had killed people, and stated he had a grenade at his house. It was the testimony of the taxi driver that helped police identify the suspect, and the hunt for him began.

Hunting a Killer

The attacker was identified as Chérif Chekatt, a 29-year-old man who police had already been looking for before the attack began, for questioning regarding an attempted murder. In the beginning of the hunt for Chekatt, 350 men from security forces were deployed, along with air units providing support. The following day, another 500 officers were added to the search, and it was decided that another 1300 would also become involved.

Many locations around the city of Strasbourg were closed, and information was relayed to the public by the police through Twitter. The security threat level was raised to the highest possible by the French government, though a declaration of a state of emergency would not be made.

A temporary shelter was formed in a sport facility, with five thousand people stranded there. The European Parliament was put on lockdown, with the President, Antonio Tajani tweeting that the European Parliament "will not be intimidated by terrorist or criminal attacks" and will "continue to work and react, strengthened by freedom and democracy against terrorist violence". The attack at the Christmas market was declared a terrorist act.

As the authorities hunted Chekatt, they questioned members of his immediate family, including his parents and two of his brothers. His father was known for his religious fundamentalism, and the brothers for their Salafist affiliation. In Algeria, a search warrant was issued for another brother who was allegedly 'very radicalized', and was believed to have contacts within Islamist circles.

At one stage In the search for Chekatt, there were fears he may have crossed the Rhine River into Germany. As a result, all highways that lead to

Germany and Switzerland were closed. Tramways between Strasbourg and Germany were also suspended.

Chekatt was finally located in Strasbourg on the night of December 13, between Neudorf and Stade de la Meinau. When police officers attempted to question Chekatt, he opened fire, resulting in the police firing back. In the gunfire, Chekatt was shot and killed.

Shortly after Chekatt's death, the Islamic State claimed him as their 'soldier'. During an interview, Chekatt's father stated his son had been a supporter of the Islamic State. Several days after he was killed, a USB key was found which contained a video of Chekatt pledging allegiance to the Islamic State.

Chekatt the 'Gangster-Jihadist'

Chekatt was a French national with Algerian ancestry and was 29 when the attack occurred. He had been characterized as a 'hardened criminal', who had converted to 'rigorous Islam'. He had been convicted of 27 crimes in France, Switzerland and Germany, and had committed 67 crimes in France alone.

The police in France referred to Chekatt as a 'gangster-Jihadist', which is a term used when those jailed for crimes are radicalized while they are in prison. When Chekatt was released in 2015 from prison in France, he was subsequently imprisoned in Germany for theft. He was released again in 2017, and expelled from Germany, and so returned to France.

The French State Security had flagged Chekatt's file with a fiche 'S', which is an extra-judiciary document that is used to keep track of suspicious individuals. He was categorized in this way because of recent 'religious radicalization' and Islamic 'extremism'. Of note, his father was also tagged with a fiche 'S'.

International Victims

Of those who were killed in the attack, two died at the scene and the other three died in hospital. Of the eleven victims who were injured, four received serious wounds. Remarkably, the victims who were murdered came from a variety of countries, and it is not known whether Chekatt targeted those he thought were foreign or if it was just a coincidence. Listed below, are those who lost their lives.

Kamal Naghchband

Naghchband was 45 years old, a father of three children, when he was shot by Chekatt. He was transported to hospital, but died two days later, having never awoken from a coma. Originally from Afghanistan, Kamal was a Muslim and had lived in France for 18 years. He worked as a mechanic and had French nationality.

Anupong Suebsamarn

Suebsamarn, 45, was a Thai national who was on holiday in France with his wife at the time of the attack. He was shot multiple times, and although his wife was also shot, she survived her injuries.

Antonio Megalizzi

Megalizzi, 29, was an Italian radio journalist, and he received a gunshot wound to the head. The bullet had allegedly lodged at the base of the skull, near the spine, and he was initially in a coma in hospital before he died on December 14. He had been in Strasbourg to follow a European Parliament session.

Unnamed Frenchman

A 61-year-old male who had previously been a bank employee, was killed at the scene.

Unnamed Polish National

An unnamed person from Poland, aged 36, was transported to the hospital but died from the injuries received on December 16.

<u>Cold Case Arrest: Murder of Lynette Dawson</u>

From rugby star to school teacher, Chris Dawson had lived a lie for nearly four decades. After many investigations by police, and two Coronial inquests, the answer to what had happened to Lynette Dawson, who disappeared in 1982, was finally uncovered with the help of an investigative podcast series.

Background of the Case

Lynette Joy Dawson, wife of Chris Dawson and mother of two daughters, disappeared on January 9, 1982. She had spoken to her mother on the telephone the day before, and had made plans to spend the following day with her mother and other family members at the Northbridge Baths, Sydney, Australia.

Her husband Chris didn't report her missing until February 18 and by that time had already moved his teenage lover into the house. He told police that Lynette had left because they were having marital problems over her spending habits. He suggested to police that she may have joined a religious organization, but this was never proven.

Her body has never been found, yet her disappearance was classified a homicide following two Coronial inquests that took place between 2001 and 2003. Right from the start, her husband Chris was considered the main suspect, though police investigators were unable to get enough evidence to prove it. The nature of his romantic involvement with one of his pupils, and the speed at which he moved her into the marital home, raised major red flags but without a body, it was extremely difficult to find the evidence needed to prosecute him.

Unraveling Chris Dawson

An investigative podcast series called 'The Teacher's Pet' had recently broadcast the case of Lynette Dawson's murder, pointing to Dawson as the killer. It isn't just any old podcast series though - it is an award-winning investigative series.

On December 3, 2018, the New South Wales Director of Public Prosecutions informed the police that they now had enough evidence for Dawson to be charged with the murder of his wife. A warrant was issued for his arrest, and around 8:00am on December 5, police approached a home on the Gold Coast where Dawson was staying. Dawson didn't put up a fight with police, and he was descried as being 'calm' and a little bit 'taken aback', but went quietly with the officers.

The family of Lynette was informed of the arrest after it had taken place, but before it was made public. Dawson was taken to the Southport watch-house, and appeared in the Southport Magistrates Court the same day. The gallery in the courtroom was packed with media representatives who Dawson would not make eye contact with. The New South Wales police requested he be extradited back to New South Wales from the Gold Coast.

Dawson, now 70 years old, blocked his ears as the facts of the murder charge were read out by the magistrate. During the bail application, the duty lawyer acting for Dawson stated he would live with his brother and hand himself in, but bail was denied, and he awaits trial following his extradition.

About Chris Dawson

Dawson was a twin, and was born in Sydney in 1948. The twin brothers had played rugby union for Eastern Suburbs for a while before switching to rugby league in 1972. They played for Newtown, both in the second row, for five seasons, and were a part of the team in 1973 who won the New South Wales Rugby League Club Championship.

Dawson and Lynette first met in 1965, then married in 1970 and had two daughters. Following his rugby career, Dawson became a Physical Education teacher at a public high school. In 1981, Dawson was teaching at Cromer High School in New South Wales when he began a sexual relationship with a 16-year-old student. The student, Joanne Curtis, was the girl who would move into the Dawson house after the disappearance of Lynette.

Dawson's twin brother, who also became a physical education teacher, was known to have sex with female students as well, at Forest High School. Joanne Curtis and Dawson married in 1984, and in 1985 they moved to Queensland, along with Dawson's twin and his family. There, Dawson worked at Keebra Park State High School, and then moved on to Coombabah State High School, where his brother was working.

In 1993, the relationship between Dawson and Curtis was no longer working, and they divorced.

It seems that whatever one twin did, the other also did, which is a disturbing thought to ponder.

Santa's Deadly Secret

Just as Christmas was approaching, the international media were shocked and saddened by the news that the bodies of two children had been discovered buried in their father's backyard. To make matters seem even worse was that the father had been employed as a Santa Claus.

The Missing Children

Elwyn Crocker Sr. had worked as a Santa at his local Walmart store in Guyton, Georgie, until a tip-off led police to the abominable secret Crocker had been keeping for years. Two years previously, his son, Elwyn Jr., 14, had disappeared, but a report was never made to police about it. Then, in October 2018, Crocker's daughter Mary, almost 14, also disappeared. Once again, no missing person's report was filed. There was also a third child with special needs, who was still living in the house.

On December 20, police had received a 911 call from a concerned person who was worried about Mary, as she hadn't been seen for a while. Police acted quickly, and went straight to Crocker's home. After talking with Crocker and his wife, Crocker, 50, lead police to the graves of his two children in his own backyard.

Crocker's wife, and stepmother to the children, Candice Crocker, 33, was also arrested on charges of concealing a death and child cruelty. Her mother, Kim Wright, and Roy Anthony Prater, Wright's boyfriend, were also held on the same charges.

Too Little Too Late

It's tragic that once the identities of the children were released, so many people came forward to say they knew or suspected abuse in the home but never did anything about it. Former neighbors stated they had seen signs of the children being abused but didn't contact the police.

A friend of Mary's, Daniella Gills, 14, said she often saw bruises on Elwyn Jr., and Mary's face was often red. Whenever she visited the Crocker home, Mary always seemed to be nervous. She said, "She would never want me to leave her. If she went to the bathroom she would want me to go with her. She wouldn't tell me why."

Daniella Gills also claimed that Elwyn Jr. was often made to sleep in a wardrobe or the bathtub as a form of punishment for behavior his father and stepmother deemed bad. There was even a lock on the refrigerator, which Crocker claimed was to stop Mary from sneaking snacks, as she was diabetic.

The father of Daniella Gills stated that Crocker and his wife were always complaining about their children's bad behavior, but he never saw any of it. He always found the two children to be respectful and well behaved.

A neighbor and former schoolmate, Gary Bennett, said Mary always had reddened hands, and they thought it was because she was being forced to work outside in the yard too much.

Where Was Their Mother?

The biological mother of the children is believed to be homeless and living in South Carolina, and police are trying to locate her. Crocker had full custody of the children because their mother hardly saw them, and wasn't really involved in the children's lives.

Terrorist Attacks in Short for December

December 1

Faryab Province, Afghanistan: The Taliban attacked security checkpoints in the Faryab Province causing clashes in which seven security forces died and eleven were wounded. Eleven Taliban insurgents were also killed.

Gujba, Nigeria: Boko Haram launched an attack on a military base in Buni Gari at Gujba, killing eight soldiers, while several were wounded in the attack. Six militants were also killed.

December 2

Nduga Regency, Indonesia: 31 construction workers were killed in a separatist militant attack in the Nduga Regency in Indonesia.

December 3

Sayyad District, Afghanistan: The Taliban stormed a police checkpoint in the Sayyad District, the attack killed 5 policemen including a district chief and also injured 7 people. 13 Taliban were also killed in the attack.

December 5

Tadmur District, Syria: The Islamic State attacked the desert area of Homs resulting in the deaths of 6 Syrian Soldiers and also the deaths of 7 insurgents.

December 6

Mogadishu, Somalia: A bomb blast struck a military vehicle leaving 7 soldiers dead and two generals killed, several others were wounded. Al-Shabaab claimed responsibility.

Beni, Democratic Republic of the Congo: 17 soldiers and civilians were killed when presumed members of the Allied Democratic Forces attacked villages near Beni with machetes.

Borno State, Nigeria: A spate of attacks by Boko Haram in the Borno State left 7 people dead including soldiers and civilians, as well as dozens of people injured. Many homes were also burnt in the attacks.

December 7

Shindand District, Afghanistan: The Taliban attacked army outposts in the Shindand District, leaving 14 Afghan soldiers killed and 21 others captive in the attack.

December 8

Hajin, Syria: An Islamic State counterattack against the SDF in Hajin resulted in 44 members of the SDF killed and 56 of the Islamic State killed.

December 9

Farah Province and Faryab Province, Afghanistan: 20 Afghan policemen were killed and 17 others were either captured or wounded in simultaneous attacks by the Taliban in the Farah and Faryab province.

Khost Province, Afghanistan: 10 security forces were killed and 3 others were wounded in a Taliban attack on a military checkpoint in the Khost Province.

Jufra District, Libya: Islamic State militants executed six hostages that had been held hostage for almost two months in the Jufra District.

December 10

Pashtun Zarghun District, Afghanistan: A Taliban attack on a police post in Herat's Pashtun Zarghun District left 6 policemen dead and 10 wounded. 10 Taliban militants were also killed and 8 others were wounded.

Oicha, Democratic Republic of the Congo: Presumed ADF rebels attacked a village in Oicha, causing the deaths of at least 10 people. The gunmen also looted several houses.

December 11

Arghistan District, Afghanistan: The Taliban attacked security checkpoints in Kandahar's Arghistan district, killing 8 policemen while 11 Taliban militants were also killed in the attack.

Paghman District, Afghanistan: A suicide bombing targeted a security convoy in Kabul's Paghman District, causing 12 deaths, including civilians and security forces, while nine others are injured. The Taliban claimed responsibility for the attack.

Ménaka Region, Mali: At least 42 Tuaregs were killed in a series of attacks by suspected jihadists in the Menaka Region; the attacks consisted of gunmen on motorcycles opening fire on the Tuareg camps.

Kunduz Province, Afghanistan: The Taliban attacked security posts in the Kunduz Province, killing 10 policemen and injuring 11 others.

December 12

Jurm District, Afghanistan: The Taliban stormed checkpoints in Badakhshan's Jurm District, killing up to seven security personnel and wounding four others.

Palma District, Mozambique: Armed gunmen believed to be from the Ansar-al-Sunna group attacked a village in the Palma District, killing 6 civilians and burning up to 14 houses.

December 14

Kech District, Pakistan: Six Pakistani security officers were killed and 14 others were injured when terrorists opened fire and bombed a security convoy in the Kech district. A Baluchistan separatist group claimed responsibility for the attack, 4 terrorists were later killed by security forces.

Aleppo Governorate, Syria: A guided anti-tank missile attack by HTS militants killed over 10 Syrian soldiers and injured several others in southern part of the Aleppo province.

December 15

Borno State, Nigeria: An attack by Boko Haram terrorists loyal to the Islamic State near the town of Gudumbali killed 12 soldiers and left dozens of other soldiers missing.

Kandahar Province, Afghanistan: 16 policemen were killed and 6 others were wounded in Taliban attacks in the Province of Kandahar, 12 Taliban were killed and 7 were also wounded in the attacks.

December 16

Jema'a, Nigeria: Militants believed to be Fulani Herdsmen attacked a village in Jema'a, killing 15 people and injuring at least 24 others. The attack occurred at a wedding ceremony.

Afrin, Syria: A car bomb exploded near a market in the Syrian city of Afrin, killing 9 people including civilians and rebel fighters and injuring at least 21 others. The Wrath of Olives group claimed responsibility for the attack.

December 19

Benishangul-Gumuz Region, Ethiopia: A roadside bomb struck a minibus, killing 10 civilians and injuring another one in a village at the Benishangul-Gumuz Region, the police blamed the attack on the Oromo Liberation Front.

Ménaka Region, Mali: Gunmen believed to be of the Islamic State, attacked a Tuareg camp in the Menaka region, killing 6 Tuaregs and 3 officers, afterwards operations were carried out by the officers in which 10 terrorists were killed.

Boni, Mali: Six civilians including four women were killed and six people were also injured when their vehicle was hit by a roadside bomb planted by suspected jihadists near the village of Boni.

December 20

Latakia Governorate, Syria: Six Syrian servicemen were killed and 5 others were wounded in shelling by militants in the Latakia Province.

December 21

Gedo, Somalia: A roadside bomb struck a military convoy belonging to Ethiopian troops in the Gedo region. Around 40 soldiers were killed and injured in the bomb attack. Al-Shabaab claimed responsibility for the attack.

December 22

Mogadishu, Somalia: Around 26 people were killed and at least 40 others were injured in car bomb attacks near the president's residence and a radio station, in Mogadishu. The attacks were done by Al-Shabaab.

December 23

Dih Yak District, Afghanistan: Seven civilians were killed in the Dih Yak District, when their minibus had struck a roadside bomb. Officials blamed the bombing on the Taliban.

December 24

Kabul, Afghanistan: A suicide bomb and a gun attack on a Kabul government compound killed 43 people and injuring 25 others, 4 attackers are said to have been killed. No group has claimed responsibility yet for the attack.

Damaturu, Nigeria: A Boko Haram ambush close to the town of Damaturu killed 14 security personnel.

December 26

Jabal al-Akrad, Syria: At least seven Syrian soldiers were killed and ten others were wounded in an attack by the "Rouse the Believers" group in the Jabal al-Akrad Mountains in Syria.

December 27

Traghan, Libya: Armed Chadian militants attacked a military camp of Libyan soldiers near Traghan, killing 7 and injuring 43 others.

Baga, Nigeria: Boko Haram attacked a military base in the town of Baga, killing 10 people and according to some reports, Boko Haram may have taken over the town.

Sourou Province, Burkina Faso: A security patrol was struck by roadside bombs and also an ambush, killing 10 officers and wounding 3 others in the province of Sourou, the Al-Qaeda linked group Jama'at Nasr al-Islam wal Muslimin claimed responsibility for the attack.

December 28

Deir ez-Zor Governorate, Syria: Cells of the ISIL organization attacked positions of the Self-Defense Forces in the Al-Omar oilfield, killing 9 people and injuring up to 5 others.

Shirin Tagab District, Afghanistan: Six Afghan civilians including four women and two children were killed as a result of an IED blast in the Shirin Tagab District, the attack was blamed on the Taliban.

December 29

Bay Region, Somalia: Eight Somali soldiers were killed in an Al-Shabaab attack in the Bay Region of Somalia, after the terrorists attacked the military base.

Conclusion

The past year has brought about the solving of many cold cases around the world, some of which have been unsolved for decades. This is a testament to the leaps and bounds that have been made in forensic technology and better cooperation between police authorities internationally. For many families of the victims, it may have taken a long time to see a result, but to finally have justice for their loved one is priceless.

It is terribly sad that mass or spree killings have continued to occur, wreaking grief and havoc on so many families and friends of victims. Tragically, the number of school shootings was high again this year, especially in America. One can only hope that sometime soon the authorities will find a collective way of bringing this terrible mass loss of life to an end.

It seems that with each year that passes, violent crime is on the increase and the reasons behind this are varied and complex. Is it a sign of the times? Can we blame the economic situation around the globe that perhaps drives people beyond their normal thinking capabilities and rationality?

As the population grows, so does crime, and although there have been numerous tragic crimes in 2018, there have been few serial murders uncovered, with most major murders being committed as a mass event. Of course terrorism is on the rise, and the global efforts to bring it to an end are yet to be successful.

Whatever the reasons for the terrible major crimes that have made international headlines in 2018, thoughts must always lay with those affected. With the children who lost their classmates; the team that lost their players; the children that lost a parent; and the parent who lost a child. All who have been touched by tragedy at the hands of another.

More books by Jack Rosewood

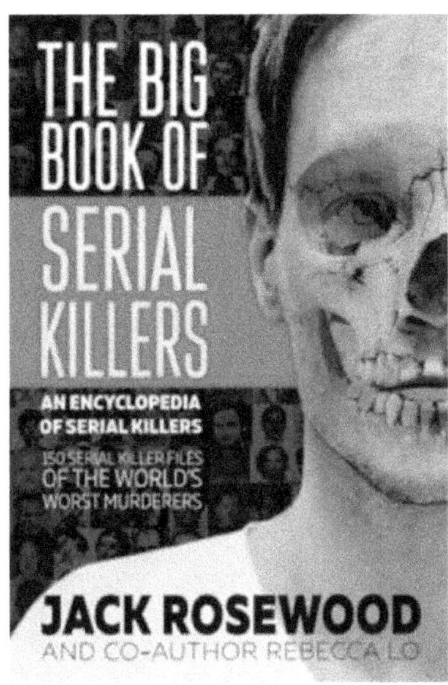

There is little more terrifying than those who hunt, stalk and snatch their prey under the cloak of darkness. These hunters search not for animals, but for the touch, taste, and empowerment of human flesh. They are cannibals, vampires and monsters, and they walk among us.

These serial killers are not mythical beasts with horns and shaggy hair. They are people living among society, going about their day to day activities until nightfall. They are the Dennis Rader's, the fathers, husbands, church going members of the community.

This A-Z encyclopedia of 150 serial killers is the ideal reference book. Included are the most famous true crime serial killers, like Jeffrey Dahmer, John Wayne Gacy, and Richard Ramirez, and not to mention the women who kill, such as Aileen Wuornos and Martha Rendell. There are also lesser known serial killers, covering many countries around the world, so the range is broad.

Each of the serial killer files includes information on when and how they killed the victims, the background of each killer, or the suspects in some cases such as the Zodiac killer, their trials and punishments. For some there are chilling quotes by the killers themselves. The Big Book of Serial Killers is an easy to follow collection of information on the world's most heinous murderers.

Open the pages of this true crime anthology and learn about twelve of the most shocking true crime cases in modern history. You will be glued to the pages as you read about high profile true crime murder cases, such as the murder of Laci Peterson, and the murder trial of actor Robert Blake, while learning about some lesser known yet equally notorious murder trials. You will follow criminal investigations into cold murder cases that were once thought to be unsolvable, but through a combination of scientific advances, good police work, and some luck, homicide detectives were able to give the victims' families closure.

Although most of the cases profiled in this book are clearly true crime stories, one case, the story of the famous doctor Jack Kevorkian, concerns changing legal interpretations of what constitutes murder in the United States of America. Other cases profiled involve privileged individuals who had plenty of money, but resorted to murder out of greed and selfishness. You will also read about one privileged woman, actress Dominque Dunne, who had her whole life in front of her, only to have it ended by a jealous lover who could not handle her success and privilege.

Open the cover of this book, if you dare, and learn about some of the most intriguing high profile crimes and true murder to happen in the last 100 years. You may want to share this book with a friend, though, because as intriguing as the following cases are, they are also shocking and disturbing.

Few serial killers in history have garnered as much attention as Jeffrey Lionel Dahmer. Although Dahmer killed seventeen young men and boys, it was not so much the number of people he killed that makes him stand out among famous serial killers, but more so the acts of depravity that he committed on the corpses of his victims. In this true crime story you will read how Dahmer transitioned from a loner to serial killer, committing numerous unnatural acts along the way such as necrophilia and cannibalism. Following in the macabre tradition of another infamous Wisconsin serial killer—Ed Gein—Jeffrey Dahmer terrorized Milwaukee for most of the 1980s until he was finally captured in 1991.

Perhaps one of the most frightening aspects of Jeffrey Dahmer's serial killer career was how easy he was able to lure his victims into his trap. Dahmer possessed above average intellect, was conventionally good looking, and usually had a calm demeanor that could disarm even the most paranoid of people. Because of these traits, Dahmer was able to evade justice numerous times, which allowed him to keep killing. Truly, Dahmer was able to fool his family, the police, his neighbors, and even the judicial system into believing that he was not a threat; but during the entire time his kill count increased and the body parts of his victims began to pile up around his apartment.

Open the pages of this book to read a story that is among the most disturbing of all true crime serial killers. You will follow the course of Dahmer's life from an alcoholic outcast in high school to a vicious predator who stalked the streets of Milwaukee. Finally, you will read about Dahmer's trial, his jail house murder, and the impact that his many crimes had on Milwaukee.

GET THESE BOOKS FOR FREE

Go to http://www.jackrosewood.com/free

and get these E-Books for free!

A Note From The Author

Hello, this is Jack Rosewood. Thank you for reading this book. I hope you enjoyed the read. If you did, I'd appreciate if you would take a few moments to **post a review on Amazon.**

I would also love if you'd sign up to my newsletter to receive updates on new releases, promotions and a FREE copy of my Herbert Mullin E-Book, www.JackRosewood.com

Thanks again for reading this book, make sure to follow me on Facebook.
Best Regards
Jack Rosewood